6

Bloom's Modern Critical Views

Bloom's Modern Critical Views

Bloom's Modern Critical Views

H.G. Wells

Edited and with an introduction by
Harold Bloom
Sterling Professor of the Humanities
Yale University

CHELSEA HOUSE
P U B L I S H E R S
A Haights Cross Communications Company

Philadelphia

A Haights Cross Communications ⬥ Company

http://www.chelseahouse.com

Introduction © 2005 by Harold Bloom.

Printed and bound in the United States of America.
10 9 8 7 6 5 4 3 2 1

Library of Congress Cataloging-in-Publication Data

H.G. Wells / [edited by] Harold Bloom.
     p. cm. — (Modern critical views)
  Includes bibliographical references and index.
  ISBN 0-7910-8130-3 (alk. paper)
  1. Wells, H. G. (Herbert George), 1866-1946—Criticism and interpretation. I. Bloom,
Harold. II. Series.
  PR5777.H17 2004
  823'.912—dc22

                              2004021453

Contributing Editor: Gabriel Welsch

Cover designed by Keith Trego

Cover photo: © Bettmann/CORBIS

Layout by EJB Publishing Services

Contents

Editor's Note

My Introduction interprets H.G. Wells's remarkable story of 1899, "The Country of the Blind," which Italo Calvino honored by comparing it to the work of Jonathan Swift.

Wells is praised by W. Warren Wagar as a pioneer of science fiction, after which Colin Manlove contrasts Charles Kingsley's *The Water-Babies* (1863) to Wells's *The Time Machine* (1895) and *The War of the Worlds* (1898).

The Time Machine is seen by Kathryn Hume as a vision of oral entropy or the triumphant return of the Sphinx, while William J. Scheick analyzes two little-known romances, *The Wonderful Visit* (1895) and *The Sea Lady* (1902).

Amorous utopianism is ascribed to the lustful Wells by John Huntington, after which Robert Sirabian returns the great womanizer to the scientism of *The Invisible Man*.

Paul A. Cantor finds *The Invisible Man* to be a contradictory blend of socialism and heroic individualism, while Bruce Beiderwell centers upon grotesque elements in the same work.

Janice H. Harris refreshingly addresses herself to three mostly forgotten Wells novels—*Marriage* (1912), *The Passionate Friends* (1913), *The Wife of Sir Isaac Harman* (1914)—and praises them for their debates on the issue of marriage.

Tono-Bungay (1909), which seems to me Wells's best conventional novel, is judged by William Kupinse to have parallels to Joyce's *Portrait of the Artist as a Young Man*, a juxtaposition that Wells cannot survive.

Philip Coupland shrewdly comments on the "Liberal Fascism" of Wells's *The Shape of Things to Come: The Ultimate Revolution* (1933), after which this volume concludes by Patrick A. McCarthy's comparison of Joseph Conrad's *Heart of Darkness* to the early novels of Wells.

Introduction

Italo Calvino concluded his wonderful anthology, *Fantastic Tales: Visionary and Everyday* with "The Country of the Blind" by H.G. Wells. To Calvino, this famous tale was "a meditation on cultural diversity." Certainly that is a possible view, though I myself tend to suspect Calvino of being characteristically ironic. Whatever Wells intended, this strange story finds its place between Borges's saturnine story, "The Immortal", and Saramago's frightening novel, *Blindness*. Borges shows us the horror of a literal, always ageing immortality, and Saramago allegorizes Fascism as a tyranny of the seeing over the sightless. Wells, for once implicitly admonishing himself, does satirize Nunez ("Bogota" to the blind) for what Calvino calls "pretensions to think oneself superior," but finally exalts his protagonist for yielding up love of a beautiful woman in order to save his eyesight. Apocalyptic womanizer as he notoriously was, Wells learns the wisdom that, in the country of the blind, only the blind can rule. All variations from the norm at last either must yield or flee.

Borges, influenced by Wells, gives us the impression that Wells is following *after* the Argentine fabulist. I have just reread "The Country of the Blind" for the first time in decades, and had to keep fighting the impression that I was reading Borges, a sensation that starts in the tale's first paragraph:

> Three hundred miles and more from Chimborazo, one hundred
> from the snows of Cotopaxi, in the wildest wastes of Ecuador's

Andes, there lies that mysterious mountain valley, cut off from the world of men, the Country of the Blind. Long years ago that valley lay so far open to the world that men might come at last through frightful gorges and over an icy pass into its equable meadows; and thither indeed men came, a family or so of Peruvian half-breeds fleeing from the lust and tyranny of an evil Spanish ruler. Then came the stupendous outbreak of Mindobamba, when it was night in Quito for seventeen days, and the water was boiling at Yaguachi and all the fish floating dying even as far as Guayaquil; everywhere along the Pacific slopes there were land-slips and swift thawings and sudden floods, and one whole side of the old Arauca crest slipped and came down in thunder, and cut off the Country of the Blind for ever from the exploring feet of men. But one of these early settlers had chanced to be on the hither side of the gorges when the world had so terribly shaken itself, and he perforce had to forget his wife and his child and all the friends and possessions he had left up there, and start life over again in the lower world. He started it again but ill, blindness overtook him, and he died of punishment in the mines; but the story he told begot a legend that lingers along the length of the Cordilleras of the Andes to this day.

What can we infer about the storyteller? Only that he is at once ancient, all-knowing, and dispassionate, and yet we may want to ask the Nietzschean question: who is the interpreter and what power does he seek to gain over the story? His rhetoric is extreme: "wildest," "mysterious," "frightful," "stupendous," "terribly" set a tonality of preparation for the weird narrative, in which a paradisal, happy valley is smitten by a disease that blinds everyone forever. And fifteen generations pass, in which the blindness becomes the given, natural and normative.

Nunez literally falls into this valley of the blind. He confronts windowless houses, and then the blind dwellers, whose hearing, through the generations, has become extraordinarily fine. Nunez, within him, hears the old proverb: "In the Country of the Blind the One-Eyed Man is King," and he deceives himself that he will reign. Soon enough, he discovers that to these blind he seems an informed savage:

It was marvellous with what confidence and precision they went about their ordered world. Everything, you see, had been made to fit their needs; each of the radiating paths of the valley area had a constant angle to the others, and was distinguished by a special notch upon its kerbing; all obstacles and irregularities of path and meadow had long since been cleared away; all their methods and procedure arose naturally from their special needs. Their senses had become marvellously acute; they could hear and judge the slightest gesture of a man a dozen paces away—could hear the very beating of his heart. Intonation had long replaced expression with them, and touches gesture, and their work with hoe and spade and fork was as free and confident as garden work can be. Their sense of smell was extraordinarily fine; they could distinguish individual differences as readily as a dog can, and they went about the tending of the llamas, who lived among the rocks above and came to the wall for food and shelter, with ease and confidence. It was only when at last Nunez sought to assert himself that he found how easy and confident their movements could be.

A permanent outsider, whose pride of sight continues, Nunez absorbs the new reality very slowly. He rebels, fights, is defeated, runs away, and returns famished. Gradually he becomes a barely accepted citizen of the Country of the Blind, and falls in love with a young woman, but cannot marry her unless he consents to be blinded. Sunrise leads him out, away from the valley and up the mountains, until: "The glow of the sunset passed, and the night came, and still he lay peacefully contented under cold, clear stars." And so the story ends.

I reluctantly dissent from Calvino, whom I personally revered, and whose writing I continue to love. But the proverb of the one-eyed man's putative kingship to me seems irrelevant in understanding this story, and may have been self-deception on Wells's part. When I remember the tale, away from its text, what comes first to mind is the solidarity and self-sufficiency of the community of the blind. They parody us, and expose *our* ability to see as only another variety of *their* blindness. Nunez is no more inward or sympathetic figure at the close, comforted by starlight, than he was when he crassly saw himself as kinging it over these formidable, banded-together blind men, women, and children. Wells, solipsistic and libido-driven, had neither the interest nor the ability to create personality and character. He was the least Shakespearean of all English writers, more so even than Daniel Defoe and Jonathan Swift. A tale-spinner and fantasist, his genius was for plot, which meant far less to Shakespeare than to modern scholars of the king of writers. Wells, confronted by the sublime fictions of Henry James, could respond only by silly parodies, which stung James but are trivial to us. And yet Wells remains a permanent and popular writer. Why?

"Liberal Fascist" no longer seems an oxymoron, in the America of 2004, where Orwell's prophecy is being fulfilled, just two decades off target. Wells who, with Poe and a few others, fathered our science fiction, hoped that history could be cured by technology, and by benign scientistic tyrannies. He clearly is a failed prophet, but like Poe he dreamed inescapable nightmares. Poe was a dreadful stylist, and Wells (at least) a drab one. As an Emersonian, I like to go on murmuring: "There is no history, only biography." Wells, heroic individualist but burgeoning Fascist, associated himself with the nightmare of history, from which I would like to awake, but cannot.

W. WARREN WAGAR

H.G. Wells and the Scientific Imagination

One of the rarest birds in the lands of literature is the scientist who writes novels. In mainstream fiction, such a creature is almost unknown. As C.P. Snow observed in *The Two Cultures and the Scientific Revolution* (1959), modern civilization is split in two. The scientists go one way, the humanists another, and those who would travel with both (like Snow himself, a novel-writing scientist) court the condemnation of both.

But one courageous band of writers straddles the two cultures ineluctably, no matter what the training or allegiance of its members. Their patron saint is H.G. Wells, and their craft is science fiction, the fiction of science.

Some few writers of science fiction are bona fide men or women of science, such as the biochemist Isaac Asimov, the astronomers Fred Hoyle and Carl Sagan, the physicists Gregory Benford and David Brin, or the experimental psychologist Alice B. Sheldon (better known by her pseudonym of James Tiptree, Jr.). Many others have no special competence in science at all, or, in curious deference to C.P. Snow's thesis, may even be hostile to the scientific world-view. But they share with their scientist-colleagues a fascination, almost an obsession, with the powers of science.

The prototypical writer of science fiction, H.G. Wells—Brian Aldiss calls him "the Shakespeare of science fiction"—started out in life not quite a scientist, but a teacher of science, educated at the Normal School of Science in South Kensington, London, now the Imperial Institute of Science and

From *Virginia Quarterly Review*, vol. 65, no. 3. © 1989 by *Virginia Quarterly Review*.

Technology. Among his teachers was T.H. Huxley, the chief apostle in late Victorian England of the theory of evolution put forward by Charles Darwin, and a tireless champion of science and scientific education. Huxley and evolutionary theory shaped decisively the impressionable intellect of the young Bertie Wells. In recent years, whole volumes have been devoted to the fierce grip of science, and evolutionary biology in particular, on Wells's imagination.

The grip is well illustrated by *The War of the Worlds* (1898), the novel that inspired Orson Welles's infamous Halloween broadcast 40 years later. *The War of the Worlds*—Wells's novel, not Welles's radio show—may be construed in various ways, as horror tale, apocalypse, political fantasia, or warning to a complacent England, basking in the warmth of Queen Victoria's 60th-anniversary Jubilee. Clearly, it owed something to the "tale of enemy invasion" popular in England from 1871 onward after the startling defeat of France by Prussia the year before. Bernard Bergonzi sees the novel as a typical product of the *fin-de-siecle* mentality, which doted on thoughts of the decadence and dissolution of modern society, and may have reflected Wells's guilty conscience, as an Englishman, about the crimes of British imperialism. There is also merit in Mark Hillegas's suggestion that *The War of the Worlds* was Wells's first experiment in forecasting the coming Great War of 1914–18, "a warning of the changes in human life to be brought by new science and technology."

But most of this is speculation and hindsight. All we can say with assurance from the available evidence is that what most forcefully engaged the mind of H.G. Wells in the early and middle 1890's was the theory of evolution and its bleak implications for the future of *Homo sapiens*. He seldom if ever referred, at the time, to the burdens of Empire or the menace to England of foreign aggressors or the prospects for global conflict in an age of soaring progress in science and technology.

The vision uppermost in the young novelist's eye was of evolution: the struggle for survival, the transformation of species resulting from environmental stimuli, the threat of extinction, and the intoxicating (yet also sinister) thought that humankind might one day become unrecognizably "advanced," all brain and no heart, like the Martians of *The War of the Worlds*. When he did ponder political matters, like most of his contemporaries, his thoughts turned to the warfare of the classes expounded by the socialists of his day and dramatized in two of his own novels of the period, *The Time Machine* (1895) and *When the Sleeper Wakes* (1899). But there is only a faint echo of such concerns in *The War of the Worlds*.

In Roslynn Haynes's recent study of Wells and the influence of the scientific world-view on his thinking, she goes to the heart of the matter.

> The Martians [in Wells's novel] are not 'evil', only amoral and highly efficient. Their fighting machines are simply their means of trapping or overrunning a more vulnerable species—a practice which Wells compares to the British colonisation of Tasmania. The *War of the Worlds* provides no answer.

Just so. There is no answer. Portrayed as coldly intelligent octopi whose only nourishment is mammalian blood, the Martians arrive in England with their overwhelming technology. They treat human beings as edible fauna, suitable (once subdued) only for rounding up and domesticating like wild cattle. One or two of the Martians are killed by their stampeding victims, but the human remnant is brought into line, and in the end the only thing that stops the invaders is yet another force of nature: the bacteria that infest the earth, to which Martians have no immunity. In Frank McConnell's phrase, *The War of the Worlds* is literally "a war of *worlds*," of competing ecologies, a Darwinian fight to the finish in which not the best but the strongest (the terrestrial bacteria) win the day. In this sense the "triumph" of mankind is wholly serendipitous, a by-product of the real triumph of earth's micro-organisms.

In most of his later work, Wells carried the logic of his biological obsessions a step further, and tried to recommend strategies for *Homo sapiens* that would spare the species from extinction without having to call in the *deus ex machina* of the bacterial microworld. Human beings, using their intelligence, their knowledge of nature, themselves, and their own possible futures, could evade destruction by fashioning a rational world state run by scientists and engineers.

But Wells had no doubt that it would be touch and go all the way. Drawing on his scientific training and his novelist's intuitions of human nature, he anticipated many of the horrors of the new century in the years before the outbreak of the First World War: the mobilization of economies for total war, tanks and bombing planes, nuclear weapons (which he was the first to call "atomic bombs"), poison gas and beam weapons (both of which appear in *The War of the Worlds* itself), and the harnessing of modern technology by totalitarian superstates to crush privacy and freedom. Nothing foreseen by the Zamyatins, Huxleys, and Orwells of later generations was missed by Wells in the science fiction and studies of the human future that he published before 1914.

II

His preoccupation in all this work was the impact on civilization of the dizzy progress of science and technology. Time and again, Wells was among the first to fathom the implications of a given advance, and the first to cheer its coming or foresee grim consequences that others, less acquainted with the human condition, failed to grasp.

Not surprisingly, he started early in his career to call for a science of the future, a disciplined inquiry into the shape of things to come, that would enable humankind to gain control of its own destiny. All contemporary futures inquiry traces its origins to Wells's *The Discovery of the Future*, a little book first published in 1902 and cited almost reverently in the work of various present-day futurists.

Much later, Wells even suggested the appointment of "Professors of Foresight," indeed "whole Faculties and Departments of Foresight," doing their best to anticipate and prepare for the consequences of the abolition of space and time made possible by modern technology. In the struggle to safeguard humankind from the dark dangers lurking in the unchecked growth of science, the only efficacious weapon available was science itself, the rational planning of the human future by scientifically trained experts. It was Wells's way—and he knew it—of bringing up to date Plato's ancient dream of philosopher-kings.

No one will be flabbergasted to learn that many of Wells's most devoted fans throughout his long literary career were scientists themselves. Quite a few were personal friends and occasionally colleagues, notably in the writing of *The Science of Life* (1930), a handsome survey of the biological sciences, which he produced in collaboration with the marine biologist, G.P. Wells (his own eldest son), and the great evolutionist Julian Huxley.

Among Wells's admirers in the scientific community, two stand out in particular. Both were physicists and both were directly inspired by the science fiction of Wells to make fateful contributions in their fields of expertise. Both men exhibit, as did Wells himself, the astonishing fertility of the scientific imagination. Both men were, like Wells, idealists with an abiding concern for human welfare and the arts of peace. Both men also uniquely share, with Wells, the distinction of having helped to usher in the nuclear age and make possible the swift annihilation of all life on earth.

The first is Leo Szilard, the Hungarian-born nuclear physicist who emigrated to the United States in the 1930's, worked with Enrico Fermi to develop the first self-sustained fission reactor fueled by uranium, and persuaded Albert Einstein to take the initiative that led to the first atomic bombs of 1945.

The story has been told more than once, but bears repeating. Szilard was familiar with Wells's writings in his earlier years and met Wells briefly in 1929. He admired both the fiction and Wells's plans for world reconstruction. In 1932 while living in Berlin, he happened on a new

German edition of one of Wells's least successful science-fiction novels, *The World Set Free*. Written in 1913 and published early the next year in book form, *The World Set Free* had taken as its central premise the speculation that radioactivity could provide a source of unlimited energy and also the means of destroying the human race. The novel was dedicated to a book by Frederick Soddy, in which the British chemist had recounted his research on radioactive isotopes, research that eventually earned him a Nobel Prize.

From the raw material supplied by Soddy's discussion of radioactivity, Wells spun an amazing tale of nuclear reactors generating vast stores of energy and the fashioning of atomic bombs from an artificial element known as Carolinum (analogous to the plutonium of later research). The bombs were dropped from airplanes in a great war that erupted in 1958 and destroyed most of the world's cities. The survivors came to their senses in the aftermath and forged a world state. But what sticks in the reader's imagination is the forceful description that Wells supplied of atomic ruin, not so very different from the devastation wreaked on London by the Martians in *The War of the Worlds*.

Not that *The World Set Free* compares even remotely as a work of art. Written in haste, it has none of the splendid shapeliness of *The War of the Worlds*. Nevertheless, Wells's grasp of the implications of scientific research was never stronger. And when Szilard read it in 1932, it made, he wrote in his memoirs, "a very great impression on me." In that same year, in a conversation with a German Wellsian named Otto Mandl, he even came to the conclusion that he should devote himself to nuclear physics and discover a source of power that would enable humankind to travel to other worlds. But for a year the seeds planted in Szilard's mind by *The World Set Free* lay dormant.

Then, in September 1933, in one of those protracted double takes that often result in great scientific discoveries, Szilard was walking down a street in London. When he stopped for a red light at an intersection,

> it suddenly occurred to me that if we could find an element which is split by neutrons and which would emit *two* neutrons when it absorbed *one* neutron, such an element, if assembled in sufficiently large mass, could sustain a nuclear chain reaction.

In no more time than is needed for a red light to turn green, atomic energy had been born.

And with it the atomic bomb. Unlike most scientists then doing research into radioactivity, Szilard perceived at once that a nuclear chain reaction could produce weapons as well as engines. After further research, he took his ideas for a chain reaction to the British War Office and later the Admiralty, assigning his patent to the Admiralty to keep the news from reaching the notice of the scientific community at large. "Knowing what this [a chain reaction] would mean," he wrote, "—and I knew it because I had read H.G. Wells—I did not want this patent to become public."

Also in 1934, Szilard tried to interest the founder of the British General Electric Company, Sir Hugo Hirst, in the possibility of the industrial application of nuclear energy. To support his case, he enclosed in his letter a few relevant pages from *The World Set Free*, admitting that Wells's story was all "moonshine" and yet likely to prove "more accurate than the forecasts of the scientists," most of whom, at this time, were adamantly denying the feasibility of wringing usable energy from atomic fission.

Szilard plunged deeply into nuclear research in the years that followed. As everyone knows, it was he who talked Einstein into signing his name to the letter to President Roosevelt that Szilard drafted in 1939 urging the U.S. government to develop an atomic bomb before the Nazis did. The work went slowly at first, but in due course, Szilard's initiative bore fruit, and the bomb intended to frustrate Adolf Hitler's plans for world conquest killed thousands of civilians on the other side of the globe.

The story does not end there. Szilard was the complete Wellsian, attracted not only to Wells's scientific prophecies but also to his vision of a new world order. As early as 1930, he had tried to organize a *Bund* or League of idealistic scientists and intellectuals from which would arise a quasi-religious, quasi-political Order capable of eventually replacing the parliamentary system of modern capitalism with something akin to technocracy. His ideas ran parallel to, and were probably influenced by, the notion of a new Order of Samurai in Wells's *A Modern Utopia* (1905) and the call for a worldwide "open conspiracy" of scientists and business leaders broached by Wells in his book *The Open Conspiracy: Blue Prints for a World Revolution* (1928), which Szilard knew and to which he sometimes referred in later years.

The *Bund* never materialized, except briefly as a small circle of German friends and followers of Szilard. But as his fame grew, Szilard continued his efforts in his adopted country, the United States. He led a group of physicists at the University of Chicago opposed to the use of the atomic bomb against Japan, drafting a petition to this effect, which was signed by 68 scientists and sent to President Truman in July 1945. He was active in launching the Pugwash movement. In 1962 he organized the Council for Abolishing War, which carries on today as the Council for a Livable World, a political action group headed by scientists that lobbies Congress and campaigns for candidates in the cause of arms control.

Szilard died in 1964, but his work continues. Scientists are still creating nuclear weapons. Other scientists, sometimes the same ones, warn humanity of their menace. This ghoulish paradox is more apparent than real: in both instances, men and women of science are acting rationally, applying their gifts of reason to the solution of problems, but in the context of a largely irrational world they do not fathom. As Einstein himself said of Szilard at the time he was forming his *Bund* in 1930, Szilard was a "fine, intelligent man," but "perhaps, like many such people, he is inclined to overestimate the significance of reason in human affairs."

III

The same pattern of inspiration, discovery, application to warfare, and humane idealism recurs in the life of Robert Hutchings Goddard. If Szilard was the father of the atomic bomb, Goddard is the father of the technology now used to deliver nuclear weapons to their targets, the rocket-propelled missile. And he, too, was a fervent Wellsian.

In 1898 the young Goddard, then 16 and living in Massachusetts, read *Fighters from Mars, or The War of the Worlds, in and near Boston*, an adaptation of Wells's novel serialized in the Boston *Post*. As Orson Welles later transferred the Martians from England to New Jersey, so the *Post* shifted them to the suburbs of Boston. Writing in 1932 to Wells, Goddard remarked that the novel "made a deep impression" on his fledgling imagination. Elsewhere he noted that his discovery of Wells's Martians and their spacecraft was

> an event ... which was destined to provide me with all the scientific speculative material that I could desire.... [It] gripped my imagination tremendously. Wells's wonderfully true psychology made the thing very vivid, and possible ways and means of accomplishing the physical marvels set forth kept me busy thinking.

But not at first. Again, as with Szilard, Goddard did a long double take. The ideas borrowed from Wells fermented in his mind for more than a year before the moment of illumination came. When it did arrive, it was not on a crowded city street but in the boughs of a cherry tree in his own backyard. On Oct. 19, 1899, Goddard climbed the tree and had a vision of a whirling spaceship capable of flying to Mars. In later years he came to regard that moment as the one that transformed his life, and celebrated October 19 as "Anniversary Day," visiting the old tree from time to time to refresh his memory. He also evolved the ritual of rereading *The War of the Worlds*, usually during the Christmas season. His letters and papers teem with references to the novel, and to several other works of Wells, including *The First Men in the Moon*, *In the Days of the Comet*, and "A Story of the Stone Age."

Over the years Goddard toiled away at the development of liquid-fuel rockets, at first with little support or encouragement. He was granted two key patents in February 1914, which contained the essential features of all the rockets that followed. Later that same year he tried to interest the U.S. Navy in military applications of his inventions, and in 1918 the Army also became briefly involved in his research. The bazooka, not employed on the battlefield until World War II, was actually a Goddard invention of 1918. In 1926 he built and successfully test-fired the world's first liquid-fuel rocket. All modern rocket artillery, jet-propelled aircraft, and of course ballistic missiles, owe much to Goddard's studies.

But although Goddard worked for the military again during World War II, it is clear from his papers that the dream animating his research was not weaponry but space flight, the same vision that sparked the parallel labors in Germany of Hermann Oberth and Wernher von Braun, the vision instilled in Goddard by reading *The War of the Worlds* in 1898. In 1932, as already noted, he acknowledged his debt in a fan letter to Wells. He followed it four years later with another congratulating Wells on his 70th birthday and enclosing a report on his latest researches. Ironically, Wells had predicted the use of guided missiles in warfare in a radio talk delivered over the B.B.C. just a few months after receiving his first letter from Goddard, although there seems to have been no connection between the two events.

Goddard also shared Wells's humanism and his hopes for a brighter future made possible by science and scientists. In his 1932 letter to Wells he confessed to

> the greatest admiration for your later work, which you no doubt feel is much more important than your writings of the nineties. What I find most inspiring is your optimism. It is the best antidote I know for the feeling of depression that comes at times when one contemplates the remarkable capacity for bungling of both man and nature.

In 1941 he added, in a letter to a friend, "I agree with you, and also H.G. Wells, that we must hope to have the race ruled by science. To continue with our present hit-or-miss policies may be disastrous."

What conclusions should one draw from all this? Were Wells, Szilard, and Goddard fools or sages? Devils or angels? Destroyers or saviors?

Actually, a little of both. They were human beings, doing what they knew best, dreaming dreams of reason in an irrational world. They were also not indispensable. Science fiction, atomic reactors, nuclear bombs, and rockets would have happened with or without H.G. Wells, Leo Szilard, and Robert H. Goddard. Perhaps not quite as soon or in quite the same way. But we cannot hold them personally responsible for what came to pass.

Yet one valuable lesson may surely be learned from their exploits. The steadfast application of reason, science, and technology to the relief of human distress is no guarantee of anything. It can lead to ruin, just as the Martians ruined London and lost their own lives in the process, victims of the mindless genocidal hunger of terrestrial bacteria. The Martians had, wrote Wells, "intellects vast and cool and unsympathetic," far in advance of those of *Homo sapiens*. But their great brains did not save them. The problems of modern civilization transcend the categories accessible to reason. In the final analysis science can assist in their solution only if guided at every step by the hearts and wills and spirits of all humankind.

COLIN MANLOVE

Charles Kingsley, H.G. Wells, and the Machine in Victorian Fiction

For what is the *Heart* but a Spring; and the *Nerves* but so many *Strings;*
and the *Joynts* but so many Wheeles, giving motion to the whole Body,
such as was intended by the Artificer?

—Hobbes, *Leviathan*

Apart from Samuel Butler in his "Book of the Machines" in *Erewhon*
(1872), there are only two Victorian writers of stature who give the machine
a central role in life and nature and try to consider its functions in human
evolution—Charles Kingsley in *The Water-Babies* (1863) and H.G. Wells in
The Time Machine (1895) and *The War of the Worlds* (1898). Beyond them we
also have a sustained critique of the mechanical in civilization in Dickens's
Hard Times (1854). That the machine is given serious treatment only in
genres we now know as fantasy and science fiction may seem to some to
relegate it to the literary periphery; to others it may seem to put it with a
subversive underculture that continually questions the complacencies of the
Victorian status quo. What is certain is that the attitudes of Kingsley and
Wells provide an insight into both the continuing and changing views of the
machine in the nineteenth century and also those views consequent upon
theistic and nontheistic concepts of the universe.

Where the machine appears in the Victorian novel—scarcely any
poetry of significance deigns to admit it, aside from Kipling's—it is rarely

From *Nineteenth Century Fiction*, vol. 48, no. 2. © 1993 by The Regents of the University of
California.

central to the work as fiction.[1] Disraeli in *Coningsby* (1844) is happy to have it occasionally, but in a context of extraliterary sermonizing: the young aristocrat Coningsby, on a visit to Manchester, views a factory as a wonder out of Arabian fable and descants on the more-than-human abilities of the machines and the apparent contentment of their operatives.[2] Mrs. Gaskell in *North and South* (1854–55), when rarely she mentions actual machinery rather than the condition of underpaid or alienated workers, uses the valetudinarian and Southern English Hale to wonder at "the energy which conquered immense difficulties with ease; the power of the machinery of Milton [again Manchester]."[3] Dickens is prepared to give the ironmaster Rouncewell in *Bleak House* (1853) a future of industrial amelioration beyond the narrative of his novel; in *Dombey and Son* (1848) he equates the rush of the railway locomotive with "Death" (chap. 20); and in *Hard Times* he shows us the effect of the machine making people mechanical.[4] In Hardy's novels the machine is subsumed in the workings of fate against the central characters, its progressive and scientific nature sweeping aside the old rural methods of Henchard in *The Mayor of Casterbridge* (1886), or, in the shape of the threshing-machine on the bleak fields of Flintcomb Ash, grinding down still further the blighted and ill-starred spirit of the heroine of *Tess of the d'Urbervilles* (1891). For Zola in *Germinal* (1895), the machinery is summed up in the name of the focal coal mine, Le Voreux, and is itself devoured by a man-engineered cataclysm at the end.[5]

And yet the Victorian period is an age that is most truly founded on the machine and the progressivism that its powers invoke. Darwin's theory of evolution might not have been formulated without the medium of mechanical amelioration in which he lived.[6] And it is fair too to say that an element of mechanism creeps back into the nineteenth-century novel despite itself. In the eighteenth-century novel the protagonist often finds out what he or she is, while in the nineteenth-century novel the process is one of learning what one may become. But that "becoming" is circumscribed by the factory of Christian teaching, and bound down as to a bench by Victorian evangelical principles. The optimism behind many Victorian novels, in which there is a tendency to turn out perfect moral products after they have been shaped in the furnace of experience or turned on the lathe of self-knowledge, makes them into spiritual manufactories in which each item of apparently contingent vicissitude is part of a production line designed to generate admiration in man and acceptability to God.

What we are dealing with, of course, is the "two nations" and the "two cultures" mentality so characteristic of Britain. *North and South* in a sense sums up one side of it: the major part of industrialism was well away from southern and metropolitan England and thus could be felt as northern and vulgar, a sentiment that persists today. But there was also the feeling among the cultured—most sharply voiced by Matthew Arnold—that machinery, with its concomitant progressivist and acquisitive philosophy, was a threat to man's human nature: "The idea of perfection as an *inward* condition of the mind and spirit is at variance with the mechanical and material civilisation in esteem with us."[7] Thus, while writers such as Carlyle, Mill, Macaulay, or Frederic Harrison might extol the wonders of the machine and its promise, and while the increased comforts and intercommunication that many Victorian poets and novelists benefited from sprang from mechanical advance,[8] there is everywhere among the "cultured" this sense of antagonism to the progress of their age, and indeed often to science itself. The emphasis of criticism is on the machine as a brutalizer of the human sensibility, the agent of a repressive society that, while it goes forward materially, is the enemy of the individual human spirit. For all those who, like Macaulay, could proclaim that "every improvement of the means of locomotion benefits mankind morally and intellectually as well as materially," or that education, sanitation, and care for the arts of life made man happier and morally better,[9] there were as many who scorned such views as philistine, as a confusion of material with spiritual goods. Yet there is real evidence that not only disease but also vice and crime were lessened by these methods.[10]

Scientifically adventurous though the age was, it was often spiritually reactionary: no accommodation of the machine to the artistic sensibility seemed possible. The result was frequent nostalgia or flight into pastoral or the past in poetry—witness Morris's escape from "six counties" of "snorting steam and piston stroke" at the start of *The Earthly Paradise*—and in the novel a reliance for amelioration solely on individual human effort rather than on any collective or mechanical aid. It seemed only at the level of analogy that a bridge could be made between the machine and human values, as in Marx's concept of a new communist society in which, via the abolition of private property, all parts would drive and be sustained by the greater whole.

It took someone who straddled both cultures—who was both "literary" and "scientific"—to show what might have been possible. Such a one was Charles Kingsley, who did it in a work now seen only as a quaint mid-Victorian children's book. Superficially *The Water-Babies* seems more a marine pastoral than a home for machines, and our eyes seem more directed to the wonderful underwater creatures of stream, river, and sea that the protagonist Tom the water-baby meets, from caddis-flies to salmon and from lobsters to whales. In fact, the book mentions machinery and engines repeatedly, and indeed sees the beasts themselves as in part machines. A close consideration of the book here will show how the mechanical could be almost invisibly fused with the natural and both, in turn, with the spiritual.

While Tom is still a chimney-sweep's apprentice in mid-Victorian Yorkshire we hear, as he and his master Grimes set out from town one early morning to clean the chimneys of a great country house, "the groaning and thumping of the pit-engine in the next field."[11] One of the first creatures Tom meets in the water (probably a species of rotifer) is like a miniature factory:

> There was one wonderful little fellow, too, who peeped out of the top of a house built of round bricks. He had two big wheels, and one little one, all over teeth, spinning round and round like the wheels in a thrashing-machine; and Tom stood and stared at him, to see what he was going to make with his machinery. And what do you think he was doing? Brick-making. With his two big wheels he swept together all the mud that floated in the water: all that was nice in it he put into his stomach and ate, and all the mud he put into the little wheel on his breast, which really was a round hole set with teeth; and there he spun it into a neat, hard, round brick; and then he took it and stuck it on the top of his house wall, and set to work to make another. Now was not he a clever little fellow?
>   (pp. 98–99)

Kingsley thus gives the machine a place in the natural order of things, breaking down the usual distinction between the mechanical and the organic.[12] He also makes it wonderful in such a context—and vital too, in that it is ever alive and active; this is also conveyed through the energetic and various syntax. Part of his interest here is similar to that of William Paley, who argued the existence of God by likening the workings of the universe to those of a watch and then claiming that a watch must suppose a watchmaker, or a design a Designer.[13] But Kingsley is also concerned to see his God as in part a scientist, "for ever at work on all phenomena, on the whole and on every part of the whole, down to the colouring of every leaf and the curdling of every cell of protoplasm."[14]

Beyond this, the machines in *The Water-Babies* become larger and more social in their effects, reflecting Kingsley's view that the whole natural order works as one great engine, driven ultimately by God. Thus the weather:

> And, as Tom and the petrels went north-eastward, it began to blow right hard; for the old gentleman in the grey great-coat,

who looks after the big copper boiler, in the gulf of Mexico, had got behindhand with his work; so Mother Carey had sent an electric message to him for more steam; and now the steam was coming....   (p. 293)

Steam and electric telegraphs: it is, of course, partly metaphor to amuse children, but it is also aimed at showing that nature is technically "up to the minute"—or, to put it another way, that every fresh scientific discovery we make will be found to have been at work in nature all along. Now the book is portraying not only machines on their own but the interconnections in nature that join them into a larger machine. Again this idea of communication occurs in the submarine volcanic action that Tom later comes across in "the white lap of the great sea-mother, ten thousand fathoms deep; where she makes world-pap all day long, for the steam-giants to knead, and the fire-giants to bake, till it has risen and hardened into mountain-loaves and island-cakes" (p. 317). Here we have the little brickmaker inverted, for where he takes in, the volcano gives to others to continue the process. And a similar idea of diffusion is present in the chemical-sifting engine, the sea "bogy" next encountered, which separates and diffuses "vapours" into "showers and streams of metal. From one wing fell gold-dust, and from another silver, and from another copper, and from another tin, and from another lead, and so on, and sank into the soft mud, into veins and cracks, and hardened there" (p. 321).

Right at the heart of the book, in the form of the Fairy Bedonebyasyoudid, who represents the operation of Newton's Third Law at both the physical and the spiritual levels, we have a force that operates throughout nature and whose action is depicted as that of an engine: "I work by machinery, just like an engine; and am full of wheels and springs inside; and am wound up very carefully, so that I cannot help going" (p. 220). Kingsley does not stop at this particular notion of nature as machine: he also has Mrs. Doasyouwouldbedoneby, who is the essential complement to her sister, the two working like different movements of a piston: "she begins where I end, and I begin where she ends" (p. 222). And beyond these two we have the futuristic creature-making factory of Mother Carey in the Arctic, a factory whose every product is induced to be self-replicating and in which the "engine" that is Mother Carey is never more busy than when she is sitting quite still with her chin on her hand "mak[ing] things make themselves" (p. 307).

In the light of these images it becomes clear that the whole of *The Water-Babies* may be seen as a kind of organic engine in terms both of its content and its style. As well as the manufacture of creatures, there is the manufacture of souls. Indeed, the two are not finally divided, for in Kingsley's view "your soul makes your body, just as a snail makes his shell" (p. 94); and thus the physical form expresses a moral state. If Tom had not morally improved, he would have degenerated from a water-baby to the form of a slimy eft, or newt (pp. 270, 375–76). The process is not just one by which he develops, but one by which he *is* developed. When Tom commits the hideous crime of stealing Mrs. Bedonebyasyoudid's sweets, he eventually grows a mass of prickles all over his body expressing his sin, and in his shame at them is driven to reform. In a sense, moral choice is finally nugatory, Kingsley believed, for the universe is so constructed that we will bend to it:

> Evil, as such, has no existence; but men can and do resist God's will, and break the law, which is appointed for them, and so punish themselves by getting into disharmony with their own constitution and that of the universe; just as a wheel in a piece of machinery punishes itself when it gets out of gear.[15]

The organic machine that is the world is an "infinite network of special providences"[16] in which nothing is random, contingent, or wasted, and in which any tendency toward divergence is corrected. Lady Why in *Madam How and Lady Why* (1869)

> will take care that you always come across a worse man than you are trying to be,—a more apish man, ... or a more swinish man, ... or a more wolfish man, ... and so she will disappoint and disgust you, my child, with that greedy, selfish, vain animal life, till you turn round and see your mistake, and try to live the true human life, which also is divine.[17]

The Water-Babies is an amazing diversity of contexts, characters, and apparent irrelevancies, all bound together by secret principles that make it a machine without being a monolithic one—indeed, it manages to fuse all the variety that Kingsley saw in nature with the purposiveness of the engine. As Tom is passed from place to place and from creature to creature we see him growing and being shaped in this factory of life. The ethic that he has to learn in life is precisely that symbolized in the machine—that the part does not live for itself, but for others. When Tom saves the lobster from the trap, he meets the water-babies; when he helps someone he does not like (Grimes), he can join the little girl Ellie. One of the prime vices attacked is greed, whether in stealing sweets (Tom), hunting too many whales (the molly-mocks, former Greenland skippers), or devouring salmon (the otter). At bottom it is selfishness: in *Alton Locke* mankind is told, "By selfishness you fell, and became beasts of prey."[18] Symbolic of this is the last Gairfowl, sitting by herself in the Atlantic on the Allalonestone, refusing all suitors out of pride until she dies and her race becomes extinct.

So too the very style of *The Water-Babies*, showing the cooperation of nature, also often shows the workings of a natural engine:

> The sea-breeze came in freshly with the tide, and blew the fog away; and the little waves danced for joy around the buoy, and the old buoy danced with them. The shadows of the clouds ran races over the bright blue bay, and yet never caught each other up; and the breakers plunged merrily upon the wide white sands, and jumped up over the rocks, to see what the green fields inside were like, and tumbled down and broke themselves all to pieces, and never minded it a bit, but mended themselves and jumped up again. And the terns hovered over Tom like huge white dragonflies with black heads, and the gulls laughed like girls at play, and the sea-pies, with their red bills and legs, flew to and fro from shore to shore, and whistled sweet and wild. (pp. 150–51)

The obvious impression here is of a simple pleasure in natural vitality extending to pathetic fallacies in which waves dance for joy and gulls laugh like girls at play. But the image is one of a living society in which breezes, waves, clouds, and birds all play their parts. It is a sort of ecosystem, but not quite so cold and autonomous as that: it partakes in joy, it could indeed be said to be fueled by joy, and all things are imbued with immanent consciousness. Moreover, there is continual reciprocity: the buoys dancing with the waves, the breakers tumbling on the shore, the birds flying about Tom and from shore to shore; and likeness too to things beyond the scene: the terns like dragonflies, the gulls like girls. These analogies take us back to the dragonfly Tom had met earlier in the book and also look forward to the playing girl he is about to meet. So there are all sorts of secret connections, and all of them are in constant motion like organic levers, rods, pistons, cogs, and pulleys. Tom, fallen in the stream as a chimney-sweep from "outside," becomes a part of that system. It is in this light particularly appropriate that at the end of the book this engine of life has turned him into an engineer, for we learn that "he is now a great man of science, and can plan railroads, and steam engines, and electric telegraphs, and rifled guns, and so forth; and knows everything about everything" (p. 374). His experience of nature has enabled him to become a Victorian scientist: nature's laboratory has created its own technician.

A reconciliation such as this between the organic and the mechanical required, as said, a mind that could compass both the religious and the scientific worldviews of the day and succeed in uniting the literary and the utilitarian approaches to experience. However, it also must be said that such a reconciliation occurs only where Kingsley has moved away from man-made machines to natural ones, operated ultimately by God. It cannot be an accident that whatever his fervor for modern inventions, Kingsley very rarely describes them or the new machines that drive them: he continually directs his gaze at sciences having to do with living nature—botany, zoology, paleontology, or geology. Apart from an occasional enthusiasm over railways,[19] he has no extended account to give in his writings of factories, marine engineering, agricultural technology, locomotives, the manufacture of gas and electricity, the chemical industry, or civil engineering projects: his main energies in the sphere of human science are in fact limited to sanitary reform.

If Dickens by contrast takes the darker view of machines in *Hard Times*, it is partly because he addresses another area of life. *The Water-Babies* soon moves us out of an urban to a pastoral and then natural landscape, but *Hard Times* remains immovable in the industrialized and non-natural darkness of Coketown. Where there is movement here, it is only the maniacal rushing of steam trains to and from the outskirts of the place. Here the machinery is demented; the nature to which it is likened is barbaric or perverted:

> [Coketown] was a town of red brick, or of brick that would have been red if the smoke and ashes had allowed it; but, as matters stood it was a town of unnatural red and black like the painted face of a savage. It was a town of machinery and tall chimneys, out of which interminable serpents of smoke trailed themselves for ever and ever, and never got uncoiled. It had a black canal in it, and a river that ran purple with ill-smelling dye, and vast piles of buildings full of windows where there was a rattling and a trembling all day long, and where the piston of the steam-engine worked monotonously up and down like the head of an elephant in a state of melancholy madness. It contained several large streets all very like one another, and many small streets still more like one another, inhabited by people equally like one another,

who all went in and out at the same hours, with the same sound upon the same pavements, to do the same work, and to whom every day was the same as yesterday and to-morrow, and every year the counterpart of the last and the next.[20]

If we put this beside Kingsley's pictures of engines or of the workings of the tide, it is in obvious contrast. To Kingsley's sense of energy, variety, and joy, it offers stasis, uniformity, and despair: the smoke-serpents trail forever, the steam-engine's piston goes up and down continually like an elephant in melancholy madness, the streets, the work, each day, each year, are all the same; individuality is destroyed. The open air has been replaced by the confined and increasingly claustrophobic, mirrored in the syntax of the last sentence.

Most of all, however, this is a picture begotten out of duality: manufactured objects are at war with the organic and particularly with the human, which the streets increasingly close in. The material is not informed by mind, but is purposeless and mad. And this is the picture in the whole book. We do not have any organic unity, but rather an assemblage of bits, whose educated product is called Bitzer. These machines neither make nor are informed by spirits: what they "make" as products is never specified but is felt to be useless; what they make of the men and women forced to serve them is dead souls. The built environment dominates the "people," who only appear in furtive and anonymous form in the last sentence. *Hard Times* is organized into three sections entitled "Sowing," "Reaping," and "Garnering," an organic analogy that stands in ironic counterpoint to the mechanized skeletons it describes. It is full, too, of fragmented and divided narratives, whether that of the louche Harthouse, the degenerate Tom, the ferocious Sparsit, the bullying Bounderby, or the worker Blackpool, all of them signifying the absence of mind that has left these several limbs incoherent with one another. In addition this signifies the absence of that very care for others and for all that is the essence of the natural machine as conceived by Kingsley. Dickens, in short, laments in his machines and their consequences the absence of the very organicism that Kingsley finds in his; and where Kingsley finds matter and spirit conjoined in harmony, Dickens sees them as at war with one another: the dualism that is supposedly so marked a feature of Victorians[21] is certainly to be seen in his work. To the picture of the town that he has given us, Dickens can only offer as remedy a flight to the itinerant circus, where imagination, idiosyncrasy, and organicism reign supreme but cannot keep their tent-pegs in the earth for longer than a week.

Dickens extends his view of the effect of factories on the proletariat to the effect of "facts" on the middle classes. The latter he depicts through a utilitarian educational system that is the correlative of organized industry and seeks to turn out uniform minds rather than objects:

> "In this life, we want nothing but Facts, sir; nothing but Facts!"
>
> The speaker [Gradgrind, Coketown worthy], and the schoolmaster, and the third grown person present, all backed a little, and swept with their eyes the inclined plane of little vessels then and there arranged in order, ready to have imperial gallons of facts poured into them until they were full to the brim. (p. 1)

Each is to know exactly the same as the others: there is to be no imagination, no individuality, for each is to be a standardized wheel in the social engine. In the same way, the workers are reduced to "hands" and any one of them who demands personal rights is rejected. The whole of society is geared—and the word is meant also literally—to the ceaseless production of ceaseless minds and bodies unendingly driven to the perpetuation of useless knowledge and the manufacture of vulgar objects.

Dickens and Kingsley may be contrasted in the way that the one directs his gaze to man-made machinery and the other to the engine of nature. Neither has a complete view, and the different environments in which they consider the mechanical could be said to go some way to determining that the one will see things optimistically, the other pessimistically. But for us the main point must be that the implied opposition between the mechanical and the organic, between technology and biology, is here shown in the very opposition of these two writers: in themselves and in the differences of their work they manifest the duality that underlies all Victorian treatments of the machine.

These novelists have one feature in common, however: they both see the machine as identified with society. For Kingsley it is part of the whole divine society of created nature, and is also the handmaid of the progressivist British nation-state. For Dickens it is the tool of a repressive commercial oligarchy aimed at subjugating its human operatives to the furtherance of productivity and wealth for those in power. The one sees the social machine as a system in which man finds his true individuality, the other sees it as a tyrannical juggernaut that reduces him to a mere cipher. But both look at the machine from the point of view of its effect on individual beings. It is to be otherwise with Wells.

The bulk of the Victorian cultural elite, of course, shares Dickens's more negative view of the machine. Its only literary home seems to be the proto-science-fictional novel, and even there (apart from a certain class of post-1871 works on the possibilities of future war between Britain and another country)[22] it is only in Verne and Wells that we find much attention given to the machine itself.[23] In other works we have the creative surgery of Frankenstein in Mary Shelley's 1818 novel, the mesmeric powers utilized in Poe's "Facts in the Case of M. Valdemar" (1845), the electrical force of *vril* in Bulwer-Lytton's *The Coming Race* (1871), or the transformative properties of the chemical powder in Stevenson's *Dr. Jekyll and Mr. Hyde* (1886). And we may note that in all these works, including those of Wells, admiration of scientific advance goes together with warning of its risks. For these novels are different from those of Kingsley and Dickens: they deal with inventions, not with machines that already exist in the form of the steam engine. They speak of what may be, while Kingsley and Dickens depict their view of what already *is*, what exists in the "real" outer world. The other works are concerned with speculative machines of the future, and thus they are inherently transgressive in content—and thereby, in their period, self-critical in orientation.

Wells writes about machines at a point when their possibilities are becoming unquantifiable. The steam engine performs evident tasks—drives ships or locomotives, drains mines, powers looms or smelters. Its actions are known, its required fuels measurable, its pressures subject to regulation. And it is this one type of engine that powers Victorian industry, through pistons, cogs, levers, belts, and ratchets. But by the time of Wells, with the discovery of the electromagnetic spectrum and the beginnings of atomic physics, a whole new generation of machines based on the seemingly invisible and immense powers of radio, electricity, magnetism, or even particle physics was poised for discovery and application.[24] Concomitant with this was an enormous excitement at the sheer boundlessness of possible invention. If Kingsley and the pro-scientific writers of his age could be thrilled still at the possibilities of the use of machines to establish a heaven on earth, or as functionaries in social betterment,[25] science by the close of the century had often leapt "beyond" such ideals to a sense of its own untested and immense powers. In Wells we see science become capable of being a law unto itself, its invented products thrown off like dangerous sparks that can threaten, not subserve, the social system.

In fact what we have here is a situation in which, from being a danger to the human individual or the soul, the machine can now be seen as a potential menace to society as a whole. From being identified with a society that variously demanded the subjection of all individuals to its collective purposes, it is now the society that becomes human and the machine that is at war with it. This to a large extent expresses the less optimistic and in particular *fin-de-siècle* view of social development; but there is also the beginnings of the modern sense that man's inventions may not work for his betterment alone, but may in ways unknown to him work rather to undermine the whole fabric of his existence on the planet.[26] There is, in short, a much greater sense of human frailty, at least registered by some of those who made it their business to speculate on the possibilities of human development.

In Wells the scientist is separate from the social fabric. Where Brunel followed the engineering demands made upon him by the revolution in public transport, or Charles Babbage sought continually to apply new science and technology to British industry, or Darwin set man among the whole society of living creatures, the inventors we find in Wells are either alone— like the invisible Griffin, the islanded Moreau, or the solitary Time Traveller—or else alien and a threat to society, in the shape of the Martians of *The War of the Worlds*. Their inventions serve to make them either more independent of their environment or able to shape it as they wish. The Time Traveller's machine flits through the lattice of the future, the changing world shimmering about it like a ghost; the invisibility of Griffin makes him free to slip through space and do as he wishes without notice; the powers of Moreau enable him to subvert Darwin and turn beasts into part-men under his control; the Martian machines are able utterly to subdue man.

With Wells we have moved on from Newtonian to pre-Einsteinian physics, expressing now a less stable reality. A literary form of the theory of relativity informs the very postulated existence of a fourth dimension in *The Time Machine*, extending reality and altering the purview on it. Indeed, much of Wells's work here is "perspectivist":[27] in *The War of the Worlds* the complacency of man is mocked in relation to the undreamed-of designs of the far-off Martians, and we are told that the Martians' treatment of man is no worse than European man's own treatment of the Tasmanian natives;[28] here too men have become as Eloi to the blood-sucking Martians. In *The Time Machine* the traveler to the future finds a baffling society for which he offers a series of hypothetical explanations until at last he thinks he arrives at the right one, but even then he has to admit, "It may be as wrong an explanation as mortal wit could invent. It is how the thing shaped itself to me, and as that I give it to you."[29] Nothing is certain: reality is plastic and elusive, shimmering and mutating as the time machine passes through it, changing form and habit as the beasts are made to do in *The Island of Dr.*

Moreau (1896). The very fact that Wells writes science fiction, creating a universe of possibilities alternative to our own, and that he writes not one but many of these tales, is a literary mode of this relativism. And of course relativism is precisely one of the purposes of Wells's invented machines: he wants to throw ironic light on our own technological pride by imagining infinitely superior technology, and equally to highlight our temporal provincialism against the perspectives revealed by a machine that may enact for the future the same Olympian view that was to be applied to the far past in his *Short History of the World* (1922).

In *The Time Machine* we also have relativism contained within the form of the journey and the story. The Time Traveller returns to the Victorian present of the book (which is now our past) to tell his tale of the future: the whole of his adventure is contained within a temporal loop within the story, where on a Thursday morning he sets off on his machine and by Thursday evening is back for supper and explanations, after having traveled thirty million years into the future. In that sense his colossal journey is contained within about ten hours of our time. Further, the futurity that he has experienced is recounted as a past event. And beyond that is the fact that the adventures the Traveller has had via the time-leaping powers of his machine may still await him: wherever he is, dead or alive, he may have to relive the future he experienced with the Eloi and the Morlocks in 802,701 and beyond as "natural" time grinds its way through to these eras; for he is now inexorably a part of that future.

Unless ... unless it is not the *only* or "the real" future—which, given relativity, may not be unreasonable. That it is contingent is implied in the Awful Warning to Victorian man in the very existence of the divided races of Eloi and Morlocks, which are the end-point of the brutal division of capitalist from laborer that to Wells had increased throughout the nineteenth century. The Time Traveller points to the dangers of the rich "haves" dividing themselves from the poor, who are increasingly thrust underground to work, and sees a "widening gulf" that will "make that exchange between class and class, that promotion by intermarriage that at present retards the splitting of our species along lines of social stratification, less and less frequent" (pp. 62–63). Clearly the point is that the future is alterable if the dangers exposed in present conditions can be corrected. Further, it is an interesting feature of the future the Time Traveller visits that one of the few buildings in it that he enters is a museum, a museum containing no identified artifact later than the late-Victorian period from which the story began (pp. 72–76). And of course we now know that the earth and sun will not run out of heat thirty million years hence (p. 85), as Kelvin's second law of thermodynamics (1868) predicted and as most scientists of the time—with the important exception of Darwin—came to believe.[30]

We can take this point further. Suppose the *machine itself* in a sense makes this future? Certainly, without it, it would never have been seen. And inevitably, at certain points in the story, the movements of the machine become assimilated to those of future history itself: "I saw trees growing and changing like puffs of vapour, now brown, now green; they grew, spread, shivered, and passed away. I saw huge buildings rise up faint and fair, and pass like dreams. The whole surface of the earth seemed changed—melting and flowing under my eyes" (p. 42); "So I came back.... The blinking succession of the days and nights was resumed, the sun got golden again, the sky blue.... The fluctuating contours of the land ebbed and flowed. The hands spun backward upon the dials" (p. 86). In 1909 E.M. Forster wrote (partly in answer to Wells) a story called "The Machine Stops": suppose that in *The Time Machine* the verb "stops" is considered as transitive? It has frequently been observed that the future the Time Traveller visits is "run down," approaching entropy. In a year whose descending numbers can be symbolic—802,701—he finds near-exhausted remnants of humankind in the disjoined segments of the effete Eloi on the one hand and the brute, near-monkey Morlocks on the other. This "civilization" is close to terminus, with the Eloi as the last and now vacuous remnants of the former ruling class, kept perhaps as cattle by a brutalized race of now purposeless workers; indeed the two could be said to be the pieces of a broken social machine. Further on into the future, life has devolved still more, with a beach populated by giant crabs: further still, life itself has shrunk to a dubious tentacled polyp flopping in the twilight by an ice-rimmed sea. The future has retraced the past, right back from the most sophisticated to the most primitive forms of life—in a sense it has swallowed itself. We may here note that eating and devouring imagery is recurrent in the story and present in its very form, whereby the story of the future is almost literally digested in the Victorian past, as the Time Traveller recounts his experience while his mutton dinner is absorbed in his stomach. More than this, we may note that the journey of the time machine is accompanied by the progressive slowing of the sun, until it becomes stationary and massively red in the sky. The further and faster the machine goes, the slower moves that symbol and stimulus of organic life, the sun. May there not be enough of a suggestion here that the transgressive technology involved in the time machine devours and deracinates the future as it traverses it?

In a sense, then, *The Time Machine* becomes an awful warning about technology even while, like much early science fiction, it also glorifies it. It is the very success of future technology that destroys man. By utterly conquering nature it renders man helpless, because he no longer has to struggle to survive, can no longer continually fashion himself on "the grindstone of pain and necessity" (p. 52). When mind has done all it can to subdue matter, it atrophies for want of material, and stasis and then decline result. There can be no question that the Time Traveller, simply by moving, by inventing a machine that transgresses the bounds of known possibility, is a kind of technological hero in the story: without his machine the future of the book would have been unplumbed. Yet technology, while it witnesses to intellectual daring, witnesses also to technical voracity: as his machine proceeds, technology declines to fading pastoral, and pastoral to the collapse of organic life altogether.

The condition of the built machine is duality. It is there from the first, even in Swift, whose adamant-driven Laputa's flight above the earth figures the dissociation of mind from body; a condition further figured in the total disconnection of the minds of Laputan thinkers from the world about them. As human construct, the machine is opposed to the organic and to nature. As product of mind, it ultimately figures the continued struggle of mind to dominate the physical and to make the universe intelligible. The mind of the Time Traveller is amply deployed in his story: first as synthetic, in the construction of the time machine; and then as analytic, in his layered interpretations of the diminished human society he encounters. In the latter role, his attempt at comprehending the future race he meets is conducted first in idealistic and pastoral terms; but later he is forced continually to modify his theories under the impact of brutal fact. Finally he is driven toward pure brutality itself, in his belief that the Eloi are the cattle of the Morlocks. Dualism remains: the last conclusion is still presented as a hypothesis (p. 82). And throughout the story, the Time Traveller glides above and through the material world, untouched by it as his machine surges through its numerous contingent manifestations, a classic image of mind's dominance of the material—if here to the point possibly of absorbing the material.

The point is put in the Traveller's own late reflection, "an animal perfectly in harmony with its environment is a perfect mechanism" (pp. 81–82). When mind and world are at one we have a perfect machine: Wells here approaches the notion of an organic machine, which at once recalls Kingsley and looks forward to his own later yearning for an organic world-state.[31] But the crux is the overcoming of duality. The Time Traveller *has* no environment: he simply travels. His inventiveness, which in itself continually throws his mind out of the present into future projections and plans, becomes, as it were, symbolized in the time machine itself. But it means that he must be perpetually mobile, with no real home. He is forced to leave the year 802, 701, he makes brief forays to the "final" future, and in the end he disappears again. Through his dependence on the machine he lacks a hold on reality: it may in fact be a mere accidental disturbance of the machine by the narrator that ensures that when the Traveller next climbs aboard it he finds himself driven once more into time, never to return. ("I ... put out my hand and touched the lever. At that the squat substantial-looking mass swayed like a bough shaken by the wind. Its instability startled me extremely, and I had a queer reminiscence of the childish days when I used to be forbidden to meddle"; and then, "I heard an exclamation, oddly truncated at the end, and a click and a thud" [p. 89].) We know the machine was heavy from the Traveller's difficulties in righting it when he first arrived in 802, 701. All this takes place just when the Traveller is about to give the narrator incontrovertible proof regarding time travel, something he strangely failed to do earlier with his prodigal party trick with the model he sent into the future (pp. 35–36). And arguably one "reason" for this is that the time machine has to remain improbable, cut off from a basis in reality, just as is its owner. And that of course could explain why the machine itself is given so little scientific explanation within the novel, but left as an uncertain and "aesthetic" construct, "a glittering metallic framework" of which "parts were of nickel, parts of ivory, parts had certainly been filed or sawn out of rock crystal" (pp. 34, 37). And beyond the Time Traveller's mind we have that of Wells himself, inventor of this book and of the explorations in it: a book that has been described as "a finely fashioned aesthetic machine,"[32] and has been presented by Wells as a mere fantasy, without the slightest basis in possible fact.[33]

The duality that Wells describes in the machine is not that of Dickens. In *Hard Times* it is the brainlessly physical that is dominant: machinery, "fact," and blind, blundering physics have crushed mind almost out of existence. But in Wells it is mind, and its child the wonderful machine, that dominates and degrades the physical, whether that "physical" be nature, society, or even the body itself. In Wells's romances the machine is no longer a tool of society: it has taken on a life of its own, which makes it a threat to the very structure of existence or to the continuation of civilization. It has become in a sense renegade. (It might even be seen as a symbol of contemporary anarchism.) Divorced from the world, with only tenuous relation to the physical bodies or times it inhabits, the machine begins to erode its environment. That environment becomes frail: in *The Time Machine* the future is made permeable, and its products are effete; in *The War of the Worlds* human society is helpless before aliens, and bodies are reduced to mere pulsating organic essentials. And yet, by strange operation of the same logic, that Olympian mind and its products are themselves made evanescent: the Time Traveller's machine is finally lost by accident, and the Martians are overthrown at the height of their power by a weakness they could not have foreseen. In parallel, the invisibility of Griffin in *The Invisible Man* (1897) makes him helpless (and itself wears off and lays him open to destruction), and the beast-men in *The Island of Dr. Moreau* revert, destroying their creator. The thrust of Wells's attack is against the overweening pride of intellect, even while he admires its products; and in this warning he is peculiarly a modern.

The War of the Worlds is, like *The Time Machine*, in part an exposure of human complacency, here against the backcloth of space rather than time. One of its satiric thrusts is effectively at the earlier Victorian belief that the application of machines would eradicate war. In this novel Wells not only shows how war and conquest are furthered by technology, but presents us with a war in part conducted between rival machines. Further, by encasing the Martians entirely within their war-machines, which they operate from inside like organic computers, Wells creates a setting in which to the beholder the machine appears capable of independent thought and action, and becomes known as "the Martian":

> the Martian's hood pointed at the batteries that were still firing across the river, and as it advanced it swung loose what must have been the generator of the Heat-Ray.
>
> In another moment it was on the bank, and in a stride wading half-way across. The knees of its foremost legs bent at the further bank, and in another moment it had raised itself to its full height again, close to the village of Shepperton. Forthwith the six guns, which, unknown to anyone on the right bank, had been hidden behind the outskirts of that village, fired simultaneously. (pp. 100–101)

But the facts of these "Martians" are that the machines are merely manufactured bodies, and the Martians themselves are physically almost helpless, especially in the denser air of Earth. They are "huge round bodies" covered with a brown oily skin, with large eyes and "a kind of fleshy beak" surrounded by tentacles: basically they are mostly brain, sustained by a heart and lungs (pp. 205–6, compare pp. 27–28). They are reminiscent of squids, but without their mobility and strength:[34] their manner of reproduction by asexual budding makes them nearer to the primitive polyp (pp. 209–10) or even to that last phase of life witnessed by the Traveller in *The Time Machine*—a bleak football-like object trailing tentacles. The Martians are in fact the product of intellectual advance, whereby "the perfection of mechanical appliances must ultimately supersede limbs, the perfection of chemical devices, digestion…. The brain alone remained a cardinal necessity" (pp. 210–11). Wells had posed a similar picture in "The Man of the Year Million" (1893), with future humanity advanced to giant brains in liquid suspension, sitting far beneath the earth in order to survive the dying of the sun;[35] but in *The War of the Worlds* the picture is far more sinister.[36] The dualism of mind and body here has gone a stage beyond that in *The Time Machine*, for mind has so developed as to discard, so far as it may, its attachment to organic body. Yet the paradox is that such dissociation has produced not more freedom but rather constriction and dependence on external aids: the Martians have in a sense rendered themselves a disabled race, wholly tied to prosthetic supports. Moreover, they are still joined to bodies: pure minds though they are, those minds are not machined computers, but work through neural streams within organic cellular structures, themselves sustained by basic organic components that cannot be repudiated. But "because" mind has refused body, body has degraded: gigantic brains inhabit the lowest shapes of physical life, and in addition the most gross and fleshly of forms.

Of course the story is long sustained on the powers and the sophistication of the Martians despite this manifest weakness, and it is not till later that analysis is made of the reasons for their physical form. What we have at first is a picture of a highly advanced mechanized civilization overcoming a more primitive one. The humans are slow to comprehend the threat, and when they do their guns and battleships are no match for the terrible heat ray or black smoke used by the Martians. In a few minutes the Martians wipe out a substantial proportion of the artillery strength of the entire British army. As the invaders converge on London, humanity panics, and the roads become choked with fleeing refugees. In a short time defeat is total, and humanity is driven into wretched hiding to await its fate. Thus Wells punctures the absurd pride of man, who complacently takes from evolutionary theory only the idea that he is the fittest, and neglects the fact that he became so only through constant struggle and watchfulness. Nor are the examples we are given of individual men very flattering: the crazed and cowardly curate is exposed for religious fatalism and effectively killed by the narrator; the apparently tough artillery man is actually a prototypic slave of the Martians pretending to be a fifth columnist for humanity; and even the narrator himself, for all his courage and love for his family, is still capable at the end of mixing Christian piety over man's salvation with anticipation of how man may now himself emulate the Martians and seek to colonize other planets.

What effectively the Martians are doing is destroying not only men and human machines but society itself, considered as a machine. The narrator asks, "Did they [the Martians] grasp that we in our millions were organized, disciplined, working together?" (pp. 140–41); but this social coherence is gone shortly afterward, as the Martians approach London and the imagery becomes that of uncontrolled nature:

> So you understand the roaring wave of fear that swept through the greatest city in the world just as Monday was dawning—the stream of flight rising swiftly to a torrent, lashing in a foaming tumult round the railway-stations, banked up into a horrible struggle about the shipping in the Thames, and hurrying by every available channel northward and eastward. By ten o'clock the police organization, and by mid-day even the railway organizations, were losing coherency, losing shape and efficiency, guttering, softening, running at last in that swift liquefaction of the social body.   (p. 150)

At the end, with the death of the Martians, this machine of society is reformed: shape, coherency, and efficiency are restored. The narrator gazes on London, "the great Mother of Cities," thinking of "the multitudinous hopes and efforts, the innumerable hosts of lives that had gone to build this human reef," rejoicing that "this dear vast dead city of mine [will] be once more alive and powerful" (pp. 285–86). The notion of an organic purposive body that is at the same time a construct of civilization and technical advance is renewed:

> The survivors of the people scattered over the country— leaderless, lawless, foodless, like sheep without a shepherd—the thousands who had fled by sea, would begin to return; the pulse of life, growing stronger and stronger, would beat again in the empty streets, and pour across the vacant squares.... All the gaunt wrecks, the blackened skeletons of houses that stared so dismally at the sunlit grass of the hill, would presently be echoing with the hammers of the restorers and ringing with the tapping of the trowels.   (pp. 286–87)

Recall the conclusion of the Time Traveller: "An animal perfectly in harmony with its environment is a perfect mechanism" (pp. 81–82). Beyond

man and his vanities and his frail machines is a far larger organic machine of
which he is a part and which, in the end, secures the defeat of the Martians.
The Earth of 802, 701 in *The Time Machine* has long been sterilized by science,
and nature has been reduced utterly to human control and manipulation: "The
ideal of preventive medicine was attained. Diseases had been stamped out. I
saw no evidence of any contagious diseases during all my stay. And I shall have
to tell you later that even the processes of putrefaction and decay had been
profoundly affected by these changes" (pp. 50–51). Not so in *The War of the
Worlds:* the Earth is swarming with bacteria, and the Martians have not been
vaccinated. It is bacteria, the very lowest forms of organic life, that defeat and
destroy the prodigiously advanced brains of the Martians. The irony of the
story is obvious: because the Martians have rejected the organic, become
"dissociated" from it, they are at its mercy, whether in their unwieldy bodies,
their pain in Earth's air and gravitation, or their deaths through infection. The
surest machines, Wells seems to be saying, are not those that divorce mind
from matter or separate technology from nature, but those that are organically
and viscerally integrated—as man, through long ages of vicissitude, has
become resistant to many germs of disease: "By the toll of a billion deaths, man
has bought his birthright of the earth, and it is his against all comers; it would
still be his were the Martians ten times as mighty as they are. For neither do
men live nor die in vain" (p. 283). In this last sentence is the law of
conservation of the organic machine: nothing is wasted, all goes to increase
efficiency. Wells seems very close here to the recent concept of the Earth as
Gaia, an ecosystem with its own immanent self-governance, even self-
consciousness: a cognitive biological machine.[37]

Technology and biology are at war in Wells. Mind has outrun body and
natural evolution (as the time machine literally outruns the temporal world).
In *The Time Machine* technology defeats biology, both in the way that the
development of science has totally subdued nature and in doing so atrophied
man, and in the sense that the time machine itself may be a factor in the later
decline of life and the death of the sun. In *The War of the Worlds* we have the
reverse process, whereby organic life renders sophisticated machines helpless
and static. There is no more vivid image of this process than the Fighting
Machines left standing about the pit of dead Martians: "The one had died,
even as it had been crying to its companions; perhaps it was the last to die,
and its voice had gone on perpetually until the force of its machinery was
exhausted. They glittered now, harmless tripod towers of shining metal, in
the brightness of the rising sun ..." (p. 285).

None of this denies the admiration that is given to the inventive powers
of mind and to the machine marvels that the mind begets. "One cannot

choose but wonder," says the narrator in *The Time Machine*; and so each novel
is framed as an experiment. But it is fair to say that in much British science
fiction there is always at least a dialogue, if not a conflict, between the impulse
to praise and the wish to restrain. It is in some American science fiction—that
of Larry Niven, Isaac Asimov, Philip J. Farmer, Greg Bear, or even of that
expatriate Briton, Arthur C. Clarke—that we find unmodified excitement at
the advanced artifact; even in Wells's own day the technical optimism of such
American utopianists as Edward Bellamy is a marked contrast.[38] The more
skeptical British have always given scant funds to research and development:
their best inventions often emerge from garden sheds.[39] Their sense of
landscape, their besotted love of animals, and their esteem for the individual
personality perhaps condition some of the British response to the machine.
Not of course that this fits Wells; but it is the substrate in which he is
nourished. In the end, it seems, nature, man, and machine must somehow be
integrated, just as within man ideally the mind does not become split from the
body it inhabits: if any one of these dominates, disaster is sure. That is why
Wells so often warns against the islanding of the self from the world, whether
in the image of Griffin's invisibility; or of the flitting time machine with its
solitary explorer; or of the actual island of Moreau; or of the blinkered
Martians, whose technical advance goes together with their organic decline
and whose lack of prior engagement with this world puts them at its mercy.
The theme that both *The Time Machine* and *The War of the Worlds* share is that
to go forward in technological isolation is to go backward biologically: a time
machine divorced from the real world and a science that defeats nature
produce devolution and solar entropy; a race that puts all premium on mind
and machine is reduced to the most primitive and frail of physical bodies. The
ultimate consequence of such divorce is a hollowing out of reality. The Time
Traveller wonders, "They say life is a dream, a precious poor dream at times—
but I can't stand another that won't fit. It's madness. And where did the dream
come from? ... I must look at that machine. If there is one!" (p. 88); and the
narrator of *The War of the Worlds* ends:

> I go to London and see the busy multitudes in Fleet Street and
> the Strand, and it comes across my mind that they are but the
> ghosts of the past, haunting the streets that seem silent and
> wretched, going to and fro, phantasms in a dead city, the mockery
> of life in a galvanized body. (p. 302)

The Time Traveller in the end is swallowed up in his dream; while the dream
that is *The War of the Worlds* infiltrates and subverts our so-solid reality.

NOTES

1. See Herbert L. Sussman, *Victorians and the Machine: The Literary Response to Technology* (Cambridge, Mass.: Harvard Univ. Press, 1968), esp. pp. 1–12, 228–33.

2. Disraeli, *Coningsby; or, The New Generation* (Leipzig: Tauchnitz, 1844), pp. 144–45.

3. Gaskell, *North and South* (London: Oxford Univ. Press, 1973), p. 69; cf. pp. 80–81.

4. Equally Butler in his "Book of the Machines" in *Erewhon* (1872) portrays an Erewhonian argument that machines have all the attributes of people and are therefore a dangerous threat that must be removed. He is actually by inversion satirizing the Huxleyan notion of likening organic life to the machine.

5. Charles Reade's *Put Yourself in His Place* (1870), which portrays improved machinery as the key to social betterment, is a lonely exception here.

6. See, e.g., Peter J. Bowler, *Evolution: The History of an Idea*, rev. ed. (Berkeley: Univ. of California Press, 1989), pp. 103–4.

7. Arnold, *Culture and Anarchy* (1869), ed. J. Dover Wilson (Cambridge: Cambridge Univ. Press, 1960), p. 49.

8. See, e.g., Walter E. Houghton, *The Victorian Frame of Mind, 1830–1870* (New Haven: Yale Univ. Press, 1957), pp. 27–45.

9. See Macaulay, *History of England*, in *The Complete Works of Lord Macaulay*, ed. Lady Trevelyan, 8 vols. (London: Longmans, Green, 1866), I, 290–91 (quoted in Houghton, p. 41). See also Houghton, pp. 35–41.

10. See Houghton, p. 41.

11. Kingsley, *The Water-Babies: A Fairy Tale for a Land-Baby* (London: Macmillan, 1863), p. 11.

12. In this he is actually following a contemporary tendency in science itself; see Sussman, pp. 135–38.

13. See Paley, *Natural Theology* (1802), chap. 1.

14. Kingsley, preface to *Westminster Sermons*, in *The Works of Charles Kingsley*, 28 vols. (London: Macmillan, 1879–84), XXVIII (1881), xxviii.

15. *Charles Kingsley: His Letters and Memories of His Life*, ed. Frances E. Kingsley, 2 vols. (London: Kegan Paul, 1876), II, 28.

16. Kingsley, *Glaucus; or, The Wonders of the Shore* (1855), *Works*, V (1879), 100.

17. Kingsley, *Madam How and Lady Why* (1869), *Works*, XIII (1880), 263; cf. pp. 298–99.

18. Kingsley, *Alton Locke, Tailor and Poet* (1850), *Works*, III (1881), 390.

19. See, e.g., *Charles Kingsley: His Letters and Memories*, I, 181.

20. Dickens, *Hard Times*, ed. George Ford and Sylvère Monod (New York: W. W. Norton, 1966), p. 17.

21. See, e.g., R.A. Forsyth, *The Lost Pattern: Essays on the Emergent City Sensibility in Victorian England* (Nedlands, W.A.: Univ. of Western Australia Press, 1976), pp. 54–55.

22. On which see I. F. Clarke, *Voices Prophesying War, 1763–1984* (London: Oxford Univ. Press, 1966), esp. chap. 2.

23. On pre-Wellsian science fiction, see Darko Suvin, *Victorian Science Fiction in the UK: The Discourses of Knowledge and Power* (Boston: G.K. Hall, 1983).

24. See Peter Nicholls, ed., *The Encyclopaedia of Science Fiction: An Illustrated A to Z* (London: Granada, 1981), p. 371. Useful accounts of technical change in the Victorian period are Lewis Mumford, *Technics and Civilization* (London: Routledge, 1934); and

Charles Singer, E.J. Holmyard, A.R. Hall, and Trevor I. Williams, eds., *A History of Technology*, 5 vols. (Oxford: Clarendon Press, 1958), vol. V, *The Late Nineteenth Century, c. 1850 to c. 1900*. For the way technological change altered the understanding of time and space in the period, see Stephen Kern, *The Culture of Space and Time, 1880–1918* (Cambridge, Mass.: Harvard Univ. Press, 1983).

25. See, e.g., Kingsley, *Sermons on National Subjects, Works*, XXII (1880), 109–10.

26. See Langdon Winner, *Autonomous Technology: Technics-out-of-Control as a Theme in Political Thought* (Cambridge, Mass.: MIT Press, 1977), esp. pp. 1–43.

27. "Perspectivism" was first promoted by Nietzsche in 1887, and formulated as a theory by the Spanish philosopher José Ortega y Gasset, who in a 1916 lecture also linked it to the theory of relativity (see Kern, pp. 150–52).

28. See *The War of the Worlds* (London: William Heinemann, 1898), pp. 4–5.

29. Harry N. Geduld, *The Definitive Time Machine: A Critical Edition of H.G. Wells's Scientific Romance with Introduction and Notes* (Bloomington and Indianapolis: Indiana Univ. Press, 1987), p. 82.

30. In his "Another Basis for Life" (22 Dec. 1894; repr. *H.G. Wells: Early Writings in Science and Science Fiction*, ed. Robert M. Philmus and David Y. Hughes [Berkeley: Univ. of California Press, 1975], pp. 144–47), Wells accepted the theory, "On the supposition, accepted by all scientific men, that the earth is undergoing a steady process of cooling ..." (p. 145): he clearly had the perspective to see that this position might be challenged in the future. See also Philmus and Hughes, pp. 4, 89–90 nn. 1, 3, 102 n. 1; and Bowler, *Evolution*, pp. 137–38, 206–7, on Kelvin and his influence.

31. E.g. in "The World Organism" (1902, 1914; repr. in *H.G. Wells: Journalism and Prophecy, 1893–1946*, ed. W. Warren Wagar [London: The Bodley Head, 1964], pp. 273–76).

32. Frank D. McConnell, *The Science Fiction of H.G. Wells* (New York: Oxford Univ. Press, 1980), p. 88.

33. See Wells's preface to *The Scientific Romances of H.G. Wells* (1933; repr. in *H.G. Wells's Literary Criticism*, ed. Patrick Parrinder and Robert M. Philmus [Sussex: Harvester Press, and Totowa, N.J.: Barnes and Noble, 1980], pp. 240–41).

34. Wells had written a story of squidlike invaders from the sea in his "The Sea Raiders" (1896).

35. Repr. in *Journalism and Prophecy*, pp. 3–8.

36. As it is again in the giant ganglion that is the Grand Lunar in Wells's *The First Men in the Moon* (1901).

37. See Lawrence E. Joseph, *Gaia: The Growth of an Idea* (New York: St. Martin's Press, 1990), esp. chaps. 1–3, 11.

38. See also Roger Neustadter, "Mechanization Takes Command: The Celebration of Technology in the Utopian Novels of Edward Bellamy, Chauncey Thomas, John Jacob Astor, and Charles Caryl," *Extrapolation*, 29 (1988), 21–33.

39. The history of the nineteenth-century inventor Charles Babbage and the Analytical Engine, his disregarded anticipation of the computer, is instructive here (see Anthony Hyman, *Charles Babbage: Pioneer of the Computer* [Oxford: Oxford Univ. Press, 1982]).

KATHRYN HUME

Eat or Be Eaten:
H.G. Wells's Time Machine

"It is very remarkable that this is so extensively overlooked," says the Time Traveller, speaking of time as the fourth dimension.[1] Similarly remarkable is the way we have overlooked the comprehensive functions of oral fantasies in *The Time Machine*. They play a fourth dimension to the other three of entropy, devolution, and utopian satire. They ramify, by regular transformations, into those other three; into the social and economic worlds of consumption and exploitation; and into the realm of gender anxieties. They transform the ideological commonplaces from which the text constructs its reality. They create a network of emotional tensions that subliminally unites the three time frames: Victorian England, the Realm of the Sphinx, and the Terminal Beach. At the same time, this nexus of related images undercuts and fragments the logical, scientific arguments being carried out on the surface of the tale.

The Time Machine is the first of Wells's scientific romances to achieve canonical status.[2] In their eagerness to elevate and assimilate this text, however, critics have lost awareness that some of its parts are not explained by their normal critical strategies. One such feature to disappear from critical discourse is the failure of any coherent social message to emerge from the world of the Eloi and Morlocks. Another partly repressed feature is the disparity between the Time Traveller's violent emotions and the experiences

From *Philological Quarterly*, vol. 69, no. 2. © 1990 by the University of Iowa.

that evoke them.[3] A third feature lost to view is the dubious logic that binds the two futuristic scenarios.

I would like to approach the text with both the oral image complex and these elided mysteries in mind. What emerges will not fill the gaps in the narrative logic; the text resists such treatment, for reasons that will be shown. Rather, I wish to explore the hidden dynamics of emotion and logic. Since the semes attached to eating, consumption, and engulfment point in so many directions, I shall start instead with the public ideologies of power, size and gender. Then we can explore their symbolic manifestations as fantasies of being eaten or engulfed; as equations involving body size, intelligence, and physical energy; and as gender attributes projected on the world. Once sensitized to these concerns, we can examine the two future scenarios and their relationship to the Victorian frame. By exploring the interplay of ideology with its symbolic distortions, we will better sense what the text represses, and why despite (or even because of) this hidden material, the book has such disturbing power.

IDEOLOGICAL ASSUMPTIONS

Ideology, used here in Roland Barthes' sense, means the unexamined assumptions as to what is natural and inevitable and hence unchangeable. One realizes these "inevitabilities" to be historical and contingent most readily by comparing cultures, for within a culture, the ideological is taken to be "real."

The part of the general ideology relevant here consists of a nexus of values that include power, body size, and gender. Separating the values even to this extent is artificial; they intertwine tightly, and in turn link to other values such as dominance, exploitation, race, physical height, and bodily strength. They also merge with political and social and military power. The form taken by this family of assumptions in England made the British Empire possible.

Let us assume you are a nineteenth-century Briton—white, male, and a member of the politically powerful classes. You are also nominally Christian and equipped with the latest weaponry. You could expect to march into any country not blessed with most of these characteristics and expropriate what you wanted, be it raw material, cheap labor, land, or valuables. Such power gives the ability to exploit and consume. The so-called inferior races had no choice, since their technology was insufficient to resist British force. The Traveller's outlook is very much that of the nineteenth-century Briton among the aliens. His strength, technological know-how, and culture elevate him in his own mind. He scribbles his name on a statue, much as other nineteenth-century Britons carved theirs on Roman and Greek temples. To the empire builders, killing Africans or Indians was not "really" murder; they were Other and hence less than truly human. While the Traveller controls his impulse to massacre Morlocks (and is even praised for his restraint by one critic),[4] he smashes at their skulls in a way he would never dream of doing in Oxford Street. He is outraged (as well as frightened) when his trespassing machine is impounded. In the "kangaroo" and "centipede" episode found in the *New Review* serialization of the novel, his immediate impulse is to hit one of the kangaroo-like creatures on the skull with a rock. When examination of the body suggests that it is of human descent, he feels only a flash of "disagreeable apprehension," evidently directed toward this proof of Man's degeneration, not at his own murderous action. His regret at leaving the body (possibly just unconscious) to the monstrous "centipede" appears to be regret at the loss of a scientific specimen, not guilt at leaving this "grey animal ... or grey man" to be devoured.[5] He protects himself from any acknowledgment of this self-centeredness by viewing his urges as scientific, but ultimately he sees himself as having the right to whatever he wants, and cherishes himself for being the only "real" human and therefore the only creature with rights.

Part of this superiority stems from physical size, the second element in the ideology and one closely linked to power. Size generally permits a man to feel superior to women, and a British man to feel superior to members of shorter races. In English, size is a metaphor used to indicate that which is valuable, good, desirable. "Great," "high," and "large" are normally positive markers.[6]

In the two paragraphs that encompass the narrator's first language lesson and his response to it, we find the word "little" used eight times. Attached in his mind to the littleness of the Eloi is their "chatter," their tiring easily, their being "indolent" and "easily fatigued," and their "lack of interest" (p. 35). Littleness and its associated debilities are so grotesquely prominent that one cannot help note this obsession with the inferiority attaching to bodies of small size. What the narrator thinks will shape and limit what he hears and sees. When he first hears the Eloi (p. 29), they look and sound like "men" running. Later, his senses register "children": "I heard cries of terror and their little feet running" (p. 46).

The ideological inferiority of littleness is reinforced for readers by the Traveller's reactions to artifacts of the prior civilization. He admires and wonders at the "ruinous splendor" consisting of "a great heap of granite, bound together by masses of aluminium, a vast labyrinth of precipitous walls" (p. 36).

He cannot describe such a building without expressing this admiration for sheer size: the buildings are "splendid," "colossal," "tall," "big," "magnificent," "vast," "great," and "huge." He never wonders whether the size was functional and if so, how. Nor does he speculate on whether it was achieved through slave labor, as were the colossal monuments of antiquity which it resembles, with its "suggestions of old Phoenician decorations" (p. 33). He simply extends automatic admiration to such remains because of their impressive size.

The third element in the common ideology, besides power and size, is gender. Power and size support the superior status of maleness. Wells extends this prejudice to the point of defining humanity as male. Early in his narrative, the Time Traveller recounts his fear that "the race had lost its manliness" (p. 28). No sooner does he identify the Eloi as shorter than himself than they become "creatures" and are quickly feminized with such terms as "graceful," "frail," "hectic beauty," "Dresden china type of prettiness." All later descriptions use codes normally applied to women or children: mouths small and bright red, eyes large and mild, a language that sounds sweet and liquid and cooing and melodious. Ultimately, he equates loss of manliness with loss of humanity.

To sum up the ideological assumptions: the text shows as natural and inevitable the interconnection of power, size and male gender. Wells was to prove capable of challenging the politics of power in later scientific romances. He questions the might-makes-right outlook of Empire in his reference to the Tasmanians in *The War of the Worlds* (1898), and in Dr. Moreau's parodic imposition of The Law on inferior beings (1896). Callousness towards non-British sentients is rebuked by Cavor, who is shocked by Bedford's slaughter of Selenites in *The First Men in the Moon* (1901). However, though power may be somewhat negotiable to Wells, size and maleness remain positively marked throughout the scientific romances. In *The Food of the Gods* (1904), size automatically conveys nobility of purpose, and this idealized race of giants consists so exclusively of men that it will have trouble propagating.

If this text merely echoed the ideology of its times, *The Time Machine* (1895) would be drab and predictable. The symbolic enlargements and distortions of these values are what create the images and tensions that make it interesting, so let us turn to them.

Symbolic Transformations of Ideology

Power belongs to the same family of values as "exploitation" and "consumption." These terms from the political and economic spheres take on added resonances when they emerge as oral fantasies about eating and being eaten. As Patrick A. McCarthy points out, cannibalism lies at the heart of this darkness, or so at least the Traveller asseverates.[7] Actually, the evidence for cannibalism is far from complete, as David Lake observes, and the narrator may be jumping to totally unwarranted conclusions. However the notion of humans as fatted kine for a technologically superior group will reappear in *The War of the Worlds*, so it evidently held some fascination for Wells. The latter book certainly makes the connection between eating people and economic exploitation,[8] a parallel made famous by Swift's "Modest Proposal."

The putative cuisine of the Morlocks is only the most obvious of the oral fantasies. "Eat or be eaten" is a way of characterizing some social systems, but in Wells's futures, the words are literally applicable, and the text regales us with variations upon the theme of eating. The Time Traveller fears that the Morlocks will feed upon him as well as on Eloi. In the extra time-frame of the *New Review* version, the centipede appears to be hungry. The crabs make clear their intentions to consume the Traveller. The Sphinx traditionally devoured those who could not guess her riddle; the Traveller's entering her pedestal constitutes but a slight displacement of entering her maw. The Victorian frame features a prominent display of after-dinner satisfactions (including drinks, cigars, and feminized chairs that embrace and support the men) and a meal at which the Traveller urgently gobbles his food. Oral fantasies also take the forms of engulfment: one can be overwhelmed, drowned, swallowed by darkness, or rendered unconscious. Both in the narrator's dreams and in his physical adventures, we find several such threats of dissolution.

Norman Holland observes that "the single most common fantasy-structure in literature is phallic assertiveness balanced against oral engulfment,"[9] exactly the pattern of *The Time Machine*. Typical of the phallic stage anxieties is the exploration of dark, dangerous, and congested places. Time travel and other magic forms of travel are common omnipotence fantasies at this stage of development. So is the pre-oedipal polarization of agents into threatening and non-threatening, and the focus on a single figure. Opposing this phallic quest are oral anxieties. One such wave of anxiety oozes forth as the engulfing embraces of night (e.g., "dreaming ... that I was drowned, and that sea-anemones were feeling over my face with their soft palps"—p. 57). Another such anxiety grips the narrator when he faces the yawning underworld; indeed, upon escaping from below, he collapses in a dead faint. The threat of being eaten, and the enfolding gloom of the Terminal Beach are two others.

The protagonist faces engulfment of body and mind. When he returns to his own time, he responds with typical defenses against oral anxieties; he eats something ("Save me some of that mutton. I'm starving for a bit of meat"—p. 18), and he tells his tale. Holland observes that "a common defense against oral fusion and merger is putting something out of the mouth ... usually speech" (p. 37).

This fantasy content forecloses many options for plot development. Within the economy of oral anxieties, the subject eats or is eaten; there is no third way. When the Time Traveller finds himself on the Terminal Beach, where nothing appears edible or consumable or exploitable, he cannot assert his status as eater. Evidently, he subliminally accepts power relationships in terms of this binary fantasy, and thus dooms himself to being devoured through sheer default of cultural imagination. His technological magic may permit him to withdraw physically, but psychically, he is more defeated than triumphant at the end. Like his strategic withdrawal from the underworld, his departure is a rout. We note that although he returns home, he does not long remain. He is swallowed up by past or future.[10]

The commonplace assumptions in this text about bodily size undergo equivalent amplifications and distortions that affect the plot. We find elaborate equations between bodily size, intelligence, and bodily energy. Some of these simply reflect the science of the day. Researchers were establishing averages for sizes and weights of male and female brains, and followed many dead-end theories as they tried to prove what they were looking for: superiority of men over women and of whites over darker races. Furthermore, many scientists were convinced that the First Law of Thermodynamics, conservation of energy, applied to mental "energy" as well as physical.

> Food was taken in, energy (including thought) emerged, and the energy was "an exact equivalent of the amount of food assumed and assimilated." In Hardaker's crudely quantitative universe bigger was definitely better, and men were bigger.[11]

If the human race dwindles in size, so will its brain size, so will intelligence, and so will physical energy. Thus much is good science of the day. The text moves from science to symbolism, however, in linking the First and Second Laws of Thermodynamics and implying that energy loss in the universe will directly diminish the mental and physical energy of humanity. Although Wells does not state this explicitly, he apparently accepted it. The loss of culture and security would otherwise have reversed the devolutionary decline as the descendants of humans had once more to struggle for existence. This reason for species degeneration remains implicit, but it clearly follows the fantastic elaboration of ideology and science.

The explicit reason given for degeneration is Darwinian. The Traveller decides that strength and size must have declined because they were no longer needed for survival: "Under the new conditions of perfect comfort and security, that restless energy, that with us is strength, would become weakness.... And in a state of physical balance and security, power, intellectual as well as physical, would be out of place" (p. 42). Such a safe society dismays him. He relishes swashbuckling physical action, and is loath to consider a world that would exclude it. Indeed the Morlocks provide him with a welcome excuse to exercise powers not wanted in London. "I struggled up, shaking the human rats from me, and, holding the bar short, I thrust where I judged their faces might be. I could feel the succulent giving of flesh and bone under my blows, and for a moment I was free" (p. 95). "Succulent" is highly suggestive, relating as it does to the realm of the edible.

The equivalence of body, mind, and energy determines major features of the futuristic scenarios. We find something like medieval planes of correspondence. As the cosmos runs down, men will lose energy individually—a linkage no more logical than the Fisher-King's thigh wound causing sterility to fall upon the crops of his realm. Given this as a textual assumption about reality, however, we can see that clever, efficient and adaptive beings are impossible, although a setting like the Terminal Beach would call forth precisely such a humanity in the hands of other writers.

Gender, the third ideological element, undergoes a different kind of symbolic transformation. The traditional semes of "masculine" and "feminine"—whether culturally derived or natural—are widely familiar and even transcend cultural boundaries. Semes of the masculine include such constellated values as culture, light, the Sun, law, reason, consciousness, the right hand, land, and rulership. The feminine merges with chaos, darkness, the Moon, intuition, feeling, the left hand, water, and the unconscious.[12] The dialogue between them in some cultures involves balance; in the West, however, we find masculine consciousness fighting off or being overwhelmed by the feminine powers associated with unconsciousness. Thus the eat-consume-overwhelm nexus also enters the story as an attribute of gender.

Much of what troubles us in the realm of the Sphinx derives its power from the text's manipulation of these values. The grotesque is frequently formed from the mingling of characteristics from two "naturally" separate sets, man and beast, for instance. Despite cultural changes since the turn of the century, the traditional assumptions about gender are well enough ingrained in us by reading, if nothing else, to give the story's grotesques most of their original power. Wells attaches but also denies "feminine" and "masculine" attributes to both Eloi and Morlocks. The resulting contradictions prevent us from resolving the tensions roused by these grotesques into the kinds of reality that we are culturally conditioned to find comfortable.

The Eloi at first appear to be the only race, and then the superior of the two. Their life consists of a pastoral idyll, sunlight, and apparent rulership. Thanks to happiness, beauty, absence of poverty, and uninterrupted leisure, their life better fits our notion of Haves than Havenots. However, closer inspection shows them to be small, lacking in reason, deficient in strength, passively fearful, ineffectual, and ultimately just not "masculine" enough to be plausible patriarchal rulers, the standard against which they are implicitly held. In the *National Observer* version the Eloi have personal flying machines, but Wells ultimately deprived them of anything so technical. For all that they are feminized, however, they lack positive identity with the feminine, so we cannot reconcile them to our sense of the real by means of that pattern.

The Morlocks, by virtue of living in the dark and underground, seem first of all sinister, but secondarily are marked with symbolism of the unconscious and hence the feminine. Their access to the innards of the Sphinx reinforces the latter. Confusing our judgment, however, is their possible control of the machines, a power linked in Western eyes with the masculine rather than the feminine. Likewise, their apparently predatory aggression, their hunting parties (if such they be) fit "masculine" patterns. However, they seem deficient in strength and size to the Traveller, and their inability to tolerate light makes them obviously vulnerable in ways not befitting a "master" race. When comparing the two races, we find that both have traits associated with ruling and exploiting. The Eloi apparently live off the labor of the Morlocks while the latter apparently live off the flesh of the former. However, both are "feminized" in ways that render them less than masterful. These ambiguities in the cultural symbol system cannot be resolved. The traits associated with each race remain in uneasy tension, and contribute to the difficulty that critics have had in putting labels to the two races.

Power, size, and gender; oral fantasies, the laws of thermodynamics as applied to bodies and thought, and the grotesque: this peculiar mixture propels the story and gives it much of its intensity, its disturbing power. However, these concepts are not entirely consistent and harmonious. The conflicts they generate undermine the narrative logic and thereby dissolve the coherence of the ideas Wells was exploring. As we move to the future scenarios, we will note the gaps in the logic.

IN THE RIDDLING REALM OF THE SPHINX

Almost any way we approach this addled utopia, we find irreducible ambiguity. Does *The Time Machine* seriously concern a possible—albeit distant—future, or is futurity only a metaphoric disguise for the present? Darko Suvin focuses on the biological elements of the story, so he views the futurity as substantial and important. Others who focus on entropy or time travel likewise assume the significance of the futurity.[13] After all, without a real time lapse, anatomical evolution would be impossible. Alternatively, the "future" settings may be read as versions of Wells's present. "If the novella imagines a future, it does so not as a forecast but as a way of contemplating the structures of our present civilization."[14] Social warnings of danger 800,000 years away will inevitably fail to grip. Hence, the reality of time in this text—Wells's cherished fourth dimensional time—depends upon whether readers are focusing on biological or social systems.

Even if the critic ruthlessly simplifies to one or the other, interpretations go fuzzy at the edges or lead to contradiction. The biological reading appears at first to be straightforward. Wells asks, "what if progress is not inevitable and devolution can happen as well as evolution?" The Traveller decides that the Eloi degenerate because they no longer need to fight for survival—an interesting argument to present to the increasingly non-physical Victorian society. The need for serious, bodily rivalry makes utopia a dangerous goal, and social restraint unhealthy. Wells thus raises a genuine problem, but does not develop it.

The social reading is yet more disturbing in its inability to satisfy the expectation of coherence. Oppressing the working class is dangerous as well as inhumane, and if we continue along such lines, the Haves will fall prey to the Havenots. At first glance, this seems like an unexceptional social warning about mistreating the Workers. Somewhat unexpectedly, Wells treats the situation not as a revolution devoutly to be desired, but as a nightmarish terror. He evidently could not work up much sense of identification with the exploited. Hence the dilemma: not improving conditions leads to nightmare, but improving them in the direction of equality gets us back to utopia and its degeneration. If one accepts the biological message—physical competition—one must ignore the social message; if one accepts the social—improved conditions—one must ignore the biological. Wells offers us no way to accept both.

Since these two approaches lead to contradiction, one might try to escape the ambiguity by generalizing the referents of Eloi and Morlocks. Then one can read this as a parable about human nature,[15] or opt for Bergonzi's approach, and see the struggle between Eloi and Morlocks as polysemous. They are Pre-Raphaelite aesthetes and proletarians, and their struggle variously resonates with "aestheticism and utilitarianism, pastoralism and technology, contemplation and action, and ultimately ... beauty and ugliness, and light and darkness" (Bergonzi, p. 305). If you are content, with Bergonzi, to call the tale "myth" and agree that meaning in myth is always multiple, you have one solution to the problem of interpretation. Otherwise, you must accept that the Eloi and Morlocks do not form coherent portraits. Their unstable identities—e.g., Morlocks as underclass or rulers—seem better likened to the duck/rabbit optical illusion, which has two embedded forms but which we are compelled to see as only one at a given time. The Eloi are an upper class in terms of pleasant material living conditions and freedom from toil, but they are an exploited class if they are being kept as cattle. The same double-identity obscures any explanation of the Morlocks. I have argued elsewhere that another possibility is that the two represent a dual assessment of the middle class alone: on the surface, we find an idealized and ineffectual claim to sweetness and light and vague aestheticism, but the vicious, exploitive side of bourgeois power, which preys upon the helpless, is hidden (Hume, pp. 286–87). We can (and will) make many other such equations because each reader's assumptions will activate different voices within the text. Resolution, though, is unlikely. The two races have been rendered permanently ambiguous through their clashing qualities.

They also resist interpretation because of the disparity between the Traveller's emotions and what he actually experiences. The Morlocks are only guilty of touching him and of trying to keep him from leaving them. They use no weapons, and they attempt to capture rather than kill him. They may be interested in studying him or in trying to establish communication. After all, as Lake points out, the Morlocks apparently visit the museum out of curiosity. The Traveller is as ready to jump to dire conclusions as Bedford is in *The First Men in the Moon*. What pushes him to such extremes of fear and loathing may be his deep uneasiness over code violations. The grotesque mixing of masculine and feminine and of human and animal seem to produce in him much the sort of panic and hostility as that felt by some people towards transvestites and physical freaks.

Even the Sphinx plays her part in such confusions. "The State" and its powers are conventionally symbolized by the masculine, the father, the lawgiver. Wells's symbols for government are patriarchal in other romances, and his heroes either rebel against this oedipal oppressor or make their way into patriarchal power and identify with it. Dr. Moreau is such a threatening father, indeed a not-very-displaced castrating father. Almost all the clashes over authority in *The Food of the Gods* are put in terms of fathers and sons. The Invisible Man's hatred for established authority causes him to act in a way that literally kills his father. The Martians allow the protagonist to project his dissatisfactions with the social system onto an enemy, and with the defeat of the enemy, take up a patriarchal role and uphold the status quo.

The Sphinx, though, is female, the spawn of chaos.[16] She looms over the landscape, evidently the symbol of a ruling power, present or past, but also a grotesque yoking of beast and woman. (The other ornaments in her realm—a griffin and a faun—are also hybrids.) Bram Dijkstra has explored the Sphinx in late nineteenth-century art. He sees her renditions there as embodying tensions between the sexes that reflect male fears of

> a struggle between woman's atavistic hunger for blood—which she regarded as the vital fluid of man's seminal energies and hence the source of that material strength she craved—and man's need to conserve the nourishment that would allow his brain to evolve. Woman was a perverse instrument of the vampire of reversion, and by giving in to her draining embrace, men thought, they must needs bleed to death. (Dijkstra, p. 332)

In the art of this era, then, we find the same configuration of man being consumed, that consumption being carried out in such a way as to diminish not only his manly strength but also his intelligence. Oral fantasies here merge with the peculiarly end-of-the-century way of construing conservation of energy in physical and mental terms. Wells's world ruled by the Sphinx is indeed one bled of its masculinity and mental power, a world of reversion.

Wells's susceptibility to such oral anxieties is underlined by another gap in the logic. The oral fears emerge in a curiously skewed form. Haves normally exploit, "eat," or consume Havenots in a capitalist system; that is how the image usually enters socio-economic discourse. In *The Time Machine*, however, the cannibalistic urges are instead projected onto the Havenots. One finds a similar reversed logic in the martial fiction of America and England in the period of 1870 to the 1920s. Those white, Anglo-American populations who were spreading empire and invading the Philippines or carrying out wars in India and Africa entertained themselves with invasion tales in which they themselves were the victims. *The War of the Worlds* is just such an invasion tale, probably the greatest to emerge out of this literary type in England. Wells likens Martian treatment of Britons to British treatment of Tasmanians. America battened on fictions about the Black Menace, the Yellow Menace, the Red Menace, not to mention fears that England, Canada, or Mexico would invade America. Throughout the same period, America was stripping Native Americans of land and lynching Blacks, and sending armies to the Philippines and Haiti.[17] Whether Wells is using this trick of mind to characterize his protagonist, or whether Wells himself is denying political guilt and replacing it with self-justifying political fears simply is not clear. The application of the cannibalistic fantasy to the exploited group remains a notable gap in the logical fabric of the whole.

What are we to make of this adventure in the realm of the Sphinx, then? A rather mixed message, at best. Utopias by most definitions eliminate competition. This proves a dangerous ideal, because so safe an environment would encourage bodily weakness, and then degeneration of mind and feminization. In other words, beware Socialism! However, the paradise of capitalists is a world in which the Great Unwashed lives underground, its misery unseen and ignored. This too leads to degeneration, as we see, because it also abolishes real struggle. Without the chance or need to compete—literally to destroy or exploit or "consume"—man devolves, according to Wells's ideology. The importance of competition comes out when we realize its relevance to power, size, and masculine behavior patterns, and its status as guarantor of intelligence. This competitive violence appears to be the most consistently upheld value in the first adventure, but even such struggle is undermined by the arguments in the second adventure, the excursion to the Terminal Beach. There entropy, by means of the planes of correspondences, cancels the energizing effect of struggling for existence.

THE TERMINAL BEACH: A JOURNEY TO THE INTERIOR

"Journey to the interior" nicely condenses what happens here. *The Time Machine* as a totality consists of a trip to the interior of some unknown land, as found in *She, Henderson the Rain King, Heart of Darkness*, and *The Lost Steps*. The foray from 800,000 to thirty million years into the future is an embedded journey to the interior, a *mise en abîme* repetition. Call the Terminal Beach a mindscape reached by being eaten. The Traveller enters the Sphinx much as Jonah or Lucian enter their respective whales.[18] Entropy may supply the logic that links the two scenarios, but the emotional unity derives from oral fantasies.

The Terminal Beach actually consists of two scenes and several fractional visions. The crab-infested litoral comes first, then the world in which life lingers in the form of a black, flapping, tentacled "football." The eclipse and snowflakes both belong to the second scene, increasing its inhospitability. However, both form a continuum of desolation and an invitation to despair.

That the Traveller's responses need not be quite so bleak becomes clear if we contrast Wells's handling this situation with what might be called the Germinal Beach in Arthur C. Clarke's *2010*. There, new life is discovered, but the physical conditions are much the same as in Wells, and Clarke clearly had both of Wells's beaches in mind. Clarke's setting consists of ice and water, where Wells has water, pebbles, and ice. Clarke's tragic snowflakes result from the ruptured space ship. Clarke offers a huge, slow-moving, semi-vegetative creature. Both authors suggest the frailty of life through flickering, flapping, flopping, intermittent movement. In *The Time Machine*, day and night "flap" as the Traveller zooms into the future; the black creature on the strand flops, a screaming butterfly flutters, crab mouths flicker, the sea surface ripples. The larval stages of Clarke's life-form remind the speaker of flowers and then butterflies, and then flop about like stranded fish. Wells eclipses the sun to squeeze the last drop of symbolic value out of the light and darkness; Clarke has his observer break their artificial light so that the phototropic life-form will return to the sea. The Time Traveller sees "a curved pale line like a vast new moon" (p. 107) and as the eclipse passes off, notes "a red-hot bow in the sky" (p. 109); Clarke's Dr. Chang notes that "Jupiter was a huge, thin crescent" (p. 81), [19] and a few pages after this scene, another character stares at a picture of Earth as a thin crescent looming above the Lunar horizon.

Even in the most distant future, the Time Traveller can breathe the atmosphere and can escape any immediate danger by pulling a lever, yet he despairs. Clarke's Chinese astronaut will die as soon as his oxygen runs out, yet he remains scientifically alert and basically excited and pleased, although the level of life visible in each scene is roughly the same: non-human, non-intelligent, and probably scarce. Clearly the two authors perceive the landscapes from different vantages. To Clarke, Europa is the key to hegemony of the outer planets, the source of "the most valuable substance in the Universe" (p. 66). With Europa's water and cold fusion, settlers would enjoy virtually unlimited power for themselves plus fuel for their spaceships. By contrast, the Time Traveller sees nothing worth colonizing in either scene, nothing to exploit or utilize, nothing to consume. Wells and Clarke are at one in valuing worlds for what we can exploit.

Again, Wells disturbs his Traveller by violating his codes for normal reality. Instead of finding light and dark, he finds all liminal and borderline colors and values: palpitating greyness, steady twilight (p. 104), a sun that glows dully, and a beach on which there are no waves, only an oily swell. An eclipse is suitably liminal as well, a state that produces neither true day nor true night. In addition to being in a permanently transitional phase, his world is also liminal with regards to land and water. The ocean has approached over the millennia; what was high land in Victorian London and 800,000 years later is about to be overwhelmed by the advancing ocean. Light and land, often mind-scape equivalents to mind and body, are threatened by the encroaching, engulfing forces of darkness and water. Insofar as sea and darkness have symbolic associations with the unconscious and the feminine, this threat repeats both the gender and oral anxieties seen in the earlier adventure.

One's first instinct upon reading the Terminal Beach chapter is to interpret it solely as a funereal rhapsody on entropy, as a look at the inevitable death of the sun and the ramifications of this eventuality for mankind. George H. Darwin provided Wells with ideas about tidal friction and slowed rotation. The Book of Revelation contributes water-turned-blood. These simple transformations, plus the narrator's depression at what he finds, make the bleakness and hopelessness seem natural and inevitable. I would argue that to some degree they are actually cultural and ideological.

One has only to look at *The War of the Worlds* or even *The First Men in the Moon* to see very different fictional responses to apparently dead-end situations. The protagonists in those stories, or various lesser characters, face new situations with the same sort of scientific curiosity and engagement shown by Clarke's Dr. Chang. They are not foolish optimists, but a bleak and threatening situation is cause for intellectual stimulation, for forming and confirming theories, for taking pride in observing new phenomena, for striving against the environment. The Time Traveller, though, seemingly suffers an entropic loss of his own energy as he observes that life in general has lost the struggle. The point of failure, however, actually came where Wells's thermodynamic fantasy overcame his Darwinian science. When the social system eventually disintegrated, the descendents of Eloi and Morlocks should have improved through survival of the fittest. His assumptions about mind, energy, and body, though, render his fictional creations helpless long before the final scenes. That helplessness was dictated by a fantastic distortion of the laws of thermodynamics, not by the laws themselves, so here again, we find the amplifications and elaborations of basic ideologies affecting plot. Mankind disappears because of one such fantasy; the Traveller's panic takes its form from another.

In superficial regards, *The Time Machine* is obviously enough a social satire to justify our expecting a reasonably coherent warning. The doubled identities of both Eloi and Morlocks turns them into the literary equivalent of an optical illusion. Coherence can no more emerge from them than from Escher's drawing of water flowing downhill in a circle. Scientifically, *The Time Machine* explores entropic decline, but refuses to give us ingenious humanity striving ever more ferociously to put off the inevitable. Humanity has already degenerated irreversibly through the exercise of what is generally considered its higher impulses. Even that would be a warning, but Wells undercuts it with his thermodynamic fantasies, which would bring about similar degeneration in any case through the links he posits among body and mind and energy. Thus do some of the rather fierce undercurrents in this romance break up its arguments, leaving them as stimulating fragments rather than logical structures. The powerful emotions both expressed by the Traveller and generated in readers are tribute to the sub-surface currents, especially the oral-stage anxieties. The torment they represent is most clearly seen in the blind, defensive, totally illogical projection of savagery and cannibalism upon the group most apparently exploited. Like the imperialistic nations fantasizing their own humiliation at the hands of invaders, Wells's Traveller, and possibly Wells himself, are projecting behavior upon others in ways that suggest considerable repressed social guilt.

The return of the repressed is important to the dynamics of this tale. I will finish my arguments with one further variant on that theme. When the Time Traveller seeks the ruler of the pastoral realm, he seeks an Absent Father, and finds instead the Sphinx, avatar of threatening femininity. Within the classical Greek world view, "man" is the proud answer to the Sphinx's riddle, and man as Oedipus vanquishes the feminine and chaotic forces from Western civilization. In *The Time Machine*, "man" is no longer as proud an answer, and man has no power to prevent the lapse from order towards entropy. One might even argue that this time-travelling Oedipus is to some degree the criminal responsible for the status quo, for the ideologies he embodies have limited his culture's vision and rendered alternatives invisible. The Greeks and their civilization based on patriarchal structures banished the Sphinx. Here, she returns, and she succeeds in swallowing humanity after all.

NOTES

1. The Atlantic edition of *The Works of H.G. Wells*, 1 (New York: Charles Scribner's Sons, 1924): 4–5.

2. Bernard Bergonzi rendered *The Time Machine* orthodox by bestowing upon it two charismatic labels: "ironic" and "myth." See *"The Time Machine:* An Ironic Myth," *Critical Quarterly* 2 (1960): 293–305.

3. See David J. Lake, "Wells's Time Traveller: An Unreliable Narrator?" *Extrapolation* 22, no. 2 (1981): 117–26.

4. John Huntington sees this mastery of his actions as index to the protagonist's superiority over both Eloi and Morlocks, since they lack such self-control. See *The Logic of Fantasy: H.G. Wells and Science Fiction* (Columbia U. Press, 1982), p. 51.

5. For details of this and many other variants, including a previously unpublished draft of an excursion into the past, see *The Definitive Time Machine: A Critical Edition of H.G. Wells's Scientific Romance*, with introduction and notes by Harry M. Geduld (Indiana U. Press, 1987), quotations from p. 179.

6. In her utopian novel, *The Dispossessed*, Ursula Le Guin calls our attention to this unthinking esteem for height by replacing commendatory terms based on size with those based on centrality.

7. See McCarthy's *"Heart's of Darkness* and the Early Novels of H.G. Wells: Evolution, Anarchy, Entropy," *Journal of Modern Literature* 13, no. 1 (1986): 37–60.

8. See Kathryn Hume, "The Hidden Dynamics of *The War of the Worlds,"* PQ 62 (1983): 279–92; Wells developed the connection more forcefully in the serialized version.

9. Norman N. Holland, *The Dynamics of Literary Response* (New York: W.W. Norton, 1975), p. 43.

10. For an argument in favor of the Traveller's being a traditional monomyth hero, and hence triumphant, see Robert J. Begiebing, "The Mythic Hero in H.G. Wells's *The Time Machine,"* *Essays in Literature,* 11 (1984): 201–10. Wells's many escape endings are analyzed by Robert P. Weeks in "Disentanglement as a Theme in H.G. Wells's Fiction," originally published in *Papers of the Michigan Academy of Science, Arts, and Letters* 39 (1954), reprinted in *H.G. Wells: A Collection of Critical Essays*, edited by Bernard Bergonzi (Englewood Cliffs, New Jersey: Prentice-Hall, 1976), pp. 25–31. Interestingly, Wells considered another kind of ending, at least in response to editorial pressures. In the version of this story serialized in *The National Observer*, the story ends with the Traveller referring to hearing his child crying upstairs because frightened by the dark. This *ad hoc* family man, however, may result from hasty termination of the serial. Henley, as editor, liked Wells's work while his replacement, Vincent, did not. See Geduld for such variants.

11. For the nineteenth-century science behind all the assumptions about body size and energy, see Cynthia Eagle Russett, *Sexual Science: The Victorian Construction of Womanhood* (Harvard U. Press, 1989), p. 105.

12. In other words, Yin, Yang, and Jung. These symbolic clusters of values are discussed and illustrated throughout both the following Jungian studies by Erich Neumann: *The Origins and History of Consciousness*, Bollingen Series 42 (Princeton U. Press, 1970) and *The Great Mother: An Analysis of the Archetype*, Bollingen Series 47 (Princeton U. Press, 1972).

13. Darko Suvin, *Metamorphoses of Science Fiction: On the Poetics and History of a Literary Genre* (Yale U. Press, 1979), chapter 10. For an analysis of time travel, see Veronica Hollinger, "Deconstructing the Time Machine," *Science-Fiction Studies* 14 (1987): 201–21.

14. Huntington, p. 41. Others focusing on social issues include Patrick Parrinder, *"News from Nowhere, The Time Machine* and the Break-Up of Classical Realism," *Science-*

Fiction Studies 3, no. 3 (1976): 265–74, and Wayne C. Connely, "H.G. Well's [sic] *The Time Machine:* It's [sic] Neglected Mythos," *Riverside Quarterly* 5, no. 3 (1972): 178–91.

15. Stephen Gill sees the Morlocks as "the bestial nature of human beings." Hennelly sees it about the failure to reconcile the contraries in the human heart, and Lake explores it as a protest against death. See Gill, *Scientific Romances of H.G. Wells: A Critical Study* (Cornwall, Ontario: Vesta Publications, 1975), p. 38, and Mark M. Hennelly, Jr., "*The Time Machine:* A Romance of 'The Human Heart,'" *Extrapolation* 20, no. 2 (1979): 154–67; and David J. Lake, "The White Sphinx and the Whitened Lemur: Images of Death in *The Time Machine,*" *Science-Fiction Studies* 6, no. 1 (1979): 77–84.

16. See Frank Scafella, "The White Sphinx and *The Time Machine,*" *Science-Fiction Studies* 8, no. 3 (1981): 255–65, p. 259. Bram Dijkstra explores the *fin de siècle* fascination with sphinxes in art in *Idols of Perversity: Fantasies of Feminine Evil in Fin-de-Siècle Culture* (Oxford U. Press, 1986), pp. 325–32.

17. For an analysis of the British version of such invasion jitters, see Cecil Degrotte Eby, *The Road to Armageddon: The Martial Spirit in English Popular Literature, 1870–1914* (Duke U. Press, 1987). For the American version, see H. Bruce Franklin, *War Stars: The Superweapon and the American Imagination* (Oxford U. Press, 1988).

18. Two mindscapes similarly reached in a physical interior are Harlan Ellison's "Adrift Just Off the Islets of Langerhans: Latitude 38° 54' N, Longitude 77° 00' 13" W," and Norman Spinrad's "Carcinoma Angels." In the latter, the protagonist psychically descends into his own body to kill cancer cells. He "finally found himself knee-deep in the sea of his digestive juices lapping against the walls of the dank, moist cave that was his stomach. And scuttling towards him on chitinous legs, a monstrous black crab with blood-red eyes, gross, squat, primeval." The Wellsian intertext enriches the cancer/crab wordplay. "Carcinoma Angels" is found in *Dangerous Visions*, ed. Harlan Ellison (London: Victor Gollancz, 1987), 513–21, quotation, p. 521.

19. The "Germinal Beach" occurs on pp. 77–82 of Arthur C. Clarke, *2010* (London: Granada, 1983).

WILLIAM J. SCHEICK

The De-Forming In-Struction of Wells's
The Wonderful Visit *and* The Sea Lady

W ells's *The Wonderful Visit* (1895) and *The Sea Lady* (1902) are even less popular now than they were when they first appeared. When they were published, both received mixed reviews, although their Swiftian satiric elements were generally appreciated; and today critics barely mention these works in passing. The subjects of these romances—the arrival of an angel from another dimension, the appearance of a mermaid from beneath the sea—seem implausible and slight in spite of their allegorical nature. This impression of triviality, however, might be the result of authorial sleight of hand, for these novels are more artistically accomplished than readers have generally suspected. In fact, if these works are considered in terms of their similar structural technique, we can begin to appreciate better what Wells invested in them as aesthetic expression.

In both romances structure, rather than characterization, is privileged, as is so often the case in Wells's fiction, early and late.[1] When fictional structure prevails over characterization in works by writers as self-aware as Wells, usually ethical concerns inform these narratives fundamentally, even sometimes are their primary *raison d'être*.[2] In *The Wonderful Visit* and *The Sea Lady* not only is structure privileged and ethical in its implication, but the one difference in authorial management of these otherwise similar structures signals a fluctuation in Wells's thought that finally highlights a difference in

From *English Literature in Transition*, vol. 30, no. 4. © 1987 by *English Literature in Transition*.

the philosophical ground of the the two novels. Generated by Wells's ambivalence concerning the ability of mankind to save itself from a more-than-likely hopeless tendency toward self-destruction, this divergence in philosophical ground can be measured in terms of a difference between Christian-humanist empathy and Schopenhauerian compassion. Since this variance in ethos is embodied in fictional structure, which is an aesthetic feature of the novels, careful attention to it will reveal something of the sophisticated artistry that can inform Wells's early writings even when they appear to be insubstantial.

I

In *The Wonderful Visit* there are two references to Max Nordau, whose *Degeneration*, in English translation, saw seven impressions in 1895.[3] Nordau focuses on the turn of the nineteenth century as a time of degenerating transition from the established order of tradition to the dehumanizing chaos of passionate egotism. Although this view is not endorsed in *The Wonderful Visit*, Nordau is mentioned because the allusion to his views suggests that the *fin de siècle* period is indeed a time of transition, a time, however, when humanity faces an opportunity to choose between a decline of the kind described by Nordau or an evolution of sensibility of the sort represented by the angel from another dimension of earthly possibility.

That humanity faces this critical choice is the message of *The Wonderful Visit*, but it is not a message readily apparent in the plot-structure of the romance. This plot-structure culminates in the near-death of Sir John Gotch, who is mean-spirited; the passing away of Delia Hardy, who evinced a capacity for sympathy absent in her elite employers; the demise of the angel, who was increasingly succumbing to the poison of human passion; and the decease of Vicar Hillyer, who "never seemed happy" again during the few months he lived after the fire that destroyed the vicarage and killed both Delia and the angel (275). Indeed, the plot-structure of *The Wonderful Visit* expresses a pessimism similar to the dark view of life depicted in Wells's early science-fiction.[4]

But *The Wonderful Visit* possesses a narrative-structure, one distinct from its plot-structure, that intimates the possibility of human development and sensibility. This structure is not optimistic; rather, it vexes the pessimistic thrust of the plot-structure by implicitly positing a human potentiality for positive change.[5] More subtle than the plot-structure, this narrative-structure is at first difficult to notice. It is the structure provided by the narrative voice, who consistently draws attention to himself and to the reader. The development of this structure implies the possibility of the evolution of the human mind by hinting at a correlation between the narrator's effort to arrive at a more advanced, informed account of events than the fragments related to him and the ideal reader's potential effort to arrive at a still more advanced, objective understanding of events beyond that of the narrator.

This narrative manner forms a tripartite pattern in which the narrator mediates between originally discordant accounts (principally rendered by Mrs. Mendham) and an exemplary sensitive reader. The pivotal importance of the narrator as a transitional figure struggling to organize data for the reader is emphasized through his numerous interruptions of his story, intrusions which draw attention to him and his function as a narrator.[6] "I am afraid it may be forgotten" (125); "I defy you to find another definition that will fit" (127); "I cannot tell you of the vision" (184); "as I think" (185); "for my own part I think" (237): such obstrusions, among many others in the text, indicate that the narrator is also a character in *The Wonderful Visit*, someone the reader might overlook if he tries to focus exclusively on the plot-structure of the account provisionally organized by the narrator. The narrator draws attention to himself not only in these relatively minor ways but also by enumerating the difficulties he encounters in trying to assemble the very story into which the engrossed reader is trying to escape. The narrator announces that he "is concerned with the facts of the case, and has neither the desire nor the confidence to explain them" (139); he at one point grumbles that he deserves a "resting place in this story" because he has "been hard at it, getting [the] story spread out" (177); and he admits that his account "is as much as anyone can tell you" (122), is as "far as [his] memory goes" (233). In short, the narrator is self-conscious and tentative, his voice negotiating between previous reporters and his readers. His voice (the text), moving between earlier accounts (the past) and the ideal thought-assembling reader (the future), symbolizes his (as well as Nordau's and Wells's) turn-of-the-century time, a crossroads, as it were, to be negotiated by the human race.[7]

The narrator's self-conscious intrusions interrupt the reader's absorption in the plot-structure and prevent his escape into the illusion of this feature of the romance. These intrusions are a deformity in the plot-structure, a deformity, a breakdown of form in the plot-structure; but this deformity/deformity gives life to an informing (message-bearing) narrative-structure through which the intrusions are in-forming (that which causes something to form). The average reader will be disturbed by these interruptions, even as Hillyer is disturbed by the angel's revelations (203); but the exemplary reader will mentally process them and the discontent they arouse—an informing/informing process urged as well by the narrator's insistent use of the pronoun *you*. The direct address evident in the narrator's frequent use of this pronoun prevents the reader from merely vicariously experiencing the story; this direct address actually includes the reader, not in the story of the plot-structure, but in the narrator's laborious effort in the narrative-structure. "You may see it for yourself," he says in the first chapter (121). Elsewhere he writes, "You would have been charmed at the couple could you have seen them"; "as the reader must admit"; "Dear Reader ..." (141, 178, 264). At another moment the narrator imagines the sort of review his "extravagant book" (131) might get from a wary reader. Indeed, the reader here is provoked into struggling with the text as much as the narrator has been wrestling with it. Like the narrator, the ideal reader becomes a character in the romance.

The presence of Mrs. Mendham and others (as sources of facts), of the narrator (as transitional organizer of the facts), and of the reader (as the next systematizer of the facts) forms a triad that vexes the dominance of the plot-structure, that vies with the importance of the plot-structure. The instruction (the incremental pulling together) of this emerging narrative-structure (sources, narrator, readers) imparts an instruction or message: that the exemplary reader should further the story by learning from it, by contributing shape to it, and by passing it on as renewed insight to others in the future. This instruction/in-struction of the narrative-structure expresses a tentative hope in the possible evolutionary enlargement of a human sensibility that might rise above the blindness and egotism which in the past and to date in the romance characterize human existence. This remains a tentative hope in *The Wonderful Visit*, not a foregone conclusion; it counters, not necessarily defeats, the pessimism of the plot-structure. The narrative-structure of this romance conveys a message about a probable potentiality within humanity to realize a higher self, symbolized by the angel.

In the angel's dimension, beings possess "wonderful imaginations" (134), and it follows that for the narrator "the angel of this story is the Angel of Art" (141).[8] The angel plays beautiful music, which awakens in humans a sense of "longing, a wish" (231), and a deep capacity to appreciate beauty:

> The study and the realities of life suddenly faded out of the Vicar's eyes, grew thinner and thinner like a mist that dissolves into air, and he and the Angel stood together on a pinnacle of wrought music, about which glittering melodies circled and vanished and reappeared. He was in the land of Beauty. (184)

The land of beauty glimpsed by Vicar Hillyer, whose soul is quickened "to beauty and delight" by the angel (252), is the dimension from which the angel has accidentally come, a dimension of human possibility where "there is nothing but Beauty" (138).

For humanity this dimension seems an imaginary realm, a place "of beautiful dreams" (143). But for the angel it is the human sphere that seems to be "the Land of Dreams" (130). This application of the same image to both worlds implies that one is integratively related to the other and, therefore, possibly one can be discarded for the other; for it is only a state of mind that separates them. Perhaps humanity will awaken from its present "dream ... that this narrow prison was the world" (258), where pain "is the warp and woof of this life" (218).

The hope that imagination and beauty are available to humanity, if it awakens from one dream to another, is the message of the narrative-structure of *The Wonderful Visit*. The tripartite pattern of this structure equating an age in transition from the past to the future, to a tentative narrative voice transmitting facts collected by others (past) to an ideal reader (future), is reinforced in the novel in a particularly pertinent passage designed to make the reader especially self-aware of his act of reading and role in the narrative-structure; in this passage the reader learns that the human and angelic dimensions lay "somewhere close together" as "near as page to page of a book" (135). The very copy of *The Wonderful Visit* in the reader's hands here becomes an instructive/in-structive emblem of epochal and narrative transition from a past page to a future page of one's life.

If the imagination and a sense of beauty are awakened, mankind will evince a greater sympathy for fellow humans. When a little girl tears her hand on barbed wire, the angel is "sympathetic, comforting, inquisitive" (237). Through the angel's tutelage, too, Vicar Hillyer comes to realize that humanity has created (dreamed up) an "unsympathetic world" (258). Indeed, in this dream of a world the angel receives no sympathy from most humans, who tend to regard him as a threat, as "an unhealthy influence" (249), as a maimed creature, or at best as a curiosity. The noteworthy exception is Delia, a servant girl who appreciates the imaginative beauty of the angel's music. When she tells the ailing angel (dying from the poison of the human dream life), "I am sorry for you, with all my heart" (261), she expresses an angelic sympathy of the sort that the exemplary reader will recognize as a model of human sensibility.

That Delia, a parlormaid, rather than her "betters," should serve as such a model is a violation of fictional convention that the narrator readily admits. He confesses that he must transgress the class stereotypes normally encountered in fiction:

> I am painfully aware of the objectionable nature of my story here. I have even thought of willfully perverting the truth to propitiate the Lady Reader. But I could not. The story has been too much for me. I do the thing with my eyes open. Delia must remain what she really was—a servant-girl. I know that to give a mere servant-girl ... the refined feelings of a human being, to present her as speaking anything but an intolerable confusion of aspirates, places me outside the pale of respectable writers. (242–43)

In fact his book has been doubly unconventional; if its heroine is a servant girl who gives her life to save something precious for the angel, its hero is also not from the upper class, but rather is a beyond-class angel, who gives his life to save "lower-class" Delia.

Such violations of convention, especially as highlighted by narrative intrusions calling attention to these infractions, reinforce the reader's discomfort, provoked elsewhere in the text by means of a well-managed narrative-structure. Such breaches of fictional conventions are, like the narrator's self-conscious interruptions, a deformity de-forming the plot-structure and contributing toward an alternative informing/in-forming narrative-structure. Instructed by this in-structing narrative-structure, the ideal reader, aroused to thought by his inclusion in this pattern (vexing the plot-structure), will not retreat into the censorious past of convention or tradition, but (as suggested by an age and a narrative in the act transition) advance toward a higher self in the future, a self awake to imagination, beauty, and active compassion. These exemplary readers will further the instruction/in-struction of the text of *The Wonderful Visit* in the text of their future lives. This is the *hope* that informs/in-forms the narrative-structure of *The Wonderful Visit*, a hope that lies behind the narrator's motivations, the "reasons [for writing] that will be more apparent as the story proceeds" (122). These reasons are never explicitly expressed, nor can they be found in the pessimistic plot-structure; these reasons are implicitly rendered in the hope embodied in the narrative-structure of the romance, a tentative hope in a vaguely possible human future of imagination, beauty, and active compassion.

II

Although the serial version of *The Sea Lady* was published six years after the appearance of *The Wonderful Visit*, its internal chronology is set in 1899, only four years later than that of the earlier romance. That *The Sea Lady* might have been written several years before it was printed is an interesting speculation since the novel is in so many ways similar to *The Wonderful Visit*.[9] Like this earlier work, *The Sea Lady* concerns the sudden appearance of a mythological figure[10]—this time it is a mermaid rather than an angel—and satirizes the lack of imagination and wonder in those who encounter her. The plot-structure of this romance, like that of *The Wonderful Visit*, eventuates in death. Harry Chatteris, an initially unimaginative politician engaged to an equally prosaic woman representing the social elite, is infatuated by the mermaid, abandons his career and his fiancée, and fatally follows the mermaid into the sea. This plot-structure, like that of *The Wonderful Visit*, conveys a pessimistic view of the possibility of human reform.[11]

The Sea Lady also possesses a narrative-structure, a tripartite pattern of organization created by a narrative voice which, at least early in the book, seems to be identical to that in *The Wonderful Visit*. This voice mediates between the reader and "broken fragments," a "poor array of collected facts," facts "vague or incomplete."[12] This voice, like that in the earlier novel, draws attention to itself as it struggles to collect these facts from others and to impose a tentative order upon them during its relation of them to the reader. Both the self-consciousness of the narrator and the tentativeness of his narration are dramatized in such equivocating expressions as "I suppose" (323, 330), "as far as I have been able to piece it together" (325), "I figure" (325), "I believe" (326), "I can't help imagining" (327), "as much verisimilitude as I can give you" (329), "I think" (345), "I fancy" (350, 410), "I falter" (377), "all I know is this much" (475), and "of the end I can only guess and dream" (478).

There is, however, an important difference between the two romances in their focus on the reader. The reader is present in the later novel, as the narrator's self-conscious equivocations imply. But whereas in *The Wonderful Visit* the reader's presence is actively evoked, especially in the narrator's use of direct address, in *The Sea Lady* the reader's presence is more passively implied. This weaker presence of the reader in *The Sea Lady* is important to note, as we shall see, because it suggests that the instruction imparted by the in-struction of the emergent narrative-structure might not be precisely identical to that of *The Wonderful Visit*.

At first glance the message of the narrative-structure of the two romances seems to be the same. Like the angel in *The Wonderful Visit*, the mermaid in *The Sea Lady* symbolizes an ideal higher human self. Similar to the angel, the mermaid (Doris Thalassia Waters) possesses the ability to "alter ... the values of things" (372) by seeming to hint at "something we never find in life.... Something we are always seeking" (447). Although mankind generally fails to respond to her "mystery" and "wonder" (458), she (like the angel) can potentially activate the human imagination;[13] this faculty of imagination is buried under humdrum human lives overshadowed by "the horrid modern spirit" (333), for which "the wonderful is utterly commonplace" and "only the familiar is really satisfying" (336, 348). Even Adeline Glendower, Chatteris' prosaic fiancée, finds her otherwise moribund "imagination was aroused" by the mermaid (347), and later when she tries to come to terms with Chatteris' infatuation with the sea lady she unwittingly, but aptly, remarks, "It is some mystery of the imagination that I cannot understand" (438). To Chatteris, Doris Waters is "like a picture ... that's— imaginary" (389-390); "it's a matter of the imagination" (399) for Chatteris, who by the end of the novel seems after all to have been "a man with rather a strong imagination" (439).

Reminiscent of *The Wonderful Visit*, this emphasis in *The Sea Lady* on imagination and a sense of wonder or beauty reveals that humanity is living in "unwholesome little dream" (401). Perhaps mankind can awaken from this impoverished dream "to other dreams" (418) symbolized by Doris Waters' deep-sea world, where its inhabitants "drift ... in dreams" (335). Precisely here, however, *The Sea Lady* differs markedly from *The Wonderful Visit*.

Whereas in the earlier story the reader is urged to complete more fully in the text of self the tentative, instructing/in-structing text of the romance, in *The Sea Lady* the reader is less actively present, his potentiality for a more highly informed/in-formed self shadowed by doubt. Whereas in *The Wonderful Visit* the reader is urged to *act* heroically, like Delia and the angel, in the tentative hope that the better dream-world of the human imagination might be realizable, in *The Sea Lady* the reader is at best invited to *contemplate* (not act to change) the limits of the dreamlike human condition. The uncertain hope present in the earlier story is absent from the later romance.[14]

This difference is indexed, in part, by allusions to the views of Nordau and Schopenhauer. In *The Wonderful Visit* Nordau's *Degeneration* is mentioned to emphasize that the reader's time is a period of transition when mankind can perhaps alter his state of mind from one dream to another, can perhaps choose between an apparent decline or a possible evolution of human sensibility. In *The Sea Lady* Schopenhauer's *The World as Will and Idea*, certainly as depressing as Nordau's book, is alluded to for the purpose of stressing the bleak fate of humanity imprisoned in a world which apparently cannot be transformed into a higher, more imaginative dream-reality. Like Nordau's volume, Schopenhauer's work, published in English translation in 1883, went through many printings during the turn of the century. The narrator's allusion to it in *The Sea Lady* is not likely a random one for Wells, who in *The Outline of History* (1927 edition) spoke of Schopenhauer's ideas as "profound and penetrating speculations" and who adapted these ideas cogently in *Brynhild* (1937).[15] Just as the structure of *Brynhild* was influenced by Schopenhauerian thought, so was that of *The Sea Lady*.

According to Schopenhauer, reality, as mankind knows it, is really *Maya*, a place of illusions governed by a blind will evident in all life, but especially manifest in human egotistical striving for gratification. Even seemingly virtuous, charitable acts are really a mode of ego gratification, as indeed the mermaid suggests in her description of Adeline's behavior toward the poor: "In her heart she does not want their dreams to be happier, in her heart she has no passion for them, only her dream is that she should be prominently doing good, asserting herself, controlling their affairs amidst thanks and praise and blessings.... Vanity of vanities" (403). According to Schopenhauer, nothing can change this reality. The best one can hope for is a profound realization of the hopelessness of existence, a recognition that might possibly result in a second birth of philosophical consciousness. This new awareness of the unmitigable pathos of human existence is the only sort of "action" available to humanity; for this insight can lead to a denial (all that is possible) of the will to live. This "act" of denial is expressed through a disinterest in and detachment from the world, through a state of mind in which we compassionately contemplate (not try to change) the forlorn human condition and quietly await our own demise and the extinction of the human race. This Schopenhauerian *contemplative* compassion contrasts with the *active* sympathy for others of the Christian-humanist sort (in Delia and the angel) engendered by the tentative hope in *The Wonderful Visit*.[16]

The allusion to Schopenhauer's ideas occurs, significantly, in the last chapter and very near the end of *The Sea Lady*. The narrator reports that Chatteris' valet last saw his master sitting and staring out an open window (an image of a wished-for imaginative escape). This "staring at nothing," the narrator says, is "indeed, as Schopenhauer observes in his crowning passage, ... the whole of human life" (472). That this remark is made by the narrator, rather than by some character in the romance, is important; it provides a key to why the narrative-structure in *The Sea Lady* differs in its implied resolution from that in *The Wonderful Visit*.

The narrator of *The Sea Lady* closes with the reader in contemplation of, not in a hoped-for active response to, the apparent futility of human existence. In lieu of the uncertain hope in *The Wonderful Visit* of a possible imaginative transformation of the world into a new dream-reality, there is in *The Sea Lady* only the "gentle ecstasy of death" (478). Chatteris' demise has none of the virtuous, heroic implications of the sacrificial death of Delia and the angel in the earlier romance. Chatteris' death follows logically from a sense of utter frustration and futility, symbolized in his defeated staring into a nothingness that cannot be transformed. This nothingness encompassing humanity is imaged by the narrator in the final paragraphs of the novel; mentioning "the margin of the softly breathing water" and "the extreme dark edge ... of the sky" (478, 479), the narrator provides two images which suggest that the edge of phenomena, of all creation, exists marginally between a sealike or skylike abyss of darkness. Indeed, the narrator's last words leave him, a policeman, and the reader staring, like Chatteris out his window, at nothing: "The interrogation of his [the policeman's] lantern must have gone out for a little way, a stain of faint pink curiosity upon the mysterious vast serenity of night" (479). With the narrator, the reader is left to contemplate (with Schopenhauerian compassion) the mystery of life, the mystery of its complete futility, that our will-driven "blind" curiosity cannot transform or even fathom.

That the narrative-structure of *The Sea Lady* arrives at a Schopenhauerian pessimism which merges with the gloom of the plot-structure contrasts with how the fragile hope of the narrative-structure of *The Wonderful Visit* keeps that structure separate from the direness of the plot-structure. In both romances the narrative-structure deforms/de-forms the plot-structure, but in *The Sea Lady* the final alliance of these two structures results in a deformity/de-formity of the narrative-structure itself. In *The Sea Lady* the narrative-structure gets out of the control of the narrator, who consistently remarks his trouble in ordering his story (e.g., 377), in contrast with the narrator of *The Wonderful Visit*, who gets his account into a transitional order in hope of its further systemization and realization by his readers. The narrator of *The Sea Lady*, unlike the narrator of the earlier novel, cannot claim that his reasons for writing the book will become more evident as the story proceeds. Instead of hope in some possible human action—a hope intimated by the mermaid's symbolization of imagination, by Chatteris' newly awakened desire to transform society (468), by the narrator's struggle to order the details of the story and communicate them to the reader, and by the example of a similar-appearing narrative-structure in *The Wonderful Visit*—instead of hope, the narrator of *The Sea Lady* can only contemplate the mystery of nothingness. Since his narrative-structure does not engender even a tenuous hope which would urge the reader to advance the text further in his self by hopefully acting for change, the direction of this structure is arrested, discontinued, finally interrupted, as the plot-structure triumphs. In fact, the narrative-structure fissures into two roughly equal parts: the first part (the seventy-two page of Chapters 1 to 5) seems to assert a narrative-structure distinct from the plot-structure; the second part (the ninety-five pages of Chapters 6 to 8) deforms/de-forms this apparent integrity by subverting the emergent narrative-structure so that its instruction/in-struction reinforces the pessimistic message of the plot-structure and thereby leaves the reader reflective rather than ready to act.[17]

As a result of this reversal, the reader's vaguely-felt expectations are frustrated, which in turn ideally should make the reader reflect upon his discontent—to contemplate. With the narrator at the end of his account, the exemplary reader will ponder the nihilistic outcome of life, as evidenced in Chatteris' suicide in spite of—or, more accurately, because of—the awakening of his imagination and sense of wonder by the sea lady. The narrator has told the story not in the hope of modifying human life, but with a contemplative Schopenhauerian compassion like that of the narrator of Herman Melville's "Bartleby, the Scrivener," when he says at the end of his narrative, "Ah, Bartleby! Ah, humanity!"[18] "Ah, Chatteris! Ah, humanity!" the narrator of *The Sea Lady* might have thought at the end of his tale, as he and the reader stare at the dark sea and dark sky, at "the mysterious vast serenity of night," at abyssal nothingness.

In *The Sea Lady* and *The Wonderful Visit* we have two works which reflect an essentially abiding pessimism characteristic of much of Wells's early writing. In *The Wonderful Visit*, however, we see another side of Wells's mind that would become more pronounced in his later writings,[19] the side that fathered a tentative hope in the possibility that life is not a Schopenhauerian void, but perhaps a dream which can be transformed into higher modes of human existence. The force of these two counter-currents in Wells's mind registers so directly in the structure of *The Wonderful Visit* and *The Sea Lady* because structure, more than any other feature of fiction, is most aligned to an author's philosophical and ethical beliefs. Read for their structural aesthetics, these two early romances can be appreciated as engaging works of art more accomplished than their present neglect by literary critics would seem to suggest.

NOTES

1. Management of structure in Wells's early fiction is considered, for example, by Darko Suvin, "A Grammar of Form and a Criticism of Fact: *The Time Machine* as a

Structural Model for Science Fiction," *H.G. Wells and Modern Science Fiction*, eds. Darko Suvin and Robert M. Philmus (Lewisburg: Bucknell University Press, 1977): 90–115. Management of structure in Wells's late fiction is treated by William J. Scheick, *The Splintering Frame: The Later Fiction of H.G. Wells* (Victoria, B.C.: University of Victoria, 1984).

2. On this correlation, see William J. Scheick, "Fictional Structure and Ethics in the Edwardian, Modern, and Contemporary Novel," *Philological Quarterly*, 62 (1984): 287–311.

3. *The Wonderful Visit* in *The Works of H.G. Wells* (New York: Scribner's, 1924), I, 156, 248. Subsequent page references to this edition will be cited parenthetically in the text. Nordau's influence on Wells is discussed by Bernard Bergonzi, *The Early H.G. Wells: A Study of the Scientific Romances* (Manchester: Manchester University Press, 1961): 4–7.

4. Early reviewers felt the force of this pessimism, as exemplified by W.L. Courtney, "Books of the Day," *Daily Telegraph* (London), 27 September 1895, p. 8, remarking the theme of the ruinous results of mixing the ideal and the practical. More recently, the ending of the romance has been interpreted as an expression of Wells's negative view of humanity, unable to achieve faith and love on earth: Antonina Vallentin, *H.G. Wells: Prophet of Our Day* (New York: Day, 1950): 112–13. The weight of the conclusion of the novel is also remarked by Norman Nicholoson, *H.G. Wells* (London: Barker, 1950). That a dark social Darwinianism informs the book is noted by Norman and Jeanne Mackenzie, *H.G. Wells: A Biography* (New York: Simon and Schuster, 1973): 124.

5. This potentiality, albeit not the distinction between plot-structure and narrative-structure, was remarked in an early anonymous review in *Literary World* (Boston), 27 (1896): 251.

6. John R. Reed's claim that the narrator's intrusions in this work and others represents Wells's satirization of the novelist's practice and Wells's need to be in the action of his works is too simplistic: *The Natural History of H.G. Wells* (Athens: University of Ohio Press, 1982): 202–3.

7. Wells used this technique as well in "In the Abyss" (1896), in which the turn of the century is presented as a time of transition when humanity can either relapse into the superstitions of the past or approach the future boldly with imagination and a sense of wonder: see William J. Scheick, "The In-Struction of Wells's 'In the Abyss.'" *Studies in Short Fiction*, forthcoming.

8. For Bergonzi, the angel is like the Eloi in *The Time Machine* (1895) in representing the insufficiency of aestheticism (91–92), a view repeated by Frank McConnell, who sees the angel as a representation of "useless beauty" in a world ignorant of beauty (*The Science Fiction of H.G. Wells* [New York: Oxford University Press, 1981]: 40–42). To assert, however, that Wells satirizes the angel's values is to miss the thrust of the narrative-structure of *The Wonderful Visit* in relation to its plot-structure.

9. *The Sea Lady* first appeared in July through December, 1901, in *Pearson's Magazine*; it was printed as a book in 1902. In *Experiment in Autobiography* (New York: Macmillan, 1934, p. 393), Wells notes that he planned the novel in 1900, but does not suggest that he wrote it this early. The question of the date of composition arises mainly as a result of a comment, in a snide anonymous review of the book, that *The Sea Lady* was an old, rejected manuscript which now was published because of Wells's increased popularity: "Novels," *Saturday Review* (London), 94 (30 August 1902): 271–72.

10. The sources of Wells's use of these two figures have interested critics. The

influences behind *The Wonderful Visit* have been said to include Swift (Alfred Borrello, *H.G. Wells: Author in Agony* [Carbondale: Southern Illinois University Press, 1972]: 62), Ivan Karamazov's "The Grand Inquisitor" (Antonina Vallentin, p. 112), and Grant Allen's *The British Barbarians* (David Y. Hughes, "H.G. Wells and the Charge of Plagiarism," *Nineteenth-Century Fiction*, 21 [1966]: 85–90), a book Wells reviewed (see *H.G. Wells's Literary Criticism*, eds. Patrick Parrinder and Robert M. Philmus [Sussex: Harvester, 1980]: 59–62). The influences behind *The Sea Lady* have been said to include Ibsen's "The Lady from the Sea" (John R. Reed, "The Literary Piracy of H.G. Wells," *Journal of Modern Literature*, 7 [1974], 537–42; reprinted in Reed, *Natural History*: 214–15) and, in Wells's own admission in *Experiment in Autobiography* (393), Mrs. Humphry Ward's *Marcella* (1894), although in both cases the endings of the earlier works have been reversed. Interestingly, both *The Wonderful Visit* and *The Sea Lady* have been identified as influences on Ford Madox Ford's *Mr. Apollo*: Arthur Mizener, *The Saddest Story: A Biography of Ford Madox Ford* (New York: World, 1971): 154–55.

11. Although John Reed asserts that both *The Wonderful Visit* and *The Sea Lady* are "trivial productions" (*Natural History*, p. 6), usually and oddly the later book has not been taken as seriously as the earlier one. For Vallentin *The Sea Lady* is evasive concerning human problems (163) and for Ingvald Raknem it is "a slight work" (*H.G. Wells and His Critics* [Torndheim, Norway: Boktrykueri, 1962]: 51). The Mackenzies refer to it as "a poor piece of work" (178), but they admit that it had a serious point to make. Just how serious both that point and the book were to Wells is indicated in *Experiment in Autobiography* (401).

12. *The Sea Lady*, in *The Works of H.G. Wells* (New York: Scribner's, 1925), V, 426, 336, 367. Subsequent page references to this edition will be cited parenthetically in the text.

13. John Reed suggests that the mermaid represents Wells's attention to the aesthetic position (*Natural History*, p. 279 n61), a point that should make us recall that the angel in the earlier romance represented the place of art (see note 8).

14. *The Sea Lady* is hardly the "jeu d'esprit" Bergonzi says it is (21); Wells's view of the seriousness of the work indicates otherwise (see note 11). Moreover, Wells elsewhere spoke of a frustrated love affair as an influence on this novel (*H.G. Wells in Love: Postscript to Experiment in Autobiography*, ed. G. P. Wells [London: Faber and Faber, 1984]: 62). The dark nature of this romance is registered still more forcefully by Geoffrey West, who thinks *The Sea Lady* incorporates Wells's thoughts about suicide (*H.G. Wells* [London: Howe, 1930]: 267).

15. William J. Scheick, "Schopenhauer, Maori Symbolism, and Wells's *Brynhild*," *Studies in the Literary Imagination*, 13 (1980): 17–29.

16. This Schopenhauerian cast of *The Sea Lady* and its sense of compassion might explain why George Gissing, who admittedly disliked the relatively more optimistic *The Wonderful Visit* (*George Gissing and H.G. Wells: Their Friendship and Correspondence*, ed. Royal A. Gettmann [Urbana: University of Illinois Press, 1961]: 193) told Wells of the darker *The Sea Lady:* "I do not pretend to interpret you with certainty; but what I *do* see is satisfying" (208). On the influence of Schopenhauerian compassion on Gissing's management of fictional structure, see William J. Scheick, "Compassion and Fictional Structure: The Example of Gissing and Bennett," *Studies in the Novel*, 15 (1983): 293–313.

17. Even some early reviewers were discontented with the conclusion of *The Sea Lady*, but they did not suspect that this disappointment might have been a deliberate Wellsian effect. One anonymous critic thought that Wells was probably as surprised at his ending

as is the reader ("Fiction," *Academy*, 63 [9 August 1902]: 155–56). Closer to the mark, another anonymous reviewer sensed a gap between the initial satire in the novel and the concluding tragedy ("Novels," *Spectator* [London], 89 [16 August 1902]: 229–30).

18. On the influence of Schopenhauer on Melville, see Daniel Stempel and Bruce M. Stillians, "'Bartleby, the Scrivener': A Parable of Pessimism," *Nineteenth-Century Fiction*, 27 (1972): 268–82.

19. Wells's struggle against his natural tendency toward pessimism is discussed in Anthony West's "Men and Ideas: H.G. Wells," *Encounter*, 8 (February 1957): 52–59; another, quite different version of this essay, with the same thesis, appeared as "The Dark World of H.G. Wells," *Harper's Magazine*, 214 (May 1957): 18–73.

JOHN HUNTINGTON

H.G. Wells:
Problems of an Amorous Utopian

H.G. Wells is probably the most significant utopian voice of the twentieth century. From 1901, with *Anticipations*, to almost the very end of his life, he worked to promote education, science, socialism, the world state, the Declaration of Human Rights, and the open conspiracy of rational and well-intentioned people. And it is the utopianism at the heart of his project that has occasioned some of the most severe criticism of Wells. F. R. Leavis speaks to a broad audience when he uses "Wellsian" as an adjective denoting all that is shallow in scientific culture; for Leavis it is sufficient to call C.P. Snow "Wellsian" to show that he is not a novelist.[1] George Orwell, in "Wells, Hitler, and the World State" (1941), while acknowledging the importance of Wells's liberating intellect early in the century, could denounce his "onesided imagination" which could treat history simply as "a series of victories won by the scientific man over the romantic man." "Wells," Orwell declares, "is too sane to understand the modern world."[2] For such critics, and they are common, the terms "Wellsian" and "utopian" are synonymous with a thin hyperrationality.

An admirer of Wells has difficulty responding to such criticisms because Wells himself declared that such rationality was the necessary and only salvation of the world. Yet, if Wells is proud of his rationality, we would not be denigrating him or his work if we observed that he is not as purely

From *English Literature in Transition*, vol. 30, no. 4. © 1987 by *English Literature in Transition*.

rational as he believes he is. On the contrary, Wells's work shows signs of a difficult struggle with a deeply selfish and irrational component of himself, and it is for that struggle, rather than for the neat conclusions he champions, that Wells's utopian work may be of greatest interest. To put it somewhat differently, Wells is greater than he himself understood, not because he achieved a pure rationality, but on the contrary, because he describes for us, if we can learn how to read him in this regard, a deep conflict between an ideal rationality and a much less admired, though not therefore contemptible, emotionality which, however much he will try to smother it, will not be quiet.

Such a reading of Wells, while it clearly opens up dimensions of his understanding that he tried to repress, is not entirely antithetical to Wells's own consciousness. In the meditation on Machiavelli which begins *The New Machiavelli*, for instance, he advocates just such a reading of the author of *The Prince*. Wells appreciates the human, even disreputable qualities revealed in Machiavelli's letters. For Wells, "these flaws complete him."[3]

I

Let us begin with the ideal that so offends many humanist critics. Toward the end of *A Modern Utopia* what Wells calls the "Voice" urges clear and bold *will* and *imagination*.

> The new things will be indeed of the substance of the thing that is, but differing just in the measure of the will and imagination that goes to make them. They will be strong and fair as the will is sturdy and organised and the imagination comprehensive and bold; they will be ugly and smeared with wretchedness as the will is fluctuating and the imagination timid and mean.[4]

This is a voice that Wells in 1905 had already practiced for a number of years and which he would continue to perfect for many more. It speaks in bold adjectives of a comfortable, efficient, tolerant, and undemanding world with understood rules. And controlling this world would be the Samurai, who would, in the slightly ironic vision of Marjorie Trafford in *Marriage*,

> lead lives of hard discipline and high effort, under self-imposed rule and restraint. They were to stand a little apart from the excitements and temptations of everyday life, to eat sparingly, drink water, resort greatly to self-criticism and self-

examination, and harden their spirits by severe and dangerous exercises.[5]

Our reading of such passages may be affected when we consider that throughout the period when Wells was publicly developing the idea of his harmonious Utopia led by disciplined will and imagination, he was finding the order his wife was so admirably sustaining at Spade House increasingly unsatisfying. The story of Wells's unconventional amatory experiments has been much retold, both by Wells himself and by later writers and biographers.[6] It is not necessary for our purposes to enter into this labyrinth in any detail beyond reminding ourselves that, according to Wells's own version of his life, within a few years of marrying Amy Catherine Robbins, his second wife, he began to have fantasies about relations with other women, and by the middle of the first decade of the century he had begun a continual series of sexual relationships, some frivolous, some serious, which remained the pattern of his life until well after the death of his wife. Wells was in his life revolting against what his own utopian voice calls its "haunting insistence on sacrifice and discipline" (234).

Wells indeed seems to have been proud of his amorous experiments, and in the late 1930s, in *H.G. Wells in Love*, he explains his persistent womanizing as a search for what he calls the Lover-Shadow. This is not a very clear concept. It resembles a Jungian archetype, a sort of *Ewigweibliche* whose proffered but never attained satisfactions are a source of desire and aspiration throughout life. Part of the difficulty Wells has talking about the Lover-Shadow is that, while it is social insofar as it draws one out of pure self-centeredness, at the same time it represents a drive that has no regard for social good. An important difference between *H.G. Wells in Love* and the *Experiment in Autobiography* is that the former depicts a Wells relentlessly intent on his private desires.

In *The New Machiavelli* Wells attempts to focus explicitly on the problem of the disjunction of love and the project to restructure society. Remington's popular phrase, "Love and fine thinking," which he poses as the solution to the political mess, turns out to be a paradox; it points to a union which contains the cause of its own disintegration.[7] The novel is a tale of tragic, toward the end rather operatic, romantic passion. The lovers admit their guilt, and the novel points to the people and causes they betray, but it finally sees them as victims of "the world-wide problem between duty and conscious, passionate love the world has still to solve" (442). Wells acknowledges the conflict, but he poses it as the world's problem, not as a contradiction within his own system of ideals. A better world, so he seems to say, would not have ostracized Remington.

The split between social ideals and personal needs is one that Wells hopes to overcome in his own experience and thought, but, even as he tries to reconcile the two, the split remains embedded in his prose. For instance, in the following passage from *H.G. Wells in Love*, the Lover-Shadow appears as something distinct from the social *persona*:

> The sustaining theme of my *Experiment in Autobiography* has been the development and consolidation of my *persona*, as a devotee, albeit consciously weak and insufficient, to the evocation of a Socialist World-State. If I have not traced the development of my Lover-Shadow, and my search for its realization in responsive flesh and blood, with the same particularity and continuity, I have at least given the broad outline of its essential beginnings.[8]

The phrase "consciously weak and insufficient" might seem to anticipate and apologize for the more narrowly personal desire expressed in the phrase "responsive flesh and blood." Wells does not state that the two aspects of personality are in conflict, but his sense of their unavoidable difference can be seen in such an image as "the *persona* and the Lover-Shadow are, as I see it, the hero and heroine of the individual drama most of us make of our lives."[9] The gender antithesis is important here, not because it puts one aspect above the other, but simply because it insists on difference.

In Wells's utopian writings—as opposed to his social novels—the Lover-Shadow is not acknowledged as significant. The usual reading of *A Modern Utopia* finds something like a parody of the Lover-Shadow in the Voice's companion, the botanist, a man apparently determined to make life in Utopia difficult.[10] He can be read as an ironic and finally irrelevant reminder of psychological stances that the utopian future will need to transcend. He comes from and drags with him the world before the Comet, a world of possessive jealousies and amorous fixations. At the end of *A Modern Utopia* a meta-voice opines that the stances represented by the Voice and the botanist are essential and incompatible, one speaking of "a synthetic wider being, the great State, mankind," the other representing "the little lures of the immediate life" (372–73). In this reading, and it seems clearly the one that Wells consciously wanted us to make, the botanist is an embarrassing figure which we have to learn to overcome.

Such a subordination of the desires of the individual to the needs of the whole society or race is one of Wells's favorite themes, and it serves as a rationale for utopian dreams throughout his work. I want to pose a stronger reading of the botanist, however, and hear him as an authentic voice of the

Lover-Shadow, a submerged voice that we can hear in one way or another throughout Wells's work, a voice that speaks for aspects of his unconscious that the rational ideals of the utopian world cannot satisfy. If we learn to hear *this* voice as "Wellsian," we shall be in a position to begin to understand some of he central texts of the Wells canon in a new way and to answer the objections of Leavis and Orwell.

II

Behind all the late works in which Wells undertakes to explain as clearly and as forthrightly as he can the amorous dimensions of his life—I am thinking especially of *Experiment in Autobiography*, the recently published *H.G. Wells in Love*, and highly autobiographical fictions such as *Apropos of Dolores* and *Brynhild*—we can point to the long affair with Odette Keun from which Wells had recently disentangled himself. This affair poses an extraordinary puzzle for Wells the rational utopian, one which he can never quite solve: why should a "free" man bind himself voluntarily over a long period of time to a person he finds thoroughly unpleasant? From early in his career as a lover, Wells had complicated his life deeply and, one has to say, compulsively. The relationships with Amber Reeves and Rebecca West are the great instances. Yet these two relationships can be explained because—there is an element of tautology here, but the language is Wells's own—Wells was "in love." But how could the affair with Keun, manifestly a source of considerable discontent, sustained by no social pressures, according to Wells never a "love" affair, continue for eight years? Clearly there is a mystery about the unconscious and about human behavior here that requires psychological explanation and must be taken into account in any rational utopian construction.

In this late period Wells himself was pointing to the importance of the unconscious as a source of unhappiness. In *The Anatomy of Frustration*, another of his attempts to put together a utopian synthesis, the author's fictional voice, William Burroughs Steele, urges that one of the main sources of "frustration" comes from "that dark undertow of unformulated or disguised impulses" which the modern technique of psychoanalysis has revealed.[11] In a loose way Steele is here picking up the theme of Freud's almost contemporaneous *Civilization and Its Discontents*, but there is a radical and significant difference between the ways Freud and Wells understand the unconscious. While Freud might agree with Steele's claim that "the psychoanalysts have opened our eyes to the artificiality of our rationalized conceptions of ourselves and our social relations" (52), he would absolutely disagree with the assertion that "our moral confusion and distress" stem for "our inability to impose any systematic direction of conduct upon the impulses from the subconscious that drive us" (60). For Freud what Wells calls the "release from instinct" (by which he seems to mean *escaping* instinct altogether rather than giving it free rein) and the "restraint upon impulse" are themselves the very sources of "discontent" in civilization. From a very early age one has emotions towards and thoughts about parents and siblings that the social code says are wrong. One has to repress these forbidden feelings and thoughts, thereby creating the guilt that is intrinsic to civilization. The "systematic direction of conduct" that Wells anticipates will, Freud would argue, increase rather than diminish discontent. Freud would warn us that what is repressed will return to plague us in ways that a Wellsian rationality will be unable to control.

For Wells the unconscious is not Freud's repressed but active system of values and desires inspired by guilt and in turn generating further guilt, but the instinctual drives that tend to disrupt the rational and ethical organization of civilization. Perhaps we may see it as something like pure *libido* without the complications created by *ego* and *super-ego*. For Wells the unconscious is simply the "primitive" that in his writings of the 1890s he loved to pit against highly evolved "civilization."[12] It is that irradicable trace of the early animal in the evolved human that must be controlled by education and will. Ultimately, Wells's theory of the unconscious is based, not on Freud, but on Darwin and Huxley.

We see this "evolutionary" conception of the unconscious in *Apropos of Dolores* when Stephen Wilbeck, the novel's narrator and the husband of Dolores, defines Dolores (the Keun figure) as "egotism" and himself (the Wells figure) as "restraint" and argues that the Dolores type must die out in the future. Dolores' egotism, Stephen contends, "is just common humanity unmitigated."[13] He concedes that he and everybody is at the core much the same as Dolores, "but tinted, mercerized..., glazed over, trimmed, loaded down," and therefore more advanced, more adapted to the utopian future. For Freud it is the frustration generated by these very overlays that is the source of civilization's discontent. Like Steele's, Wilbeck's analysis, which we have no reason to think of as different from Wells's own, treats the unconscious simply as the evolutionary primitive that must, somehow, be tamed.

Such an "ethical" conception of the unconscious may simplify the utopianist's project, but it makes it extremely difficult for Wells to account for his own behavior in the affair with Keun. In order to allow *Apropos of Dolores* to generate a utopian message rather than a message of despair, Wells must depict Stephen Wilbeck as different from himself in ways that seem minor in the text but are significant given the issues of "egotism" and "restraint." Stephen maintains a strict monogamy. When his first wife has an affair, he promptly divorces her. In his thirteen years of marriage to Dolores he is never unfaithful with another woman. Wells himself, as he makes clear in the *Autobiography*, *H.G. Wells in Love*, and in his utopian writings, was never committed to monogamy, and in the last years of his affair with Keun he had resumed his passionate relationship with Moura Budberg. The difficult question must arise here: if in the self-justifying fiction of *Apropos of Dolores* he finds it necessary for his moral and social point to make Stephen Wilbeck doggedly and self-sacrificingly "restrained"—and we should note that most of Wells's heroes share these traits of pointed fidelity and rigorous restraint—then what did Wells think of his own comparative "unrestraint"?

From a utopian perspective, Wells's love life poses a double contradiction. It is, first of all, unrestrained. And yet, and this comes out most clearly in the affair with Keun, it is subject to a mysterious restraint that prevents him from breaking off a relationship he claims he detests. Such a contradiction is common enough in human experience. In Wells's case the experience of his distant and disapproving mother, briefly but movingly depicted in the early scenes of *Tono-Bungay*, may in part account for his clinging to a relationship which seems to offer him very little reward.[14] Nevertheless, my aim here is not to perform an analysis of Wells himself, but to show a point of crisis in Wells's utopian vision. A novel like *Apropos of Dolores* is interesting in this context because in its twistings it reveals some of the strain Wells is undergoing in trying to bring into harmony his own life and his utopian ideals. Wells's anger at Keun and his sense of himself as long-suffering seem to have blinded him to the deeper implications of the affair. But such a work can alert us to issues which we can then find Wells working on, more or less consciously, in his earlier writings. An unstated mystery, which his utopian Voice would like to ignore but which his own life repeatedly brings to his attention, is why, in a world in which happiness should be there for the taking, do people make themselves unhappy. Wells addresses this question quite explicitly even when he is writing about a utopia beyond Sirius or an invasion from Mars.

III

We can all agree that the botanist in *A Modern Utopia* serves as an increasingly foolish challenge to the main utopian speculations of the book. But the botanist also expresses the "unrestrained" aspect of Wells himself that we have been looking at, which he cannot acknowledge openly, perhaps even to himself, but which he is unable to deny.

This confused and double quality of the botanist, his paradoxical burden of being mocked by the author for speaking matters that are deeply important to the author, is rendered repeatedly in the text. From the beginning the Voice complains about the botanist in terms that suggest there is more going on here than can be said: "It is srange, but this figure of the botanist will not keep in place. It sprang up between us, dear reader, as a passing illustrative invention. I do not know what put him into my head" (25). This admission of ignorance is casual, but important. It is an acknowledgment that, for the moment at least, the unconscious is dictating. Somewhat later the Voice will again complain that

> "when my whole being should be taken up with speculative wonder, this man should be standing by my side, and lugging my attention persistently towards himself, towards his limited futile self. This thing perpetually happens to me, this intrusion of something small and irrelevant and alive, upon my great impressions." (54)

Such a passage, behind its comedy, speaks to deep issues in Wells's own life and work; if we can read it from the proper angle, the passage warns us that the botanist's presence is not trivial: it is recurrent, important, and, most significantly, "alive." It is essential to Wells's honesty even as he strives to develop his Utopia of *will* and *imagination*. The botanist's "paltry egotistical love story" (124; cf. also 69) is, after all, a sketch of the situation Wells will elaborate without comedy in *The Passionate Friends.* "I suppose," the Voice confesses, "I had no power to leave him behind" (179; cf. also 343).

The botanist, then, is an absolutely essential figure for *A Modern Utopia*. Without him, the Voice itself becomes hollow. It might be argued that to attribute so much to such an apparently peripheral figure is to misread the comedy and the repeated trivializations of him in the text. But, as Freud has taught us to see, these very gestures of disregard may be significant; they allow Wells to approach the issues of obsessive and irrational love that the botanist represents and of which Wells himself cannot speak freely and openly.

When the Voice laments, "Is not the suppression of these notes [of amorous sentimentality] my perpetual effort, my undying despair?" (178), he may be acknowledging Wells's own powerful erotic urges in the very act of attempting to exclude them. And the botanist has his own insights into this restrictive aspect of the Voice. At one point, near the end, he complains of the Voice, "You are always talking as though you could kick the past to pieces; as though one could get right out from oneself and begin afresh" (359). This statement is more than just an obstructional balking at utopian energy. In 1904 when he was writing this, Wells may have wished very much that he could "begin afresh" in a number of ways. There are the manifest utopian beginnings, but Wells is also feeling trapped in his marriage. Something here needs to "begin afresh." He is in despair about the power of his amorous impulses, and he dreams of a new, more controlled, utopian self. *A Modern Utopia* can be seen as an attempt to rationalize his frustrations, to keep the botanist in himself, who cannot be entirely denied, at least in his place.

It is a nice irony that a year or two later, when Wells began to meet Amber Reeves at Cambridge, it was the utopian Voice's ideas of group marriage that seem to have, as Wells put it in *H.G. Wells in Love*, "provided all that was necessary for a swift mutual understanding" (75).

IV

I am suggesting that part of the power of Wells's work derives from the repressed recognitions in it of desires which he cannot acknowledge and which are incongruent with his rational, utopian ideals but which he is unable to explain away. To put it another way, it is Wells's hypocrisy as a utopian that makes him an honest artist: as he advocates an order of self-controlled Samurai, "advanced" people who will repress and control their egoistic desires, he himself is exploring ways to escape just such repression and control. His writings depict, however covertly, his emotional desires along with his rational ideals.

This complex surface which renders latent and private meanings in terms of a narrative about public events and policies can be seen in fiction that antedates Wells's explicitly utopian formulations of the first part of the century. *The War of the Worlds*, for instance, while on the surface a tale of imperialist guilt and of civilization restored, is also a more private consideration of the emotional drawbacks of the couple. The main symbol of civilization lost and recovered is the narrator's wife, but the attitudes towards the wife are fraught with unexplained negative emotions. It is remarkable that a figure of such profound symbolic import and of such recurrent obligation should be unnamed and undescribed. She is a counter to be moved, an abstract value to be lost.

We get our first clues to the emotional subtext of the novel in the strangely labored quality of the narrator's self-justifications. When he gets his wife to Leatherhead he gives, over the course of two paragraphs, three different explanations for why he must leave her again: he has his "promise to the innkeeper," he is "feverishly excited," and he admits "in my heart I was not so very sorry that I had to return to Maybury that night."[15] Any one of these excuses would be adequate; the three of them suggest that the real one is being covered up. Much later he finds himself "praying that the Heat-Ray might have suddenly and painlessly struck her out of being" (428). Of course the manifest meaning here is a humane desire that she be spared suffering, but given the general coolness running through the relationship in the novel, we may well hear a more selfish wish-fantasy in these words.

It is telling that anxiety over the narrator's wife is closely connected with the entrance of the curate. That appearance is a strange narrative moment with an almost hallucinatory quality to it:

> It is a curious thing that I felt angry with my wife; I cannot account for it, but my impotent desire to reach Leatherhead worried me excessively.
>
> I do not clearly remember the arrival of the curate, so that probably I dozed. I became aware of him as a seated figure.... (360–61)

The claim to be anxious about reaching Leatherhead has all the earmarks of a rationalization to prevent further inquiry into the sources of anger that he has just declared to be unaccountable. At this moment of explicit but inexplicable anger at the narrator's wife, the curate appears.

For the middle part of the novel the curate replaces the wife as the narrator's housemate. Now the "anxiety" for the *absent* companion converts to a declared anger at the *present* one, as can be seen in the subtle movement of the following paragraph:

> My mind was occupied by anxiety for my wife. I figured her at Leatherhead, terrified, in danger, mourning me already as a dead man. I paced the rooms and cried aloud when I thought of how I was cut off from her, of all that might happen to her in my absence. My cousin [at whose house she was] I knew was brave enough for any emergency, but he was not the sort of man to realize danger quickly, to rise promptly. What was needed now was not bravery, but circumspection. My only consolation was to

believe that the Martians were moving Londonward and away from her. Such vague anxieties keep the mind sensitive and painful. I grew very weary and irritable with the curate's perpetual ejaculations; tired of the sight of his selfish despair. After some ineffectual remonstrance I kept away from him.... (399)

The elision of the two figures of the wife and curate that the prose performs here is carried out in the plot. The narrator and the curate live together, squabbling over household economics, until the narrator, in self-defense, to prevent the curate from revealing their hiding place, clubs him and leaves him to be taken by the Martians. It is a moment of ambiguous responsibilities,[16] not unlike that which terminates Dolores' life in the novel written forty years later.

The expressions of irritation at the curate are echoed in the contemptuous descriptions of Mrs. Elphinstone's yearning for her husband "George," which is, of course, Wells's own name. Mrs. Elphinstone, like the narrator's wife, has become separated from her competent husband, and instead of rising to the occasion (like her sister-in-law), she falls into helpless whinings. She is a completely gratuitous figure as far as the plot of the novel goes, but she is an important presence insofar as she allows the novel to complain about wives without admitting that *the* wife is an object of complaint.

If the curate and Mrs. Elphinstone represent a bitter commentary on the trap of domesticity, the Artillery Man, in his satire on the ordinary man's "little miserable skeddadle through the world" (433) becomes, momentarily, a powerful critic of the domestic ideal: "No proud dreams and no proud lusts; and a man who hasn't one or the other—Lord! what is he but funk and precautions?" "Dreams" here probably means, not utopian ideals, but something like the ambitions of uncle Teddy Ponderevo. Here is a real promise to "begin afresh"! But then the novel takes another twist and renders the vision of amorous liberation as empty boasting. At the same time it treats as impossible the Artillery Man's other dream of an organized underground, a sort of prefiguration of the Open Conspiracy. The amorous and the utopian promises all collapse, and the narrator again leaves home.

The War of the Worlds is an extraordinary work for the way in which it manages to combine creative exuberance and deep pessimism. We can partially account for this combination by observing that the Martians, at one level, offer a fantasy of freedom from the snare of domesticity. Like the Voice in *A Modern Utopia*, they seem to offer an opportunity to "kick the past to pieces" so that the sane man can "begin afresh." The emptiness the narrator feels at the death of the last Martian may be partly caused by his sense that his liberation has been frustrated.[17] And the joy of the final reunion of husband and wife is severely muted. The novel's final words tell, not of promise and renewal, but of the hostile and forbidden thoughts that the novel has lived out: "And strangest of all is it to hold my wife's hand again, and to think that I have counted her, and that she has counted me, among the dead."

V

I do not mean to suggest that Wells was unusual or immoral for having such fantasies. Freud tells us that it is not the fantasies, but the failure to find some outlet for them, that is the cause of "discontent." Wells, of course, went beyond fantasy, not to the point of killing his wife, but certainly to the extent of escaping domesticity. As he became a more active and promiscuous lover, however, he must have had a difficult time reconciling his behavior with his ideals of utopian discipline.

Early in *A Modern Utopia* the Voice, considering for a moment how energetic and charismatic personalities will fit into Utopia, wonders, "What, for instance, will Utopia do with Mr. Roosevelt?" (28) This is, of course, a serious question in itself, but we may be missing the real implications if we do not see that behind it lies an even more difficult, though private, question: "What will Utopia do with H.G. Wells?" In his fiction we can see Wells, obliquely to be sure, but relentlessly too, considering the difficulties his powerful emotions create. Wells is half conscious of these difficulties, but he also, for perfectly understandable reasons, is not likely to be the first person to point to them. After all, his utopian ideal of discipline and restraint was not advanced by the complex and disruptive awarenesses his own life and experience generate. If we are to understand the totality of his enterprise, we need to see past the efficient and persuasive rhetorical surface to the more complex dynamics of each individual Wellsian text. This project does not mean denying the surface meaning, but it does involve inspecting it closely, questioning it, and relating it to Wells's own life.

NOTES

1. F.R. Leavis, *Two Cultures? The Significance of C.P. Snow. Being the Richmond Lecture, 1962* (New York: Pantheon Books, 1963).

2. George Orwell, "Wells, Hitler, and the World State," *The Collected Essays,*

Journalism and Letters of George Orwell, ed. Sonia Orwell and Ian Angus (New York: Harcourt, Brace, and World, 1968), II: 139–45.

3. H.G. Wells, *The New Machiavelli* (New York: Duffield & Co., 1910): 6. All further references to this text are noted in the text in parentheses.

4. H.G. Wells, *A Modern Utopia* (1905; Lincoln, NE: University of Nebraska Press, 1968): 368. All further references to this text are noted in the text in parentheses.

5. H.G. Wells, *Marriage* (1912; London: Hogarth Press, 1986): 222.

6. Wells described his mode of life in somewhat abstract terms in his *Experiment in Autobiography* (1934) and in rather more explicit terms in *H.G. Wells in Love* (published posthumously, 1984). For other angles on this matter, see Norman and Jeanne MacKensie, *H.G. Wells* (New York: Simon & Schuster, 1973); Anthony West, *H.G. Wells: Aspects of a Life* (New York: Random House, 1984); and David Smith, *H.G. Wells: Desperately Mortal* (New Haven: Yale University Press, 1986).

7. Even as he makes the lovers in the novel out to be "bad" people who injure friends and destroy the promise of utopian reform in England, Wells here, as he will do later in *Apropos of Dolores*, finds it necessary to vary from the reality of his own situation. Remington, though he has engaged in some brief sexual escapades before his marriage, is a faithful husband until after his wife locks him out and he falls passionately "in love" with Isabel Rivers.

8. H.G. Wells, *H.G. Wells in Love: Postscript to an Experiment in Autobiography*, ed. G. P. Wells (Boston: Little, Brown and Co., 1984): 55.

9. *Ibid.*: 55.

10. The botanist has been discussed by Mark Hillegas in his introduction to the Nebraska reprint of *A Modern Utopia*, by David Hughes in "The Mood of *A Modern Utopia*," *Extrapolation*, 19 (1977): 56–57, and by myself in *The Logic of Fantasy: H.G. Wells and Science Fiction* (New York: Columbia University Press, 1982): 168.

11. H.G. Wells, *The Anatomy of Frustration: A Modern Synthesis* (New York: Macmillan, 1936): 51.

12. *The Logic of Fantasy*: 16–17.

13. H.G. Wells, *Apropos of Dolores* (New York: Scribners, 1938): 159.

14. See Nancy Steffan-Fluhr, "Paper Tiger: Women in H.G. Wells," *Science-Fiction Studies*, 37 (1985): 313.

15. H.G. Wells, *The War of the Worlds* in *Seven Science Fiction Novels of H.G. Wells* (New York: Dover Publications, 1934): 340. All further references to this text are noted in the text in parentheses.

16. Discussed in *The Logic of Fantasy*: 75.

17. *Ibid.*: 63, 81.

ROBERT SIRABIAN

The Conception of Science in
Wells's The Invisible Man

Whoever, in the pursuit of science, seeks after immediate practical utility, may generally rest assured that he will seek in vain. All that science can achieve is a perfect knowledge and a perfect understanding of the action of natural and moral forces.

—Herman Ludwig Ferdinand Von Helmholt
Academic Discourse, Heidelberg (1862)

Various film adaptations of Wells's *The Invisible Man—The Invisible Man* (1933), *Abbott and Costello Meet the Invisible Man* (1951), *Memoirs of an Invisible Man* (1992), and *Hollow Man* (2000) to name a few—attest to its hold on the popular imagination. Like *Frankenstein*, Wells's novel is a part our culture, and film versions represent various perspectives about the possibilities of science and its place in society. The most accessible meaning of *The Invisible Man* is its moral warning about the individual's desire to transgress human boundaries in the name of science. While many film versions portray Griffin, the novella's protagonist, as a madman who practices science without controls, they also raise other concerns, some explicitly and others often implicitly or in passing, that Wells held important. The imaginative thinking that scientific discovery depends upon, the humorous ironies inherent in some scientific discoveries, and the nature of science itself are powerful and relevant ideas that Wells explores in his early

From *Papers on Language and Literature*, vol. 37, no. 4. © 2001 by the Board of Trustees, Southern Illinois University.

scientific romances. Like *The Time Machine*, *The Island of Dr. Moreau*, and the *War of the Worlds*, *The Invisible Man* reveals provocative ideas about the relationship of science, (human) nature, and society below the surface of its imaginative plotting.

As Richard Altick points out, science as a prestige branch of learning came about at the end of the Victorian period, when *The Invisible Man* was written, as Britain's trade position was threatened by Germany's emphasis on science (261). Early in the period, amateur scientists paved the way for the rise of science as a legitimate field of study in schools, but even as science became a respectable discipline and developed as a field of inquiry, there was a fear that the legitimization of science could erode culture and obscure literature. Tied to the period's utilitarian bents, scientific study was often valued for its practical uses of improving society, and with the development of evolutionary geology and biology in the nineteenth century, a quantitative, inductive (i.e. Baconian) methodology became well established (Mason 146). Yet during the nineteenth century, Bacon's status and scientific method are increasingly questioned, and the debate over inductive methodology and over the nature of science itself became increasingly focused and vociferous.

The achievement of *The Invisible Man* is Wells's treatment of science beyond its oversimplified conceptions, either as a purely imaginative, speculative pursuit or as an analytical activity concerned only with facts. Although an integrated conception of science is taken for granted in the twentieth century, in England during the nineteenth century scientific method was a significant issue for discussion. The romantic conception of science pursued by Griffin challenges a prevailing Victorian notion of science, defined as the finding of truth for social good through the factual recording and observation of nature. But while the novel clearly shows the dangers of uncontrolled speculative science, it more subtly reveals the limits of scientific thought based solely on factual observation, reason, and utility. By the end of the nineteenth century, Baconian methodology, with its perceived emphasis on "fact collecting" rather than imagination, was viewed as a faulty approach to scientific inquiry. According to Jonathan Smith, "Far from repudiating the imagination, then, nineteenth-century scientists and philosophers saw it as an indispensable component of scientific method. Hypotheses could not be formed, analogies could not be recognized, inferences could not be made without it" (37).

Griffin's experiments with invisibility are irrational when viewed through the lens of rational science, but *The Invisible Man* also reverses this critique. Rational science, which reinforces socially informed boundaries of acceptable thought, can be rigid and irrational too. The novella ultimately moves beyond its popular status as moral fable to suggest a more complex process of scientific inquiry—a process that combines imaginative/speculative and analytical/practical conceptions of science. What commentators on the novella have overlooked is that Wells situates his work within the nineteenth-century debate over scientific methodology, incorporating that debate's two main concepts in his text both thematically by juxtaposing Griffin's narrative to the novella's main narrative and artistically by blending vivid, imaginative storytelling and authentic science themes. Scientific discovery and the imagination were interdependent in both the scientific writing and literature of the period,[1] and it is an exploration of the tensions caused by trying to reconcile two seemingly opposite conceptions of science that makes *The Invisible Man* more than a scientific romance.

Of course, *The Invisible Man* is not the only literary work to explore the conflict between respectable, rational science and the "irrational" scientist. In *Dr. Jekyll and Mr. Hyde*, Dr. Lanyon dismisses Dr. Jekyll's scientific research as "'unscientific balderdash'" that "'would have estranged Damon and Pythias'" (9), Greek Pythagoreans who to Dr. Lanyon exemplify legitimate, factual science grounded in mathematical reasoning. In the early chapters of *Frankenstein*, Victor's father scolds him for reading cabalist Cornelius Agrippa, explaining to Victor that Agrippa's principles "had been entirely exploded and that a modern system of science had been introduced which possessed much greater powers than the ancient, because the powers of the latter were chimerical, while those of the former were real and practical ..." (24). At Ingolstadt, M. Krempe also tells Victor, "'I little expected, in this enlightened and scientific age, to find a disciple of Albert Magnus and Paracelsus'" (31), other "irrational scientists" in whom Victor has taken great interest. The science practiced by Victor Frankenstein and Henry Jekyll is viewed as imaginative speculation—fantastical and divorced from reason and practicality.

Distinctions between science and poetry made by many Romantic and Victorian writers reveal influential distinctions between imagination and reason as they relate to science. Wordsworth, in his *Preface to Lyrical Ballads*, explains that "the knowledge both of the poet and the man of science is pleasure; but the knowledge of one cleaves to us as a necessary part of our existence, our natural and unalienable inheritance; the other is a personal and individual acquisition, slow to come to us, and by no habitual and direct sympathy connecting us with our fellow-beings" (149). Victorian Matthew Arnold articulates a similar sentiment in "Literature and Science":

They [men of science] will give us other pieces of knowledge, other facts, about other animals and their ancestors, or about plants, or about stones, or about stars; and they may finally bring us to those great "general conceptions of the universe, which are forced upon us all," says Professor Huxley, "by the progress of physical science." But still it will be *knowledge* only which they give us; knowledge not put for us into relation with our sense for conduct, our sense for beauty, and touched with emotion by being so put; not thus put for us, and therefore, to the majority of mankind, after a certain while, unsatisfying, wearying. (495; Arnold's emphasis)

In both expressions, the goals of science are relevant to the individual scientist, not to humankind, and science is, furthermore, viewed as disconnected from human emotions and senses, from those qualities that enhance life. Many writers viewed science as missing that imaginative quality that transcends the quantifiable, practical nature of everyday life. Coleridge distinguishes poetry from science by arguing that "a poem is that species of composition which is opposed to works of science by proposing for its *immediate* object pleasure, not truth" (*Biographia Literaria* 101; Coleridge's emphasis). Here, science's truth is understood to be its correlation to facts that document the physical world.

It would be an oversimplification, however, to conclude that these statements are antiscience or that science has no place within society and culture. While the above writers subordinate science to poetry, they do not dismiss science or see it as an invalid form of knowledge. Nor do they exclude the possibility that science might be conceived of in a way that is complementary to poetry. Indeed, many Victorian and Romantic writers use scientific language and concepts in their poetry and prose. Coleridge's theory of organic forms is an obvious example. Even though science lacks poetry's social function for Wordsworth, poetry has the ability to assimilate science's discoveries thorough the imagination and to present them in a more meaningful and striking way. Shelley's *Defense of Poetry* acknowledges that science can benefit humankind, even though poetry protects society from the excesses of science that destroy the moral imagination of human beings. Thomas Huxley, whom Wells admired, rejected the usefulness of a classical education for the student of physical science and argues, in "Science and Culture," that the study of physical science can "confer" culture and "[touch] the higher problems of life" (528).

The apparent dichotomy between science and literature in the nineteenth-century literature, fueled by perceived conceptions of science, tends to be overstated, as much of the scientific writing of the period offers a view of science that transcends the practical and observable world, much like poetry. Prevailing social attitudes shaped the discourse about science and its practice. The literature/science schism underlies a key consideration—both literature and science are cultural constructions shaped by conceptions of the imagination and reason. Victor Frankenstein's scientific pursuits emphasize imaginative speculation over the concerns of rational science:

> He [the most learned philosopher] had partially unveiled the face of Nature, but her immortal lineaments were still a wonder and a mystery. He might dissect, anatomize, and give names; but, not to speak of a final cause, causes in their secondary and tertiary grades were utterly unknown to him. I had gazed upon the fortifications and impediments that seemed to keep human beings from entering the citadel of nature, and rashly and ignorantly I had repined. (25)

For Victor, science includes the imaginative vision that reaches beyond the directly observable features of nature to its invisible secrets. Unlike the traditional methods of scientific investigation popular throughout the nineteenth century, Victor's investigations are not focused on proofs and facts that lead to theory but on speculation and theorizing that will be later tested. Likewise, in *The Invisible Man* Griffin expresses this same emphasis in his scientific pursuits: "'Fools, common men, even common mathematicians, do not know anything of what some general expressions may mean to the student of molecular physics. In the books ... there are marvels, miracles! But this was not a method, it was an idea, that might lead to a method by which it [invisibility] would be possible ...'" (79). Jonathan Smith reveals that in *The Friend* Coleridge discusses the inadequacy of some theories of electricity that derive from the idea of polarity. But Coleridge also argues that the "'theories and fictions of the electricians' nonetheless 'contained an idea, ... which has necessarily lead to METHOD ...'" (qtd. in Smith 68).[2] The similarity in the language used by Coleridge and Griffin and the closeness of their interpretations suggest that Wells has the debate over scientific method in mind in his novella. Their descriptions underscore two points: scientific method must include theories and hypotheses, and it should incorporate theories that are eventually tested and grounded in facts. Griffin's view of science, along with Victor Frankenstein and Henry Jekyll's, challenges the notion of traditional science by making the imagination a vital component of scientific method. Whereas for them traditional or classical science is burdensome and mentally confining, speculative science contains all of the potential for intellectual freedom and discovery. Yet *The Invisible Man* also demonstrates that unrestricted and untested speculation is equally problematic.

The novella does not begin with an explanation of Griffin's predicament and how he becomes invisible. Instead, it introduces readers to Griffin through the eyes of the villagers. Anthony West remarks that what is strange about the opening chapter ("A Strange Man's Arrival") "is not his [Griffin's] invisibility so much as the way in which he is dressed" (xiv). Appareled in theatrical garments, Griffin looks odd if not ridiculous to the Iping villagers. The humor prevalent in the first half of the novel results from the villagers's reactions to Griffin. As Bernard Bergonzi suggests, "Instead of seeing a society, albeit a small one, through the eyes of a strange visitor ... we see the strange visitor—to begin with—through the eyes of the society. And as Wells emphasizes, it is a smug, settled and apparently prosperous little community" (116–17). By having readers view the Invisible Man through the eyes of the villagers, Wells constructs an interesting experiment that demonstrates the process of scientific inquiry.

In this first section of his novella, Wells links the phenomenon of the unknown to scientific investigation, reconstructing the nineteenth-century debate over Baconian methodology. As the villagers are initially confronted with the strange looking and mysterious Griffin, they attempt to formulate a conclusion about his identity, relying on a form of deductive reasoning in the spirit of the scientific approach popularized by Conan Doyle's Sherlock Holmes in the late part of the nineteenth century. In the absence of any facts, however, their hypotheses fail to reveal anything concrete about him. In chapter one of *The Invisible Man*, Griffin's arrival piques Mrs. Hall's curiosity immediately. Confronted with an unfamiliar sight, she immediately attempts to make sense of Griffin, to understand him within the frame of her own experience and environment. She makes sense of his bandages by intuiting that he must have been in an accident, a reasonable assumption that elevates her own sense of learning when she informs acquaintances that he is an "experimental investigator," someone who "'discovered things'" (18). Not concerned with the ideas that inform his science, Mrs. Hall sees science as an occupation, however mysterious, and uses her self-proclaimed knowledge of science to elevate herself above her peers.

But aside from some initial, vague impressions of their visitor, the villagers gain no information about who he might be, so they decide to try an "inductive approach" by attempting to gather information in order to determine the stranger's identity and situation. Mrs. Hall devises an excuse to visit Griffin's room with clockjobber Teddy Henfry under the pretense of looking over the clock. Asleep when they first enter the room, Griffin has forgotten to bandage the lower part of his face, and Mrs. Hall is mystified at the appearance of the blank space. The dim lighting, though, makes it difficult to see clearly, and she can only say that what she observed looked strange. Mr. Henfry tries to talk with Griffin while he fiddles needlessly with the clock, but Griffin defies any penetration. Leaving Griffin's room foiled and upset, he can only tell Mr. Hall later that the bandages look like a disguise. When Mr. Fearenside's dog bites Griffin as he unloads his baggage, Griffin retreats to his room to repair his clothes. Following Griffin to check on him, Fearenside sees a handless arm and Griffin's face without his goggles—black holes in his white bandages. Processing what he sees as best he can, he theorizes from his observation that Griffin is a piebald. As he tells Mr. Henfry, "'He's kind of a half-breed, and the colour's come off patchy instead of mixing. I've heard of such things before'" (16). Even Mr. Cuss, the general practitioner who has some science background, cannot clearly account for what he witnesses—an empty sleeve that stays open and the feeling of a hand tweaking his nose. Just as their hypotheses fail to reveal anything about Griffin's identity, the few facts the villagers gather do not provide them with clear understanding of Griffin either. Induction as scientific method is hampered when data cannot be obtained or is inconclusive.

In addition to critiquing the limits of rational scientific methods, Wells also introduces in these early chapters the humor inherent in scientific discovery or in the creation of odd phenomena. Never having encountered anyone like Griffin before, the villagers try to construct hypotheses based on their direct observations of him, but what they observe is inadequate. The theories about Griffin range from his having been in a bad accident, to being a fugitive, a piebald, and a harmless lunatic. And there are some who see him as a supernatural phenomenon, a "Bogey Man." Scientific discovery can be a source of humor, and Wells shows the humorous results of science that is at odds with a community unable to fathom science's implications—an element absent in *Frankenstein* and *Dr. Jekyll and Mr. Hyde*. The fact that Griffin's pranks occur during Whit Monday adds a humorous irony to a day of celebration and gaiety. In a practical sense, Griffin looks ridiculously festive in his costume. And the villagers's reactions to the odd occurrences are funny to observe. As the butt of Griffin's jokes, however, the villagers are also sympathetically portrayed. Their wild conclusions about Griffin function not as an indicator of their ignorance so much as an indication of reason's limits to comprehend what lies outside of direct observation. Scientific method itself becomes silly when it leads to untenable truths. His pursuit by the villagers takes on the guise of slapstick comedy at times as they try to swing at or capture him. Science can be a source of pranks, albeit sometimes mean spirited. But comedy also humanizes Griffin because it shows his ability to see the possible effects of science in intellectual as well as common terms. Humor also reveals that scientific study is a human activity rather than an isolated process.

The Invisible Man is able to carry out pranks at the villagers's expense, which utterly confuse and amaze them since they cannot fathom the truth of his situation. He tolerates them for a while and then becomes more condescending as they become more intrusive. If humor lightens the tone of the novel, it also reveals the bitter irony of Griffin's situation. As he later tells Kemp, "'The more I thought it over ... the more I realized what a helpless absurdity an invisible man was, in a cold and dirty climate and a crowded city'" (110). Henry Jekyll's transformation is an absurdity as well when his transformations into Hyde occur beyond his control and, in one instance, Hyde's facial distortions are a source of humor for a cabman. When a phenomenon cannot be understood, one response is to laugh.

The first section of *The Invisible Man*, then, reveals the limits of a scientific methodology based solely on inductive reasoning. Roslynn Haynes notes that Wells has been criticized in his scientific romances for departing from a strict inductive method, instead advocating "an educated guess, which leaps beyond the observed facts and suggests a further hypothesis or a new synthesis of previously known facts" (53). The reliance of the villagers on reason or facts, constructs of the senses, becomes a critique of a narrowly defined, inductive scientific method that shows Wells's assessment of narrowly practiced Baconian methodology. As Jonathan Smity explains, "Paradoxically, Baconian methods eventually came to be seen not as an 'organ' of discovery, but as an impediment to it" (19). Similarly, hypothesis alone is equally inadequate, an idea underscored in Griffin's narrative.

Between the comic first section of the novella and its darker last section lies a middle narrative in which Griffin reveals to Kemp the particulars of his experiment and the sequence of events that turn Griffin into a hunted outcast. Bernard Bergonzi suggests that "Griffin's lengthy recapitulation of his discovery and adventures ... seems a somewhat clumsy device" (113), and John Batchelor argues that this middle section of the novella weakens its purpose of enlisting our sympathy for Griffin by turning him into an "obvious maniac" (22). While Griffin's narrative may lend itself to easy moral interpretation, it more importantly presents a contrasting conception of science to that presented in the first section of novella—science conceived of as imaginative vision.

Bengonzi explains Wells's early works this way: "Wells's early novels and tales are romances in the traditional sense, insofar as they contain an element of the marvelous, which may have a scientific—or pseudo-scientific—explanation, but which may equally originate in a supernatural happening, or in some disturbance of the individual consciousness" (17). While Stevenson and Shelley's novels question the nature of science and its role within society, Wells makes scientific method integral to plot and theme. The creation scene in *Frankenstein* is one sentence, and in *Dr. Jekyll and Mr. Hyde*, Jekyll's chemistry is never explained. Griffin explains that his invisibility is rooted in the theories of optics, not the result of secret potions as many of the movie versions suggest. Although invisibility is never suggested as an actual scientific possibility, Wells makes it appear to be possible so that the science itself is never an afterthought when its effects are explored. Whereas Stevenson and Shelley focus on the effects of science, as does Wells, credible scientific method itself is always foregrounded in *The Invisible Man*.

Griffin is driven by the same pursuit of knowledge as Victor Frankenstein and Henry Jekyll. Victor has a "thirst for knowledge" (22), while Henry Jekyll labors for the "furtherance of knowledge" (53). Griffin tells Kemp that "'I beheld, unclouded by doubt, a magnificent vision of all that invisibility might mean to a man,—the mystery, the power, the freedom. Drawbacks I saw none'" (82). His romantic pursuit of knowledge is a largely personal one, which is explained by his background. Victor Frankenstein and Henry Jekyll are men of means from affluent families. Their scientific exploration is initially motivated by a desire to serve society. Griffin does not come from a background of privilege and social status: "'And I, a shabby, poverty-struck, hemmed-in demonstrator, teaching fools in a provincial college, might suddenly become this'" (82–83). He also works at night to avoid being bothered by "gaping, silly students" (82). Like his scientist counterparts, however, Griffin was hampered in his pursuits by an academic system unable to appreciate his intellectual vision, and, in the same vain as Huxley's criticisms, the novella specifically targets the way science was taught in the nineteenth-century English educational system. As Griffin tells Kemp, "'I had to do all my work under frightful disadvantages. Oliver, my professor, was a scientific bounder, a journalist by instinct, a thief of ideas,—he was always prying. And you know the knavish system of the scientific world'" (82). Griffin's scientific pursuits are a means of freeing himself from social constraints of class and of narrow thinking. The romantic appeal of invisibility is the power and freedom it provides him in thwarting those conditions that have impoverished him, both economically and intellectually.

The problem with a romantic practice of science is perhaps best expressed by the narrator: "Great and strange ideas transcending experience often have less effect upon men and women than smaller, more tangible considerations" (43). Griffin's science isolates him because no one is able to understand the significance of his discovery. Even after his science becomes a reality, there is no one who can appreciate its profundity. He tries to establish a relationship with two persons, but even the scientist Kemp, who is in the best position to understand Griffin's discovery, can only see the unconventionality of his science.

Griffin's first confidant is the reluctant Mr. Marvel, whose physical description ironically recalls Griffin's in the novel's opening chapter:

> You must picture Mr. Thomas Marvel as a person of copious, flexible visage, a nose of cylindrical protrusion, a liquorish, ample, fluctuating mouth, and a beard of bristling eccentricity. His figure inclined to embonpoint; his short limbs accentuated this inclination. He wore a furry silk hat, and the frequent substitution of twine and shoe-laces for buttons, apparent at critical points of his costume, marked a man essentially bachelor. (37)

Is Mr. Marvel any stranger in appearance than Griffin in the opening chapter? The similarity in general appearance here underscores an important point—that Mr. Marvel, like Griffin, is an outcast, but Mr. Marvel is an acceptable anomaly within the community. Griffin upsets the villagers's environment because he does not belong to it. When he defies their attempts to make sense of him, they become increasingly alarmed until their surprise and fear turn to hatred and violence. When Mr. Marvel first encounters the Invisible Man, he refuses to believe he exists, but even after Griffin proves he is real, Mr. Marvel is only interested in touching him to establish his existence. Mr. Marvel is unable to believe what his senses cannot measure and is incapable of understanding the true significance of an invisible man. In the end, he can only flee from Griffin. Kemp, however, a legitimate man of science, becomes the one person capable of understanding the significance of Griffin's discovery, yet he cannot accept the practice of science divorced from its established practice and ethical norms.

Like the Iping villagers, Kemp, too, cannot comprehend an invisible man, but after his initial credulity, Kemp is able to go beyond the immediate questions surrounding invisibility to grasp its larger scientific significance. Griffin helps him to see that the universe abounds with invisible creatures and organisms, and his concrete description of the optics that explain visibility makes the unbelievable believable. Able to think beyond the boundaries of the "rational" to envision other possibilities, Griffin demonstrates the power and delight of his imaginative vision. Science's contribution to progress lies in its ability to make new discoveries and to envision new possibilities that can become workable methods and solutions, a view held by those who argued for the necessity of hypothesizing as part of scientific method in the nineteenth century. Coleridge's "Essay IV" from *Treatise on Method* (from Section II of *The Friend*) acknowledges the importance of method in the "formation of understanding and in the constructions of science and literature" (141). The excellence of Shakespeare's method, he argues, is "that union and interpenetration of the universal and the particular, which must ever pervade all works of decided genius and true science" (147; also qtd. by Smith). Here, Coleridge not only defines scientific method as relying on the proportionate use of hypothesis (imagination) and factual observation, but also he shows that the method is important to the common interests of science and literature. Kemp, however, compartmentalizes scientific method, believing that it must rely on fact and reason, so he recoils at Griffin's application of science.

Kemp initially promises to keep Griffin's confidence, but as he reads accounts of Griffin's actions, he concludes that "'he's mad! Homicidal!'" (77). Thinking about his course of action, Kemp decides to warn the authorities: "'For instance, would it be a breach of faith if—No!'" (77). As a mainstream scientist, who hopes for fellowship in the Royal Society, Kemp's traditional view of science is the alternative to Griffin's romantic scientific vision. His strict sense of ethics makes him question the limits of a promise to an Invisible Man. Griffin threatens social order, and even the provocative nature of his discovery must be subordinated to reason and morality.

Ultimately, Griffin's narrative exposes the danger of science without controls. Just as science based only on analytical method fails to enlarge human understanding, a romantic notion of science can become subject to the whims of the individual scientist. The moral reading of *The Invisible Man* and other science narratives points to the hubris of the lone scientist whose ambition exceeds and threatens the interests of human society. Because Griffin's thinking is ahead of any available institutional or educational agenda, he is forced to pursue his work alone and in secret, a condition he shares with Victor Frankenstein and Henry Jekyll. But without any thought of the practical and social concerns of his science, Griffin is ruled by the idea itself. His description of his state of mind echoes that of Frankenstein and Jekyll: "'The fixed idea still ruled me'" (88), and "'Drawbacks I saw none'" (82). Immersion in his research creates waves of euphoria and moments of depression, but the final success of his project creates a mood of "exaltation." Soon, however, this exaltation turns to disappointment when Griffin begins to realize that the practical realities of living as an invisible man strip away the grandeur of the idea.

In his passion to complete his experiments, Griffin, like Victor Frankenstein, never considers the day-to-day concerns of his discovery. His outline can be seen if covered by dirt or only partially clothed, and undigested food in his system is visible. Kemp's betrayal of Griffin ends his final hope of securing a companion to help him with the practical necessities of being invisible. This betrayal also leaves Griffin alone, completely isolated from society. Angry, tired, and frustrated, Griffin realizes that there will be no place in society for him. He can only think of ruling over everyone, of getting revenge on a world that cannot appreciate his scientific contribution. His mostly harmless pranks and property destruction in the novella's first section become a deadly reign of terror in the last section of the novella, and, ironically, Kemp uses what Griffin tells him to inform the police about how best to counter the advantage of his invisibility. Although the capture and killing of Griffin seems to be the result of science gone astray, the mob that kills Griffin, members of a reasonable society, is also out of control.

The narrator, far from condemning Griffin, tries to win readers's sympathies for him. Take, for instance, the explanation of the circumstances surrounding Wicksteed's murder:

> Now this, to the present writer's mind at least, lifts the murder out of the realm of the absolutely wanton. We may imagine that Griffin had taken the rod as a weapon indeed, but without any deliberate intention of using it in murder. Wicksteed may then have come by and noticed this rod inexplicably moving through the air. Without any thought of the Invisible Man—for Port Burdock is ten miles away—he may have pursued it. It is quite conceivable that he may not have even heard of the Invisible Man. One can then imagine the Invisible Man making off— quietly in order to avoid discovering his presence in the neighborhood, and Wicksteed, excited and curious, pursuing this unaccountably locomotive object,—finally striking at it.... But this is pure hypothesis. The only undeniable facts—for the stories

of children are often unreliable—are discovery of the body, done to death, and of the bloodstained iron rod flung among the nettles.... (120–21)

The narrator clearly wants readers to see Griffin as someone other than a bloodthirsty murderer, but what is more interesting is his appeal to the use of imagination. Like the romantic scientist, readers are asked to "imagine" what the "facts" might suggest. Against this type of speculation, the narrator undercuts his own "hypothesis," suggesting that it is not "undeniable fact." He brings together in this passage the two conceptions of science that the novel presents, showing that each by itself is incomplete. The facts tell as little as the hypothesis. Only the use of both—imagination and facts—can possibly lead to an explanation of what might have happened.

This merging of two conceptions of science is also seen in the numerous references to game playing in the last section of the novel. In his letter to Kemp after he has been betrayed, the Invisible Man tells him that "the game is only beginning" (122), and Kemp himself describes Griffin's pursuit of him as "'a game,' ... 'an odd game, but the chances are all for me'" (123). When Policeman Ayde is intercepted in front of Kemp's house by Griffin and is told to get Kemp to open the door, Ayde wants Griffin to promise not to rush the door if Kemp opens it: "'Don't push a winning game too far. Give a man a chance,'" to which Griffin replies, "'You go back to the house. I tell you flatly I will not promise anything'" (127). "Game," as it used here, takes on meaning beyond its common function as metaphorical comparison. According to cultural historian Johan Huizinga, play is a "voluntary activity" (7) associated with freedom and choice by the player. It creates structure through the use of simple rules and conduct (13). Most controversially, Huizinga claims that play involves "a stepping out of 'real' life in to a temporary sphere of activity" (8). As more organized forms of play, games emphasize freedom and choice, but this increased structure (created by rules) and the tension associated with game playing challenge the player's freedom.

Kemp's description of Griffin's reign of terror as an "odd game" reflects Huizinga's notion of play. He views Griffin's actions as divorced from real life, from the thinking of reasonable, moral people. Because it is separate from real life, his game threatens the social and moral order of society. When Kemp tells Ayde to spread broken glass in the roads to slow Griffin down or injure him, Ayde replies, "'It's unsportsmanlike'" (117), but both agree that desperate measures warrant drastic action. The game ideology, both as strategy and as chance,[3] has a strong cultural influence on how individuals process the world in which they live. Both Ayde and Kemp are socially and culturally conditioned to abide by rules that define fair play in a competitive contest, but they also count on chance since Griffin may not "play fairly" and has the advantage of invisibility. By thinking of game playing in terms of its reason-based emphasis on strategy and in terms of chance, they are able to confront an unfamiliar situation and make sense of it within a familiar cultural framework.

For Griffin, game playing takes on a different dimension and challenges Huizinga's notion of play as separate from everyday life. Rethinking the idea of play, Jacques Erhmann challenges Huizinga's assertion that play can be measured against the "backdrop of reality": "Play is not played against a background of a fixed, stable, reality, which would serve as its standard. All reality is caught up in the play of the concepts which designate it. Reality is thus not capable of being objectified, nor subjectified. However, it is never neutral. Nor can it be neutralized" (56). Rather than exist apart from reality, the game is inseparable from everyday life. For Griffin, the game is reality; game playing offers him the freedom and creativity to reshape and control a world that tries to isolate him. Although games are characterized by rules, an attraction to a Victorian society that sought structure and order, these rules can be revised to allow for spontaneity and imagination. Griffin mediates an existence through a game he constructs, one that offers him, within its boundaries, an identity that has meaning. Furthermore, Griffin's idea of scientific investigation values imaginative speculation as play, as a postulation of ideas that are not immediately supported by experiment or observable facts. For Kemp, science that privileges playful speculation is frivolous. Serious science deals in reason and practical application. The notion of play, then, has a direct bearing on the nineteenth-century debate over scientific method. The Victorian play/work dichotomy devalues play as frivolous just as hypothesis was considered "unscientific." Towards the end of the century, however, hypothesis through imaginative speculation was seen as an essential component of scientific method.

The game Griffin devises, however, cannot overcome the reason and moral order that defines social organization. His romantic vision of conquering the world, which he pursues through the game, only creates the illusion that he can recreate a world using his own moral or ethical codes. But if his game is an illusion, the moral and social order that will serve as its alternative is also questionable. Finally caught by a mob in his obsessive pursuit of Kemp, the Invisible Man is kicked and beaten until the mob cannot hear him breathing. As he slowly becomes visible again, the result of the mob's violence becomes visible as well: "There lay, naked and pitiful on the ground, the bruised and broken body of a young man about thirty'" (136). Kemp is the one voice of reason who tries to stop the mob's brutality, but to no avail.

If the mob represents the reasonable members of society who Griffin has threatened, then their moral and ethical authority is seriously questionable. Are their actions less violent and threatening to the social order than Griffin's? An interesting offhand detail mentioned twice in the novel is that Griffin is an albino. His whiteness symbolically suggests the effects of invisibility, but more pointedly underscores his outcast status, an individual who looks different, who is not "normal." The impulse to reject the unfamiliar is very powerful. Griffin's scientific vision challenges and threatens the rational view of science, but the novel shows, with equal vividness, the limits of reason in dealing with the unknown.[4] The answer, however, lies not in a choice between the imaginative and practical views of science but in a conception of science that mediates these views and that reexamines the social and cultural attitudes about that shape its practice.

Although the ending of the novella shows the potentially destructive power of the mad scientist and mob justice, the Epilogue to *The Invisible Man* reemphasizes the idea that scientific method must integrate imagination and reason, hypothesis and fact. Here, "Wells achieves his effects with an economy and humour he rarely excelled" (Hammond 90), but those "effects" are more than artistic and thematic symmetry. Readers learn that Griffin's notebooks are in the possession of no other than Mr. Marvel, whose appearance has suggestive parallels to Griffin's in the novel's opening. In this sense, the novel ends where it begins, with a strange looking man puzzling over a scientific mystery: "'Full of secrets,' he says. 'Wonderful secrets! Once I get the haul of them—*Lord!* I wouldn't do what he did; I'd just—well!' He pulls at his pipe. So he lapses into a dream, the undying wonderful dream of his life" (138). Although ill-equipped to understand the significance of his findings, Marvel can still dream about the possibilities this secret offers. Like Griffin, he harbors romantic notions of science's possibilities.

Whereas Kemp would be the most logical choice for the owner of Griffin's books, it is humorously ironic that the local outcast whose greatest asset is his ability to dream possesses the secrets of invisibility. According to Frank McConnell, Marvel is the appropriate recipient of the books because he "is the embodiment, not of a utopian intelligence, but of an antiutopian, generous ignorance that knows its own limits, and in recognizing its own limits asserts or incarnates something important about the limits of human capability" (122). The choice of Marvel as the owner of the notebooks is humorous irony as well as a comment upon scientific excess, and the juxtaposition of Marvel and Kemp underscores Wells's awareness that scientific method was an important issue for the Victorians and for the next century.

The concept of science *The Invisible Man* ultimately presents, and that becomes a prevailing view of scientific methodology by the late nineteenth century, is articulated by twentieth-century scientist Peter Medawar. Discussing two conceptions of science, he explains one as an "imaginative and exploratory activity" and the other as a "critical and analytical activity" (30–31). Or in other words, the two modes can be understood as "what might be true" and as "testing it" or "trying it out" (33). For Medawar, these two seemingly contradictory views of science are in fact "*two* successive and complementary episodes of thought that occur in every advance of scientific understanding" (33; Medawar's emphasis). This view suggests that science is not just concerned with how phenomena are composed but also with how they come to be understood. The nineteenth-century debate over science suggests that like literature, science is a cultural construct, subject to the same ideologies that shape discourse and capable of presenting alternative, yet credible truths. Wells, by choosing to express ideas about science in literature, shows that art and science are involved in the interaction of similar imaginative and analytical processes.

WORKS CITED

Altick, Richard D. *Victorian People and Ideas.* New York: Norton, 1973.
Arnold, Matthew. "Literature and Science." *Prose of the Victorian Period.* Ed. William E. Buckler. Boston: Houghton, 1958. 486–501.
Batchelor, John. *H.G. Wells.* Cambridge: Cambridge UP, 1985.
Bergonzi, Bernard. *The Early H.G. Wells: A Study of the Scientific Romances.* Manchester, Eng.: Manchester UP, 1961.
Coleridge, Samuel Taylor. *Biographia Literaria. Prose of the Romantic Period.* Ed. Carl R. Woodring. Boston: Houghton, 1961. 91–121.
———. *The Friend. Prose of the Romantic Period.* Ed. Carl R. Woodring. Boston: Houghton, 1961. 139–47.
Erhmann, Jacques. "Homo Ludens Revisited." Trans. Cathy and Phil Lewis. *Yale French Studies* 41 (1968): 31–57.
Hammond, J.R. *An H.G. Wells Companion: A Guide to the Novels, Romances, and Short Stories.* New York: Barnes & Noble, 1979.
Haynes, Roslynn. *H.G. Wells: Discoverer of the Future.* New York: New York UP, 1980.
Huizinga, Johan. *Homo Ludens: A Study of the Play Element in Culture.* Boston: Beacon P, 1955.
Huxley, Thomas. "Science and Culture." *Prose of the Victorian Period.* Ed. William E. Buckler. Boston: Houghton, 1958. 526–37.

Mason, Stephen F. *A History of the Sciences.* New York: Collier, 1962.

McConnell, Frank. *The Science Fiction of H.G. Wells.* New York: Oxford UP, 1981.

Medawar, Peter. *Plato's Republic.* New York: Oxford UP, 1958.

Shelley, Mary. *Frankenstein.* New York: Bantam, 1981.

Smith, Jonathan. *Fact and Feeling: Baconian Method and the Nineteenth-Century Literary Imagination.* Madison: U of Wisconsin P, 1994.

Stevenson, Robert Louis. *The Strange Case of Dr. Jekyll and Mr. Hyde and Other Famous Tales.* New York: Dodd and Mead, 1961.

Wordsworth, William. *The Preface to Lyrical Ballads. Prose of the Romantic Period.* Ed. Carl R. Woodring. Boston: Houghton, 1961. 49–68.

Wells, H.G. *The Invisible Man.* New York: Bantam, 1983.

West, Anthony. Introduction. *The Invisible Man.* By H.G. Wells. New York: Bantam, 1983, vii–xvi.

NOTES

1. See Paradis, James, and Thomas Postlewait, eds. *Victorian Science and Victorian Values: Literary Perspectives.* Annuals of the New York Academy of Sciences. Vol. 360. New York: The New York Academy of Sciences, 1981, and Chapple, J.A.V. *Science and Literature in the Nineteenth Century.* Houndmills, Eng.: Macmillian, 1986.

2. In *Fact and Feeling: Baconian Science and the Nineteenth-Century Literary Imagination,* Jonathan Smith traces the nineteenth-century debate over scientific method, revealing the links between scientific method (i.e., Bacon) and the literary imagination. In addition to Romantic and Victorian literary artists, Smith discusses writers such as William Whewell, John Hershel, David Brewster, and James Spedding, all of whom reassess Baconian methodology, particularly the relationship between fact and theory (scientific observation and hypothesis). Both groups show how nineteenth-century writers, both literary and nonliterary, reevaluated the role of the imagination in science and the relationship between science and literature.

3. Roger Callois makes the distinction between competitive games (agôn) and games of chance (alea). See his essay "The Structure and Classification of Games" (*Diogenes* 12 [1955]: 62–75).

4. See Singh, Kirpal. "Science and Society: A Brief Look at *The Invisible Man.*" *Wellsian* 7 (1984): 19–23.

PAUL A. CANTOR

The Invisible Man *and the Invisible Hand:* *H.G. Wells's Critique of Capitalism*

W hen H.G. Wells died in 1946, his place in the history of twentieth-century literature seemed assured. At his funeral, J.B. Priestley referred to him as the "great prophet of our time." Shortly thereafter, Prime Minister Clement Atlee headed a Service of Public Homage for Wells, at which Winston Churchill spoke to honor his memory. During his long literary career, Wells had been one of the most popular and financially successful writers in the English language. Moreover, he was admired by the general public as a sage or visionary, so revered that in his later years he could command audiences with Stalin and Roosevelt. But today Wells is seldom taken seriously, and if he is discussed in literary circles at all, it is almost always among specialists in science fiction. In the long run, authors are remembered for what literary critics say about them, and Wells was never embraced by the professional literary establishment. As popular as his books were (or perhaps precisely because they were popular), they have at best hovered on the periphery of the academic canon of twentieth-century literary classics. Most critics concluded that Wells was the loser in the famous debate on the nature of fiction that he carried on with Henry James in a series of essays, reviews, and letters. Advocating an aesthetic perspective, James emerged as the champion of modernist fiction, above all its sophisticated handling of point of view, while Wells, who valued content over

From *The American Scholar*, vol. 68, no. 3. © 1999 by Paul A. Cantor.

form and social message over artistic technique, seemed like a throwback to the nineteenth century, incapable of appreciating the epistemological subtlety of the avant-garde novel.

We are left with a paradox: as the founder of the genre of science fiction, Wells is perhaps the greatest prophet of modernity, and yet literary critics classify him as the antithesis and antagonist of modernism. No one wrote more extensively or prophetically about characteristically twentieth-century developments, from air power to the atomic bomb (Wells coined the phrase), from international finance capital to experiments in socialism, from world wars to the horrors of colonialism. From the literary critics' point of view, Wells's sin was to write about modernity, but not in the style of modernism.

As we near the end of the century whose course Wells did such a good job of predicting back in the 1890s, the time seems ripe for a reassessment of his reputation, or at least a re-examination of his importance in modern (if not modernist) literature. Whatever Wells's fate has been within the academy, the general public has never deserted him. His great science fiction novels have stayed in print continuously and, made and remade as motion pictures, they have helped shape the consciousness of twentieth-century humanity around the globe. *The Time Machine, The Island of Doctor Moreau, The War of the Worlds, The Invisible Man:* if any works can lay claim to the title, these are the myths of our modern world. *Independence Day*, the blockbuster hit of the summer of 1996, was a transparent rip-off of *War of the Worlds*, with a computer virus cleverly substituted for the bacteria that defeated Wells's invading Martians. However unsophisticated Wells's stories may be in narrative technique, they evidently have a power that keeps them alive in the minds and hearts of the public.

Moreover, at a time when literary criticism has come to focus increasingly on economic, social, and political issues, Wells may deserve a fresh look. In economic terms, he was one of the most influential writers of the twentieth century. He did as much as anybody to shape the course that socialist theory and practice took in modern Britain; he may also be regarded as one of the architects of the welfare state. Wells believed that the only rational economy is a command economy, one in which a board of experts scientifically plans, directs, and coordinates all economic activity from its central position, thereby keeping entrepreneurs from pursuing their individual interests. He hoped that the twentieth century would be the century of socialism, the era when humanity finally took responsibility for its destiny and planned centrally for its future. As we come to the end of the twentieth century, the cause of socialism—in both theory and practice—is, to say the least, not looking as robust as Wells would have hoped. Thus our re-evaluation of Wells should include a critical look at his socialist ideas, to see how accurately he foresaw economic developments in the twentieth century. If his prophetic powers in economic matters were not as great as they were in science and technology, it is worth considering what may have distorted his vision in that area.

As a first step in this reconsideration of Wells, I have chosen to discuss one of his most enduring novels, *The Invisible Man*, which turns out to be one of the most interesting from an economic perspective. Though ultimately critical of Wells's achievement in the novel, I believe that, like many of his works, *The Invisible Man* has a greater depth of content and seriousness of purpose than has hitherto been realized.

First published in 1897, *The Invisible Man* tells the story of Griffin, the University College student who finds a way to make himself disappear. Driven to his experiments by an ambition that has always been fierce, Griffin grows increasingly megalomaniacal once he becomes invisible. He thus takes his place in a line of literary portrayals of mad scientists that stretches back to Mary Shelley's Victor Frankenstein. Interest in *The Invisible Man* has understandably tended to focus on the scientific aspects of the tale, especially the questions Wells raises about the ethics of modern technology.

But as often happens in Wells's work, the science fiction situation he creates in *The Invisible Man* provides a vehicle for exploring a larger set of economic and political problems that preoccupied him throughout his career. In particular, though Griffin's invisibility has scientific causes, it largely has economic effects—above all, on the movement and transfer of money. To put it bluntly, the chief use Griffin makes of his invisibility is to rob people of their cash:

> The story of the flying money was true. And all about that neighbourhood, even from the august London and Country Banking Company, from the tills of shops and inns ... money had been quietly and dexterously making off that day in handfuls and rouleaux, floating quietly along by walls and shady places, dodging quickly from the approaching eyes of men. And it had, though no man had traced it, invariably ended its mysterious flight in the pocket of that agitated gentleman.

Wells calls attention to the difficulty of tracing the movement of money. In our age of offshore banking and money-laundering schemes, we hardly need to be reminded that the circulation of money can be mysterious even without a literally invisible man behind it. Perhaps, then, Wells's *The Invisible Man* is an economic as well as a scientific parable, with money as its central subject.

For Wells, Griffin's invisibility symbolizes the working of an impersonal, decentralized, and—in Wells's view—dangerously chaotic market economy that fails to respect the dictates of either traditional communal ties or established government authorities. In effect, what is most significant about Griffin is his invisible *hand.* In his *Wealth of Nations* (1776), Adam Smith had argued that in an unfettered market economy, an invisible hand guides the self-seeking actions of individual entrepreneurs for the good of the community as a whole. As a socialist visionary, Wells uses his parable of the Invisible Man to call Smith's economic theories into question, presenting Griffin as a monster of egoism and finding chaos and catastrophe where Smith had seen order and progress. Thus, *The Invisible Man* offers an opportunity to examine Wells's critique of capitalism, both the substance of his arguments and the motives behind his hostility to the free market.

The key to understanding *The Invisible Man* is the dual setting of the story. Most of the novel takes place in the rural village of Iping and other rustic parts of England. But in Griffin's flashback narrative of how he became invisible, the scene shifts to the urban metropolis of London. Wells juxtaposes the tradition-bound, community-oriented existence of a rural village with the *anomie* and rootless cosmopolitanism of a modern city. In moving from London to a country village, Griffin creates the novel's dramatic tension, a confrontation between antithetical ways of life. As Wells describes Griffin's situation: "His irritability, though it might have been comprehensible to an urban brain-worker, was an amazing thing to these quiet Sussex villagers." Wells portrays Iping as a tight-knit community: everybody knows everybody else and everybody minds everybody else's business. The citizens of Iping are closed-minded and superstitious, easily upset by anything that might disturb the regularity of their existence. In the opening pages of the novel, Griffin arrives in Iping as the quintessential stranger, unknown to anyone in the village and visibly alien by virtue of his grotesque appearance.

In these circumstances, the only thing that can guarantee Griffin's acceptance in Iping is money. The novel opens with a prototypical market transaction. Griffin gets a room at the inn, not because of "human charity," as he at first suggests, but because of his ability to "strike [a] bargain" and pay the going rate. Money in and of itself already confers a kind of invisibility on him. Even in a town of busybodies, he is able to remain anonymous; as nosy as the innkeeper is, she does not even bother to learn Griffin's name as long as he pays his bills on time. We thus see how money transforms a traditional community. The citizens of Iping are used to dealing face to face and only with people well-known to them—as one of the villagers says: "I'd like to see a man's face if I had him stopping in *my* place." But a complete stranger is able to live among them by virtue of the power of money, which stands for the impersonal working of the market.

One would think that Wells would welcome this power as a force for progress. As he himself demonstrates, a market transaction allows perfect strangers, who may even have reasons to be hostile to each other, to cooperate in a limited way for their mutual benefit. Money seems to be a way of greatly expanding the range of social interaction. And in Wells's portrayal, villages like Iping certainly could use some broadening of their horizons. On the whole, Wells treats the villagers comically, making us laugh at their conventionality and superstitiousness. Nevertheless, he seems to take their side, accepting their way of life as the measure of normality and presenting the Invisible Man as the sinister figure, the one who in his secretiveness and obsessive concern for privacy disrupts the peaceful functioning of the village community. Wells reserves his truly sharp criticism for the modern city—London.

In the London section of the narrative, Griffin's invisibility oddly comes to symbolize the weakness and vulnerability of modern man, the way he becomes a nonentity under the pressure of mass society, the way he gets lost in the shuffle of the urban crowd. Griffin has of course high hopes for what his invisibility will allow him to do, but once he actually becomes invisible, almost the first thing he discovers is how much trouble his new condition is going to cause him. Emerging triumphantly into the streets of London, expecting to "revel in [his] extraordinary advantage," Griffin finds himself instead buffeted by the mass of people in the big city: "But hardly had I emerged upon Great Portland Street ... when I heard a clashing concussion and was hit violently behind.... I tried to get into the stream of people, but they were too thick for me, and in a moment my heels were being trodden upon." Hoping to be a god in the eyes of his fellow Londoners, Griffin at first finds that he is quite literally nothing to them. They walk right into and over him.

Griffin's invisibility thus becomes a striking image for everything Wells is trying to show about the impersonality of the market economy. In the small village of Iping, Griffin's problem is that all eyes are upon him: everybody wants to butt into his business. His problem in London is just the opposite: he is completely ignored. In London, no one knows anybody else, or at least a man can be virtually unknown to his next-door neighbors. Wells seems to suggest that even without his fiendish experiments, Griffin would be, in effect, invisible in London. The modern urban metropolis is a peculiarly attenuated form of community, in which people live together but have very little in common. Wells emphasizes this point by choosing as Griffin's London landlord "an old Polish Jew" who speaks Yiddish at a key moment. London is not simply a paradoxical community of strangers; it is a community of foreigners who sometimes do not even speak the same language.

For Wells, then, to be invisible in London is to be an individual in a vast, impersonal market economy that provides no genuine roots or community and hence turns a man into a purely necessitous being. Throughout the story Griffin is surprisingly obsessed with the basic human needs: food, clothing, shelter. He ends up embodying everything Wells finds wrong in capitalist existence. With nothing to stabilize his life, Griffin is always on the go, unable to find rest. He is continually scheming against his fellow human beings, always trying to take advantage of any situation. He encounters all the problems of the emancipated individual in the modern, enlightened world. In this context, it is highly appropriate that Griffin is a scientist, a man who tries to live by reason alone and who rejects all traditional religious beliefs. The villagers are particularly upset by his "never going to church of a Sunday."

Cut off from any sense of community, the Invisible Man becomes a monster of egoism, governed only by his own will and desires. As his colleague Dr. Kemp describes him: "He is pure selfishness. He thinks of nothing but his own advantage, his own safety." Thus Griffin serves as Wells's representation of *homo economicus*, the man who pursues his rational self-interest to the exclusion of all other considerations. In particular, the Invisible Man becomes Wells's symbol of the pure consumer. In a marvelous scene, Griffin invades the bastion of bourgeois consumerism, a department store. The phenomenon was sufficiently novel in Wells's day for him to feel compelled to have Griffin explain the concept: "[I] found myself outside Omniums, the big establishment where everything is to be bought,—you know the place,—meat, grocery, linen, furniture, clothing, oil paintings even,—a huge meandering collection of shops rather than a shop." Griffin's invisibility gives him access to the full panoply of consumer goods capitalism produces. But Wells adds a twist to his myth of the Invisible Man to suggest the self-defeating character of the capitalist economy and its consumer rat race. Although Griffin is able to acquire anything he wants, Wells dwells upon the difficulties he encounters consuming those goods. If he eats the food he craves, it renders him temporarily visible to his enemies until his body can assimilate it. If he puts on the clothing he covets, he becomes similarly vulnerable.

Griffin himself formulates his dilemma precisely: "I went over the heads of the things a man reckons desirable. No doubt invisibility made it possible to get them, but it made it impossible to enjoy them when they are got." Here Wells anticipates later, post-Marxist critiques of capitalism, particularly that of the Frankfurt School. Capitalism may succeed in allowing consumers to acquire the goods they want, but it prevents people from enjoying them. Indeed, by generating an infinity of desires and involving consumers in an unending process of acquisition, the market economy, in this view, dooms them to perpetual dissatisfaction.

However cleverly Wells employs the figure of the Invisible Man to develop a critique of capitalism, I believe that his critique fails. For one thing, its target is broader than he realizes. In most of *The Invisible Man*, Wells is not criticizing capitalism in particular but modernity in general. The aspects of life he questions—large-scale organization, urban existence, the masses of people, cosmopolitanism, rationalist and anti-traditional behavior—characterize all modern regimes, socialist as well as capitalist. If anything, capitalism mitigates the negative effects of mass society by dispersing economic power and preserving private pockets of resistance to the Leviathan state. The experience of socialist communities in the twentieth century suggests that in a centrally planned command economy, human beings are in fact more likely to feel like zeros, with even their rights to private property and private initiative taken away. As for Wells's point about consumption under capitalism, it rests on a false analogy. Nothing in the real world corresponds to the difficulties Griffin encounters in enjoying what he acquires; they are entirely peculiar to his situation as an invisible man. In fact, most consumers under capitalism want their consumption to be *visible*. Ever since Thorsten Veblen, critics of capitalism have been complaining about "conspicuous consumption." Wells may have a point in his critique of capitalist consumption, but his particular fictional vehicle for expressing it does nothing to prove it.

Indeed, Wells's central metaphor fails to work in one respect so fundamental that it obviates the need for a detailed, point-by-point refutation of his position. There is only *one* Invisible Man in Wells's story. Far from functioning in a market system, he enjoys a kind of monopoly. Hence he operates without the checks and balances that are vital to Adam Smith's notion of the invisible hand. Smith never denied that human beings are egoistic. But his point was that as selfish as individual people may be, when that selfishness is made to operate within the system of a market economy, it is forced to serve the common good. Thus Wells's science fiction parable fails to offer a fair test of Smith's economic principles. In fact, Smith would be likely to agree that making a man invisible would turn him into a monster of egoism, for it would set him free from the normal discipline of the market, where businessmen keep each other in check precisely by observing each other's actions, ever on the lookout for any competitive advantage. In Smith the individual entrepreneur is *not* invisible; indeed the working of the invisible hand depends entirely on the visibility of businessmen as they meet in open competition.

I prefer therefore to concentrate on analyzing not the logic of Wells's position, which is weak, but the motives behind his hostility to the market economy. The most peculiar aspect of *The Invisible Man* is the atavism of Wells's position. He generally sides with the backward, unsophisticated villagers against the forward-looking scientific genius, Griffin. Wells seems in fact to be guilty of economic and political nostalgia in *The Invisible Man*, looking back longingly to an earlier and simpler age when communities were small and tightly knit and human beings could count on directly cooperating with each other to solve their problems. Wells fundamentally distrusts the central insight of Smith and capitalist economics: that the market provides a way of rationally ordering the productive activities of human beings without the need for central direction or even without the actors knowing each other personally.

Wells shares the suspicions and fears of capitalism that typically grip the citizens of pre-modern and economically undeveloped communities. As Friedrich Hayek has argued in *The Fatal Conceit*, to such people the operation of the market economy looks like magic. The merchant, the entrepreneur, the financier—all these basic actors in the market economy apparently produce wealth out of nothing and thus, to the common man, seem like sorcerers. Wells's portrait of Griffin confirms all the common man's suspicions of the businessman: that he is unproductive, that he is secretive in his dealings, that all he does is move around money that belongs to other people, that essentially his acquisition is a form of theft, that he lives off the work of others. Like many people, Wells cannot understand or appreciate the special contribution that the entrepreneur makes to the good of the economy as a whole. In *A Modern Utopia*, he makes the revealing statement that "trade is a bye-product and not an essential factor in social life." In fact, the entrepreneur, by means of his special knowledge of market conditions and his willingness to assume risks in an uncertain world, makes it possible for goods to be available when and where people want them. Anyone who believes that the entrepreneur does not earn his profits is essentially claiming that we live in a risk-free world.

Like many nineteenth-century Englishmen with socialist leanings, Wells had trouble accepting the messiness and apparent disorder of the complex system of the market economy, which works precisely by dispersing economic knowledge, power, and control. Wells was not overtly nostalgic for the Middle Ages and its feudal system in the way Thomas Carlyle and William Morris were, but he did, in effect, return to medieval ways of thinking in his insistence that order has to be imposed on society from above—that only with leaders centrally directing economic activity can it take a rational form. Throughout *The Invisible Man*, we can see that Wells does not like the idea of a character operating outside the ken of any central authority and hence beyond any centralized control. The Invisible Man personifies everything Wells distrusts in the spontaneous order of the market. Griffin is the least predictable of human beings. He can appear anywhere at any time and throw a wrench into the working of the most elaborate government plan. He is indeed the bureaucrat's worst nightmare: how can you regulate a man if you cannot even see him?

Toward the end of the story, Griffin begins to behave like the arch-enemy of government authority, the terrorist. He hopes to undermine the power of the government by means of random acts of violence that will demonstrate its inability to assert its authority and maintain order. Thus *The Invisible Man* builds up to a confrontation that reveals Wells's vision of the well-ordered society. Faced with the threat of murderous violence from Griffin, the community finally organizes—into a huge manhunt from which even an invisible man cannot escape. Griffin has been a challenge to what Foucault and others call the panoptical character of government, its ability to see into every corner of society and thus to oversee all the activities of its citizens. With a nationwide dragnet, Wells's authorities will make sure that Griffin can no longer elude their surveillance:

> Every passenger train along the lines on a great parallelogram between Southampton, Winchester, Brighton, and Horsham, travelled with locked doors, and the goods traffic was almost entirely suspended. And in a great circle of twenty miles round Port Burdock, men armed with guns and bludgeons were presently setting out in groups of three and four, with dogs, to beat the roads and fields. Mounted policemen rode along the country lanes, stopping at every cottage.

Wells inadvertently shows his true colors here. This vision is profoundly totalitarian. Hostility to the Invisible Man easily passes over into hostility to ordinary commerce and indeed to the free and spontaneous movement of any individual.

The nationwide dragnet lays bare what has all too often been the nightmare result of the socialist dream: society turned into an armed camp, what Wells himself describes as a "state of siege." Nothing in the country is to move without the government knowing about it; all rights to privacy have been suspended. At a number of points earlier in the story, Griffin is protected by the traditional Anglo-Saxon regard for civil rights. Even when the authorities suspect him of having committed crimes, they punctiliously observe the procedures designed to protect the individual against unjustified government intrusion into his life, such as the requirement for search warrants. Initially contemplating cruel methods to snare Griffin, including "powdered glass" on the roads, the local police chief worries that these might be "unsportsmanlike." But by the end of the story, all sense of the individual's rights has been dissolved and the government conducts an all-out war against one of its citizens. Wells is able to make a case for the unique danger of an invisible man, but one may still be struck by the disproportion between the power of a solitary individual like Griffin and the vast forces mobilized to capture and destroy him. In the end, Wells shows the rebellious individual literally crushed by the weight of the community arrayed against him: what Wells calls "the pressure of the crowd."

At just the point when the Invisible Man threatens to elude the control of the authorities in England, he momentarily escapes Wells's control as a novelist as well. In chapter 26, Griffin finally becomes invisible even to his author. Up to this point, Wells has generally maintained the stance of an omniscient narrator, able to recount all the movements of his characters and even to give us access to their inmost thoughts. But suddenly he loses sight of his own creation:

> Thereafter for some hours the Invisible Man passed out of human perceptions. No one knows where he went nor what he did. But one can imagine him hurrying through the hot June forenoon, ... and sheltering ... amid the thickets of Hintondean.... That seems the most probable refuge for him.... One wonders what his state of mind may have been during that time, and what plans he devised.... At any rate he vanished from human ken about midday, and no living witness can tell what he did until about half-past two.

This is an odd moment in Wells's fiction. He is usually content to tell his stories in a straightforward manner, not troubling himself over issues of perspective or point of view. But here he calls attention to the fictionality of his story, and indeed throughout the rest of this chapter he presents himself uncharacteristically as a limited narrator who is forced to resort to rank speculation: "We can know nothing of the details of the encounter" or "But this is pure hypothesis." Wells seems uncomfortable with his new situation. For once he is not in total control of his story; he cannot supply the full explanation of the action in which he usually delights. Thanks to the elusiveness of the Invisible Man, Wells's own story threatens to become a mystery to him.

In this rare moment in his fiction, we get a glimpse of what unites H.G. Wells the novelist and H.G. Wells the socialist: both believe in central planning. As a writer, Wells was used to plotting his novels carefully so as to maintain strict control over their structure. Even among novelists, he is distinguished, at least in his early science fiction works, by the leanness of his plots, the fact that he generally excludes extraneous matter and keeps a tight focus on his thematic concerns. He almost never grants freedom to his characters. They exist only to carry out his plot and express his ideas. One reason Wells has not been a favorite among literary critics is that his novels strike many of them as thematically didactic and technically unsophisticated—which is another way of saying that he does not go in for the sort of modernist fiction that grants a certain autonomy to the characters and their points of view. The world of a Wells science fiction novel may be beset by chaos and cataclysms—dying suns, rebellious beast-men, invading Martians, giant insects run amok—but the book itself is always well ordered and clearly under the author's command.

This obsession with control seems to have carried over into Wells's attitude toward politics and economics. He expected society to be as orderly and centrally planned as one of his novels. As a novelist, Wells was always looking for closure, for the artfully plotted story that would take shape once and for all time. But in the free market, stories do not work out with the clear shape and neat outcomes of well-written novels. The market is always in flux, continually adapting to changing circumstances in the natural world and to the changing desires and attitudes of consumers. Hence Wells's dislike for the market. Like that of many artists, Wells's socialism has an aesthetic dimension. As a novelist, he had one model of order constantly in front of him: if a novel has a shape, the reason is that a single consciousness planned the work. Wells's aesthetic distaste for contingency prejudiced him against the spontaneous order of the market economy. He was used to the static perfection of a work of fiction, in which nothing is left to chance and the author takes responsibility for tying up all the loose ends before he reaches the conclusion. In speaking of his own temperament in *A Modern Utopia*, Wells describes how "the mere pleasure of completeness, of holding and controlling all the threads, possesses [him]." This ideal of control provides an excellent blueprint for fiction (a tautly plotted story) but a poor one for society (totalitarianism).

To understand Wells's hostility to the Invisible Man and the capitalist order he represents, we must return to his characterization of Griffin. In the Frankenstein tradition, Griffin is a portrait of the scientist as a young artist. Wells deliberately eliminates all the collaborative aspects of scientific research by presenting Griffin as a solitary creative genius, operating, like a Romantic artist, alone and on the fringes of society. As we have seen, Wells is highly critical of his Invisible Man, to the point of imaginatively siding with his enemies. And yet, like most authors, Wells cannot help sympathizing to some extent with his protagonist. Indeed, it would be odd if Wells, the visionary science fiction writer, did not in some way identify with Griffin, the scientific visionary.

Thus, in addition to providing a symbol of the capitalist order, the Invisible Man can be viewed as a self-portrait of Wells. Like his creator, Griffin is a man ahead of his time, so far ahead that the public fails to appreciate his genius. Griffin may thus give us a glimpse into his creator's dark side by revealing more than Wells intended about his own psychology. Griffin thinks of himself as a god among men—indeed, he plays that role to the servant he adopts, Thomas Marvel, who even addresses him as "Lord." Specifically, Griffin thinks of himself as a Nietzschean superman, raised above the conventional moral restraints that ordinary men feel compelled to observe. But at the same time, Griffin is a brilliant study of what Nietzsche calls *ressentiment*. In many ways, his invisibility scheme is an attempt to compensate for his deep feelings of inferiority, inadequacy, and powerlessness. Coming from humble origins, perpetually short of money, Griffin is a classic case of a man who tries to rise in the world by virtue of his wits; he wants desperately "to become famous at a blow." By his own account, he is jealous of other researchers and paranoid that they will steal and take credit for his discoveries. Griffin reveals himself to be obsessed with petty frustrations, chiefly the drudgery of his career as a teacher, surrounded by "gaping, silly students" and under constant pressure to publish or perish.

In short, Griffin feels woefully undervalued by society. He knows that he is more intelligent than the people around him, but many of them make more money or hold more honored positions. Society does not reward intelligence sufficiently to suit him. When he figures out how to become invisible, he is using his intelligence to obtain the rewards and privileges that society has been denying him. Griffin is out to prove something, as he tells the ignorant villagers of Iping: "'You don't understand,' he said, 'who I am or what I am. I'll show you. By Heaven! I'll show you.'" Griffin has a profound contempt for ordinary humanity, which he regards as well beneath him in the one quality he esteems: intelligence. That is why he is frustrated by the fact that an ordinary man like Marvel can interfere with his plans: "To have worked for years, to have planned and plotted, and then to get some fumbling purblind idiot messing across your course! Every conceivable sort of silly creature that has ever been created has been sent to cross me." Griffin's contempt for the stupidity of the common man means that he has contempt for the market economy and the way it distributes wealth. After all, it is the market economy that has denied Griffin the rewards he thinks he deserves. The principal use Griffin makes of his invisibility is to redistribute wealth, taking it away from the established owners of property and sending it in his own direction. To the extent that the Invisible Man seeks to undo the injustice of a market economy that in his view does not adequately reward merit, he may be said to be a socialist himself.

I have presented Wells's Invisible Man as at one moment a symbol of capitalism and at another a symbol of socialism: an obvious contradiction. But I believe that this contradiction lies in Wells's novel itself—that he portrays his central figure inconsistently. In many ways Wells was trying to give a portrait of the capitalist mentality in the figure of the Invisible Man, but he evidently invested too much of himself in his protagonist and ended up simultaneously portraying the mentality of a political visionary, a man who tries to remake the world to fit his image of a just social order. Indeed, at several points in the novel, the Invisible Man sounds a lot more like a radical revolutionary than like a capitalist businessman. He conceives the idea of a Reign of Terror to establish and consolidate his power: "Port Burdock is no longer under the Queen, ... it is under me—the Terror! This is day one of year one of the new epoch,—the Epoch of the Invisible Man. I am Invisible Man the First." This is hardly the language of the free market. As Griffin's proclamation of a new era indicates, it is in fact the language of revolutionary totalitarianism.

Claiming to be able to spy into any corner of society and arrogating to himself the right to execute anyone he chooses, the Invisible Man becomes the mirror image of the panoptical, totalitarian regime arrayed against him. His model of order is not the free market but absolute monarchy. In proclaiming himself "Invisible Man the First," Griffin is only drawing the logical conclusion from his belief in his mental superiority. He is smarter than all other men, hence he ought to be able to rule them and order their lives. In his own way, the Invisible Man becomes a profoundly atavistic force, wanting to return England to its illiberal past, substituting one-man rule from above for any spontaneous ordering of market forces from below.

As a brilliant case study of *ressentiment*, Griffin provides remarkable insights into the psychology of the modern, alienated intellectual and his typically anti-capitalist mentality. In his feeling that the market economy treats him unjustly by insufficiently rewarding his talent and his genius, Griffin is indeed the prototype of the modern intellectual. This attitude helps explain why so many artists, scientists, academics, and other members of the intellectual and cultural elite have rejected capitalism and embraced socialism. They fantasize that a socialist order would undo the injustices of the market economy because, like Griffin, they secretly imagine that they will somehow be in charge of the centrally planned economy and thus able to redirect the flow of rewards as they see fit. Wells himself provides a perfect example of this mentality, and this may explain why he does such a good job of portraying Griffin. Like Griffin, Wells came from a humble background, spent time as a teacher, and used his wits (a good deal more successfully) to rise in the world and make himself famous. Moreover, despite his socialist leanings, Wells had a great deal of contempt for the common man and believed that society must be ruled from above, by an intellectual elite.

These attitudes surface prominently in *The Invisible Man*. We have already seen that although Wells ultimately sides with the villagers against Griffin, he presents them in a negative light, ridiculing their simplemindedness. On their own, they would clearly be incapable of protecting themselves against a genius like Griffin. They would be doomed without the intervention of Dr. Kemp, the medical associate Griffin tries to enlist in his cause but who quickly turns against him. As Wells sets up the situation, one man of intellect is required to counteract the nefarious schemes of another man of intellect. Kemp shows his superior intelligence in the way he immediately sizes up Griffin and grasps the full extent of the threat an invisible man constitutes to England and humanity. Moreover, it is Kemp, and Kemp alone, who comes up with all the plans for organizing society to capture Griffin.

Kemp's role in *The Invisible Man* reflects the peculiarly aristocratic form that socialism took in late-nineteenth-century England. Socialist doctrine offered a way of clamping down on all the productive forces that had been unleashed by free-market policies, forces that looked chaotic and anarchic to fastidious Englishmen like Wells and seemed to threaten the lingering ascendancy of cultural elites left over from the aristocratic past. Wells hoped to replace the old aristocracy of birth with a new aristocracy of talent, particularly intellectual and artistic talent, but his basic attitude remained aristocratic and anti-democratic nonetheless. One can detect in Wells a strong element of the socialist equivalent of noblesse oblige; his concern for the common man is mixed with a good deal of condescension, if not outright contempt. By virtue of his superior intellect and cultivation, Wells thought himself entitled to show Englishmen how they should live, how they should organize their social and economic existence. This is the peculiar Nietzscheanism of Wells's socialism. Like his contemporary, George Bernard Shaw, Wells managed to combine faith in socialist doctrine with the belief that only a kind of Nietzschean superman could successfully implement it. He believed that if society is to be saved, it cannot be by a collective effort, but only by the work of a single great man, or perhaps a band of great men, an elite brotherhood.

If, then, I have given a contradictory account of *The Invisible Man*, the reason is that a fundamental contradiction lies at the core of Wells's thinking. He upheld a socialist ideal of community, yet at the same time he saw a form of heroic individualism as the only way of bringing about socialism. Wells's vacillation between socialism and heroic individualism helps explain his conflicted portrayal of the Invisible Man and the basic incoherence of the Invisible Man as a symbol. But it is precisely this incoherence that makes *The Invisible Man* such a richly rewarding work to analyze. Wells may have set out to present a critique of capitalism, but in the process he ended up providing the materials for a critique of his own position and more generally of the artist-intellectual's predilection for socialism. Above all, Wells's portrait of the Invisible Man teaches us how contempt for the common man and contempt for the market economy actually go hand in hand. Wells's socialism is ultimately aesthetic and aristocratic in nature; it is rooted in nothing so much as his conviction of his superiority, as an artistic visionary, to the ordinary mass of humanity. Evidently, Griffin was not the only megalomaniac in town.

BRUCE BEIDERWELL

The Grotesque in Wells's The Invisible Man

Regarding *The Invisible Man*, Joseph Conrad wrote to H.G. Wells: "One can always *see* a lot in your work—there is always a 'beyond' to your books—but into this (with due respect to its theme and length) you've managed to put an amazing quantity of effects."[1] Apparently not many critics have seen as much as Conrad saw, but a few have sought the source of the "beyond" in *The Invisible Man*. Bernard Bergonzi considers it a tale of the progressive alienation of a scientist-magician figure from a very solid and real social world.[2] Jack Williamson insists that the novel's two central characters represent opposing extremes in an inner conflict we all share: the lawless individual (Griffin, the Invisible Man) against the social man (Kemp).[3] Frank McConnell takes the lead Williamson offers and reads *The Invisible Man* as a psychologically and politically intelligent representation of the terrors of anarchy.[4] And, most recently, David Lake examines the novel's color imagery in relation to themes of death and damnation.[5]

These essays are suggestive, but none really considers the many curious tensions or oppositions that Wells plays upon throughout the book. Over thirty years ago, Norman Nicholson touched upon *The Invisible Man*'s "peculiar attraction," which arises from "the way it hovers between the incredible predicament of the invisible man and the humdrum life of *The Coach and Horses* at Iping near Bramblehurst."[6] My argument will begin with

From *Extrapolation*, vol. 24, no. 4. © 1983 by The Kent State University Press.

the "peculiar attraction" of the unexpected, incongruous, and disorienting oppositions of *The Invisible Man*. These oppositions suspend the reader between a sense of playful exuberance and a sensation of the grimmest terror.

Such a suspension puts us in the world of the grotesque—a world where the familiar is made strange. Wolfgang Kayser in *The Grotesque in Art and Literature* states that the grotesque expresses "our failure to orient ourselves in the physical universe."[7] By fusing realms which we habitually perceive as separate, the grotesque calls into question our basis for discrimination and challenges our sense of reality and personal identity. Kayser maintains that the nineteenth century reduced the power of the grotesque by depriving it of its ominous dimensions. He notes that the grotesque became little more than a comedy of fantastic invention as a result of a stubbornly optimistic rationalism, an insensitivity to myth, and an unwillingness to acknowledge its inhuman and alienating qualities.[8]

Wells seems distinctly modern in his employment of those qualities. *The Invisible Man* consistently undercuts our optimism in either the knowledge we possess or the knowledge we hope to acquire. It mixes the fantastic and the familiar. It blurs the animal and the human. It disturbs our sense of proportion by introducing the comic or petty when we expect the tragic or heroic. And finally, it expresses the two-sided terror of the stranger—the terror he experiences and the terror he inspires.

But the Victorians were not entirely oblivious to the power of the grotesque. Pater characterized modern art as "subtle and penetrative, yet somewhat grotesque"—distinct from the "blithe and steady poise" of the classical age.[9] Earlier, Ruskin had demonstrated a keen awareness of the unsteady poise of the grotesque. His chapter in *The Stones of Venice* on the grotesque in Renaissance art stands as perhaps the most exacting and certainly the most well-known nineteenth-century English discussion of the word. He notes that the grotesque is composed of two complementary elements, "one ludicrous, the other fearful." The difficulty in distinguishing between these two elements, Ruskin maintains, arises from the fact that "the mind, under certain phases of excitement, *plays* with *terror*, and summons images which, if it were in another temper, would be awful, but of which, either in weariness or in irony, it refrains for a time to acknowledge the true terribleness."[10] A tension between play and terror (along with a resistance to the full recognition of terror) functions as the central technique in *The Invisible Man*.

Ruskin's own sense of the playful grotesque provided Wells with the idea for his early tale "The Wonderful Visit."[11] But Wells seems to have appreciated the more serious possibilities as well. Ruskin cites Dürer as exemplifying the "noblest forms" of the grotesque; in *The First Men in the Moon* Wells describes one of the Selenites as "a monster [such] as Dürer might have invented."[12] The link between the grotesque (the most often used adjective attached to the Selenites) and Dürer suggests that Ruskin's influence extended farther than "The Wonderful Visit."

It seems that Wells consciously developed the aesthetics of the grotesque. *The Invisible Man*, subtitled *A Grotesque Romance*, appeared in 1897, one year after *The Island of Doctor Moreau*, "a theological grotesque."[13] In *Moreau*, Wells provides a textbook example of the essential characteristics of the grotesque—characteristics which Wells again adopts in *The Invisible Man*. The two novels are, of course, very different in tone. *Moreau* is more savagely satiric, even more fantastic, and certainly less funny than the later book. But the starker horrors of *Moreau* serve to clarify the grotesque elements which give the seemingly lighter book its disturbing undercurrent.

Prendick, the protagonist of *Moreau*, is physically weakened by an ordeal at sea and thrown into an unfamiliar and isolated land. Despite his need for rest, he is driven from his room by the horrible screams of one of Moreau's laboratory animals. Outside, Prendick experiences the grotesque: "in spite of the brilliant sunlight and the green fans of the trees waving in the soothing sea-breeze, the world was a confusion, blurred with drifting black and red phantasms" (M, p. 45). He first sees what he takes to be a man running on all fours and lapping up water from a brook. Soon after that, he comes across a freshly killed rabbit. Finally, when Prendick comes upon three "grotesque human figures," he realizes the source of the disturbing sensations he has felt since first seeing a "native" of Moreau's island:

> I perceived clearly for the first time what it was that had offended me, what had given me the two inconsistent and conflicting impressions of utter strangeness and yet of the strangest familiarity. The three creatures ... were human in shape, and yet human beings with the strangest air about them of some familiar animal. Each of these creatures, despite its human form, its rag of clothing, and the rough humanity of its bodily form, had woven into it, into its movements, into the expression of its countenance, into its whole presence, some now irresistible suggestion of a hog, a swinish taint, the unmistakable mark of the beast. (M, pp. 50–51)

Prendick, however, misinterprets what he sees. He assumes Moreau has turned men into beasts—not beasts into men. In an effort to escape the supposed threat that Moreau represents, Prendick allows a beast-man to lead him down into a dark, hellish den where the monsters congregate. Prendick imagines himself as "already dead and in another world" (M, p. 72). But he is not dead and not really in another world.

Moreau represents a greater threat than Prendick first realizes, for by turning beasts into men he destroys man's distinct, special identity. Moreau states it tersely: "A pig may be educated" (M, p. 91). Prendick cannot escape Moreau's meaning even if he can escape his island. When he returns to England, Prendick (rather like Gulliver) sees man differently:

> I could not persuade myself that the men and women I met were not also another, still passably human, Beast People, animals half-wrought into the outward image of human souls.... I would go out into the streets to fight with my delusion, and prowling women would mew after me, furtive craving men glance jealously at me, weary pale workers go coughing by me ... like wounded deer dripping blood, old people, bent and dull, pass murmuring to themselves and all unheeding a ragged tail of gibing children. (M, pp. 170–72)

Under his first, mistaken impression of Moreau's experiments, Prendick fears for his life; when he realizes the truth, he fears life itself. Kayser notes this distinction as central to the nature of the grotesque, for it is not an other-world which is terrifying and strange, but our world—at least our world as we are forced to experience it under the pressure of new ideas or facts which we cannot process within our old world view. Surprise or shock is an essential part of the grotesque; both *Moreau* and *The Invisible Man* illustrate this point.

But the shock of the new does not necessarily lead anywhere. Darko Suvin's discussion of Wells's "ambiguously disquieting strangeness" is relevant here. The grotesque destroys meaning without offering new meaning in return. It estranges us from our world without suggesting an acceptable alternative. The final chapters of both *Moreau* and *The Invisible Man* express a broken confidence in established values or knowledge, but those worn-out abstractions remain as viable as any. As Suvin puts it, Wells is a virtuoso at having it both ways ideologically.[14]

Or perhaps we can substitute "neither way," for the sudden disorienting effects and the shock which arise from the breakdown of coherence and stability can often provoke the kind of laughter which edges towards a reaction to the absurd. In the beast-men's parody of a worship service, Wells explores this darkly comic potential of the grotesque. When

Prendick first arrives at the creatures' gathering place, an especially hideous sloth-man confirms Prendick's human identity by comparison to its own humanness. The creature speaks in a thick, rather peculiar voice, "but its English accent is strangely good" (M, p. 71). This touch makes us laugh while it draws us closer to the beast/man confusion which is at the center of the nightmare. It should also be noted that this entire scene puts Prendick in the position of seeking acceptance into a community. Prendick may choose to be a "man alone," but both he and the Invisible Man discover that a "man alone" is a contradiction in terms. Man can only be identified as a creature within a group and that group encompasses a frightening breadth. Prendick nearly joins the fervor of the beast-men's mad litany, but he feels "deep down" within himself the struggle between "laughter and disgust" (M, p. 73).

For most readers of *Moreau*, disgust effectively stifles laughter. The comic fares far better in *The Invisible Man*. But the difference should not obscure an essential similarity. In some respects *Moreau* mirrors *The Invisible Man*; both books rest upon the structure of the grotesque, but the latter book reverses the tension between the strange and the familiar. In *Moreau*, Prendick—a "man alone"—is brought to a world which shows him things he cannot accept. Moreau's creatures force the profoundly ominous element upon Prendick's vision. In *The Invisible Man*, Griffin—a "stranger"—is the ominous element. He intrudes into our familiar world and upsets our faith in it. This reversal accounts for the unrelentingly grim and disturbing tone of *Moreau*. We are forced to identify exclusively with Prendick, the sole narrator, and fully share his nightmare. In *Moreau*, a lone man confronts terror; in *The Invisible Man*, a lone terror confronts man. In *Moreau*, only Prendick (and the reader with him) experiences the power of the grotesque; in *The Invisible Man*, the power of the grotesque is more diffused. Griffin commands a portion of our sympathy by his reckless individuality, but only a portion. He remains a nameless stranger throughout the first half of the book and achieves full human identity only in death. Faced with the threat Griffin represents, we can always retreat to the relative security of belonging to the mob.

Such a retreat offers little comfort since the mob is scarcely more human than Griffin, but as Williamson points out, the mob is at least identified with the necessary, social workings of a community.[15] The numerous references to games underscore this idea. People work together against a common foe:

> Hall sent the knife sliding along the table to Wadgers, who acted
> as goal-keeper for the offensive, so to speak, and then stepped

forward as Jaffers and the stranger swayed and staggered towards him, clutching and hitting in.[16]

In the final battle, "there was a simultaneous rush upon the struggle, and a stranger coming into the road suddenly might have thought an exceptionally savage game of Rugby football was in progress" (IM, p. 199). Griffin comes to realize that he needs a teammate. Poor Mr. Marvel cannot fill the role, so Griffin turns to Kemp: "What I want ... is a goal-keeper, a helper, and a hiding-place" (IM, p. 169). But Kemp, like Marvel, has a shrewd sense of the odds. It will take more than a single confederate to play "a game against the race" (IM, p. 170). The race responds to Griffin's threat with equal savagery and greater numbers. By cutting himself off from his own kind, Griffin may threaten the community, but he can only destroy himself.

Griffin's narrative marks his radical alienation. He keeps every step of his experiment a secret. He scorns "teaching fools in a provincial college" (IM, p. 124). When money to continue his work runs low he robs his father, who, in desperate straits himself, commits suicide. The funeral, familiar sights, a girl out of his past—all fail to engage his concern or even his attention:

> "It was all like a dream, that visit to the old places. I did not feel then that I was lonely, that I had come out from the world into a desolate place. I appreciated my loss of sympathy, but I put it down to the general inanity of things. Re-entering my room seemed like a recovery of reality." (IM, p. 127)

Once he achieves invisibility, Griffin begins to sense subconsciously that his human identity has disappeared. He dreams that he is buried with his father:

> "I struggled, shouted, appealed to the mourners, but they continued stonily following the service; the old clergyman, too, never faltered droning and sniffing through the ritual. I realised I was invisible and inaudible, that overwhelming forces had their grip on me." (IM, p. 150)

When he awakes, Griffin is almost as terrified by his invisibility as others are. Clothes become not only his disguise and protection against weather, but also his link to a solid self. He keeps the clothes he has stolen in the emporium, even at the risk of capture: " 'Odd as it may seem—it did not occur to me at the moment to take off my clothes as I should have done. I had made up my mind, I suppose, to get away in them, and that ruled me'" (IM, p. 151). Similarly, Griffin considers it a "queer fancy" that he likes to be dressed when he eats, but we do not mistake his motivation (IM, p. 108).

Griffin's alienation from his species is further emphasized by the animal/human confusion so vital to the grotesque. Despite the savage potential of the mob, most of the animal associations in the book are attached to the Invisible Man. Williamson touches upon this point and calls attention to the name: Griffin.[17] The grotesque confusion is certainly apparent here, but it is possible Wells had more than the mythical creature in mind. The *OED* notes that a griffin is a species of vulture, a vulture that, as one nineteenth-century naturalist claims, must disgorge itself of its prey in order to escape when surprised by other predators. The Invisible Man suffers from a similar weakness. Griffin must be careful when he eats because his undigested food shows. He also discovers the obvious—dressed in his costume he cannot eat without exposing his invisible face. Even more to the point, Griffin must often leave behind things that he wants, needs, and momentarily holds, for when he steals he is marked by what he steals. Griffin finds his grandest ambitions are trivialized and frustrated by the very discovery that spurred those ambitions.

In relation to the animal/human confusion, it should also be noted that, unlike Aeschylus' silent "dogs of Zeus," this Griffin barks. And, befitting an agent of the grotesque, it is a cruel bark of laughter: "The visitor laughed abruptly, a bark of a laugh that seemed to bite and kill in his mouth" (IM, p. 9). Griffin savors jokes which are as terrible as they are funny. In this respect he seems rather like the author of *Moreau*. Prendick's naive reflections in the final chapter of that novel lend the whole work the character of an elaborate practical joke on Wells's part. Griffin's jokes (like Wells's) play upon the shock or surprise of the grotesque and leave those they are directed against in a state of panic. Mr. Cuss is the first victim of such a joke. Griffin gets a "bark of laughter" at Cuss's expense by nipping his nose with an invisible finger and thumb. The incident (first vaguely overheard by the landlady, then told with great sincerity and detail by Cuss) is beautifully paced as a good joke should be; but Cuss's terror is real, even if it is occasioned by the ignominious tweak which suddenly breaks the spell of looking into an empty, but animated sleeve (IM, pp. 29–33).

Griffin's barking laughter is a small part in the pervasive role dogs or dog imagery plays in *The Invisible Man*. Dogs are a special curse to Griffin because they detect him by scent, not sight. Still, this faculty does not account for the antipathy dogs express toward Griffin. It cannot be that dogs are merely angered by smelling what they cannot see; in the third chapter, a fully costumed, visible Griffin is bitten by a dog. It seems that dogs instinctively dislike Griffin. But the grotesque allows for no categories defining dogs, Griffin, and man. As is clear from *Moreau*, confusion is the rule. Griffin uses the word "cur" several times towards those people who betray him and yet he tells Kemp: "I've a particular objection to being caught by my fellow-men" (IM, p. 111). The roles of hunter and hunted shift about during the pursuit scenes which close the novel, and when Griffin is finally taken down, his "fellow-men" are indeed represented as a pack of dogs:

> Then came a mighty effort, and the Invisible Man threw off a couple of his antagonists and rose to his knees. Kemp clung to him in front like a hound to a stag, and a dozen hands gripped, clutched, and tore at the Unseen. (IM, p. 199)

The simile likening the rational, respectable, and responsible Kemp to a hound extends the discomforting associations that Wells has developed around Griffin. I have stated that the reader of *The Invisible Man* may take refuge from the horrors of the grotesque, but that refuge can at best be tenuously held against the suggestions which are inherent in such savage scenes.

The very things that make *The Invisible Man* a lighter book than *Moreau* for most readers make it more subtly terrifying for a few. The threat represented by the grotesque may be more keenly felt because the familiar and the commonly assumed are more fully projected. Here, more than in *Moreau*, it is our world which is estranged, our world which becomes horrifying to live in. The third-person narrator is as attentive to ordinary details as he is to the extraordinary. The dispassionate, even tone the narrator maintains throughout further heightens the grotesque tension. Griffin, of course, narrates a part of his own story, but only within a frame established by the third-person narrator, which prepares us for what Griffin will relate. In addition, Griffin's narrative is regularly interrupted by Kemp's blunt, common-sense reactions, which help keep us, at least in part, grounded in the ordinary.

That ground is not easily shaken. The stranger who arrives in Iping on the twenty-ninth day of February has a hard time disturbing the stubbornly matter-of-fact Sussex villagers and peasants.[18] Simple disbelief in the fantastic protects one from the implications of the grotesque, but when the evidence of one's senses affirms the fantastic, disbelief comes only at the cost of some anxiety:

> After the first gusty panic had spent itself Iping became
> argumentative. Scepticism suddenly reared its head,—rather
> nervous scepticism, not at all assured of its back, but scepticism
> nevertheless. It is so much easier not to believe in an invisible
> man. (IM, p. 64)

Even at the moment when Griffin unveils his invisibility (if one can unveil
invisibility), Jaffers, the village constable, and Huxter, the store keeper, stick
to what they know in spite of what they don't see:

> "Invisible, eigh?" said Huxter.... "Who ever heard the likes of
> that?"
> "It's strange, perhaps, but it's not a crime. Why am I assaulted by
> a policeman in this fashion?"
> "Ah! that's a different matter," said Jaffers. "No doubt you are a bit
> difficult to see in this light, but I got a warrant and it's all correct.
> What I'm after ain't no invisibility,—it's burglary." (IM, p. 52)

Until we are brought to consider what Jaffers refuses to acknowledge, such
scenes remain purely comic. But the man's invisibility presses for
recognition; two pages later, Jaffers lies near death, pummelled by the man
he could not see. The juxtaposition of this grim note with the comic scene
which precedes it does not allow the reader (or anyone else) to maintain an
easy naiveté. Wells uses this stategy of quickly shifting moods throughout
The Invisible Man. Our reactions as readers are rather like those of the
villagers; we are a step behind the ominous message Griffin brings to us.

The village people are slow to respond to the uncanny, but they
eventually react with the appropriate panic and confusion.[19] Griffin unveils
himself on Whitmonday, but this stranger who "fell out of Infinity into
Iping" brings a confusion of tongues, not a sharing of them as was brought
by the Holy Spirit: "Every one seemed eager to talk at once, and the result
was babel" (IM, p. 49). And later, for emphasis: "A perfect babel of noises
they made" (IM, p. 53). Whitmonday, not Whitsunday, is an especially
telling choice for it both reduces and negates the events of the Pentecost by
placing them in the same realm of the grotesque which Griffin introduces.
The incredible happens, Wells implies, in a sequence which defeats
coherence. The fantastic events of one day turn the fantastic events of
another upside down. The mix of biblical associations in the topsy-turvy
Pentecost this scene presents suggests that Wells did not abandon the
"theological grotesque" when he finished *Moreau*.

The grotesque play upon theological matters is important in understanding the character of the fantastic in Wells. Paradoxically Wells's sense of the fantastic continually forces us to a grim materialism. The fantastic does not mean the supernatural in either *Moreau* or *The Invisible Man;* it does mean that the natural is far more vast than man comprehends, and that man is far less significant in relation to that vastness than he generally supposes.[20] Wells's more reflective characters confront the grotesque and glimpse their own pettiness and their own animality. They are not well suited to sustain the confrontation. Moreau and Griffin die. Prendick takes to his study. Kemp takes to his heels. In the world Wells presents, the latter two actions are to be preferred.

NOTES

1. Joseph Conrad, A letter to Wells, 4 December 1898, in *H.G. Wells: The Critical Heritage*, ed. Patrick Parrinder (London: Routledge & Kegan Paul, 1972), p. 60.

2. Bernard Bergonzi, *The Early H.G. Wells* (Manchester: Manchester Univ. Press, 1961), pp. 112–22.

3. Jack Williamson, *H.G. Wells: Critic of Progress* (Baltimore: Mirage Press, 1973), pp. 83–88.

4. Frank McConnell, *The Science Fiction of H.G. Wells* (Oxford: Oxford Univ. Press, 1981), pp. 113–24.

5. David Lake, "The Whiteness of Griffin and H.G. Wells's Images of Death, 1897–1914," *Science-Fiction Studies*, 8 (1981), 12–18.

6. Norman Nicholson, *H.G. Wells* (London: Arthur Barker, 1950), pp. 32–35.

7. Wolfgang Kayser, *The Grotesque in Art and Literature*, trans. Ulrich Weisstein (Bloomington: Indiana Univ. Press, 1963), p. 185.

8. Kayser, pp. 103–04.

9. Walter Pater, *The Renaissance: Studies in Art and Poetry*, ed. Donald L. Hill (Berkeley: Univ. of California Press, 1980), p. 178.

10. John Ruskin, *The Stones of Venice*, Vol. XI of *The Works of John Ruskin*, ed. E.T. Cook and Alexander Wedderburn (London: George Allen, 1904), p. 166.

11. Norman MacKenzie and Jeanne MacKenzie, *The Time Traveller: The Life of H.G. Wells* (London: Weidenfeld and Nicholson, 1973), p. 107. Published in America as *H.G. Wells: A Biography* (New York: Simon and Schuster, 1973).

12. H.G. Wells, *The First Men in the Moon*, in Vol. VI of *The Works of H.G. Wells* (New York: Scribners, 1924), p. 108.

13. H.G. Wells, *The Island of Doctor Moreau*, in Vol. II of *The Works of H.G. Wells* (New York: Scribners, 1924), p. ix. All further references to this work appear in the text with the abbreviated title M. See Gorman Beauchamp, *"The Island of Dr. Moreau as Theological Grotesque," Papers on Language and Literature*, 15 (1979), 408–17; and Robert M. Philmus, "The Satiric Ambivalence of *The Island of Doctor Moreau,*" *Science-Fiction Studies*, 8 (1981), 2–11. Beauchamp convincingly argues that Moreau's island represents "God's great one." His concern, however, is focused more on the theological than the grotesque. Philmus'

argument is actually more relevant to mine. He pays close attention to Wells's revisions which enrich the confusion between beast and man.

14. Darko Suvin, *Metamorphoses of Science Fiction: On the Poetics and History of a Literary Genre* (New Haven: Yale Univ. Press, 1979), pp. 217–18.

15. Williamson, pp. 84–87.

16. H.G. Wells, *The Invisible Man*, in Vol. III of *The Works of H.G. Wells* (New York: Scribners, 1924), p. 50. All further references to this work appear in the text with the abbreviated title IM.

17. Williamson, p. 83.

18. There is some confusion as to when Griffin arrives in Iping. The first sentence in the novel states that the "stranger came early in February," but Wells fixes upon a more appropriate date in the first sentence of the third chapter: "Thus it was that on the twenty-ninth day of February, at the beginning of the thaw, this singular person fell out of infinity into Iping Village."

19. Freud's discussion of the uncanny is especially relevant to Prendick's slow recognition of the beast in man. The terror and strangeness of the world is central to both the grotesque and the uncanny. See "The 'Uncanny,'" in *Collected Papers*, IV, trans. Joan Riviere (London: The Hogarth Press, 1950), pp. 368–407.

20. "A Talk with Gryllotalpa" (1887) suggests that Wells held this idea from an early point in his career. See reprint in *H.G. Wells: Early Writings in Science and Science Fiction*, ed. Robert M. Philmus and David Hughes (Berkeley: Univ. of California Press, 1975), pp. 19–21.

JANICE H. HARRIS

Wifely Silence and Speech in Three Marriage Novels by H.G. Wells

In *Experiment in Autobiography* (1934), H.G. Wells predicts that his Edwardian "Writings About Sex" will be the first of his works to be swallowed by the waters of oblivion.[1] "If any survive they will survive as a citation or so ... They had their function in their time but their time has already gone by ... No one will ever read them for delight" (p. 392). Wells' prediction was off on several counts. Certain of those Edwardian writings have survived. In particular, The Hogarth Press reissued a trio of Wells' marriage novels in 1986, *Marriage* (1912), *The Passionate Friends* (1913), and *The Wife of Sir Isaac Harman* (1914), each with a feisty feminist introduction by Victoria Glendinning. To read them is to realize that their time has not gone by, for they still provide the kind of delight one feels in the company of an inquiring mind wrestling with a difficult problem.

Still engaging, still pertinent, still holding their own against oblivion: these are good reasons to look again at Wells' early twentieth-century writings about sex, in this case a trio of his novels on marriage. In a more tentative voice, I would add a further reason. While recognizing that three novels by Wells do not the modern British novel make, in reading them I found myself questioning several recent, and not so recent, critical assessments of modern British fiction's treatment of marriage. That marriage has fared ill in the modern British novel is an opinion of long standing. In

From *Studies in the Novel*, vol. 26, no. 4. © 1994 by the University of North Texas.

"Marriage Questions in Modern Fiction" (1896), Elizabeth Rachel Chapman feared for the very institution, so powerfully in her view were novels of the 1890s representing marriage as a degradation.[2] Some eighty years on, Heilbrun, Gilbert, and Gubar see much the same thing: marriage in modernist literature consistently represented as a disaster, an analogue for death, a site of anger and violence.[3] These critics construct careful arguments; but like any generalization, the one they share regarding modern literature's grim representation of marriage oversimplifies. Mainly, it obscures the liveliness of the debate being conducted in the modern British novel of marriage, a liveliness one sees as well in the legal, medical, and theological discourses of the time. In each arena, the flaws that were being perceived in the institution were set alongside the joys, virtues, and apparent economic necessities, the remedies against potential new sufferings.[4] At the least, the complexity of the conversation about marriage one traces in Wells' trio of novels may urge us to look for a similar complexity—for the sense of genuine debate, of a jury still out—elsewhere in modern British fiction.

In the following essay, I argue that tracing the vision of marriage Wells develops in these novels is best accomplished by emphasizing their sequential character: *Marriage* (1912) concludes with questions that *The Passionate Friends* (1913) subsequently attempts but fails to solve; *The Wife of Sir Isaac Harman* (1914) then turns on both previous novels, fundamentally rescripting both of their plots. Further, I propose that the debate Wells enacts as he writes his way from text to text is reflected in the figure he develops in all three novels to represent marriage, a figure of marital intercourse that calls attention to textual exchange: talking, listening, interrupting, writing, reading.[5]

More specifically, preoccupying Wells in each of these novels is a contradiction that Lévi-Strauss comments on at the end of *The Elementary Structure of Kinship* and that Gayle Rubin and Nelly Furman have explored[6]: to wit, the contradiction that arises when conceptualizations of marriage that define women as homogeneous, silent objects of exchange circulated among men within masculine discourse systems are set alongside opposing, often simultaneous conceptualizations that recognize that women have voices, originate signs, and receive their very worth from their individual "talent— before and after marriage—for taking part in a duet" (Lévi-Strauss, p. 496). As indicated above, in Wells the opposition between wifely silence and speech develops within an array of interests related to marital discourse. He explores the ways in which old stories and/or new stories are capable of offering useful scripts for modern marriage, the way in which interpretive communities play a role in shaping the voices of wives and husbands, and the close link between cultural story-lines and plots of domestic ground, i.e., the link between homelessness and plotlessness.

Readers familiar with Wells' biography will recognize that his marriage novels were written during a difficult stage within his second marriage. His first marriage had ended in a divorce in 1895. As Anthony West sees it, Wells' affair with Amber Reeves and its break-up was a source of lingering grief and bitterness.[7] At the same time, the early stages of his affair with Rebecca West were both exciting and troublesome.[8] Undoubtedly, continuing feelings about the Reeves affair, the beginning of the liaison with West, and their respective places within Wells' marriage to Amy Catherine (Jane) Robbins lie behind this sequence of fictions on marriage.

A further impetus for writing these marriage novels may have been Wells' growing conception of himself as an ally of the feminists, indeed a feminist himself.[9] Like other social activists during the decade, Wells viewed woman suffrage as an obvious necessity but more important was a reconceptualization of men's and women's working, parenting, and sexual lives.

Reinforcing the sense that these novels reflect an on-going conversation in Wells' thinking about his own marriage and that they are related to his identification with Edwardian feminists is an additional possible impetus for this sequence: that is, the existence of a pair of notable wifely silences in two of Wells' earlier works. In Chapter Five of *A Modern Utopia* (1905), Wells sets out his scheme for improving the lives of women.[10] But what an odd chapter it is. Grandly titled "Women in a Modern Utopia," it could have examined women's education, work, health care, sexuality. Instead, it takes as its key topic the relationship between mothers and the government. So bold in promise, this chapter ends up representing women only within the context of Wells' interest in a state-funded endowment for motherhood. Although the endowment scheme remained attractive to Wells for decades (see *Experiment in Autobiography*, p. 394), one can imagine him sensing the inadequacy of this vision of modern married women's lives and the many additional ways those lives might be represented.

The silence of *Ann Veronica* (1909) is more conventional.[11] Like other "modern girl" novels of the period, *Ann Veronica* ends with a marriage. Once combative and articulate, the newly married and still quite young Ann Veronica subsides into domestic silence, closing the novel with a sigh: "the great time is over ... the petals have fallen" (pp. 389–90). That the great times are far from over becomes the argument of Marjorie Pope, heroine of the upcoming *Marriage*. *Marriage* opens with the courtship of Marjorie and Rag Trafford, but their wedding bells chime within the first third of this long novel. Wells left himself over 300 pages to explore all of the petals yet to unfold, all the female speeches yet to be enunciated.

If we follow Henry James's judgment of *Marriage*, we will read it not as a breaking of female silence but a continuation. In James's view, *Marriage*, like most of Wells' fiction, is essentially a monologue as Wells by-passes the play of all of his characters' consciousnesses and delivers an energetic lecture on better ways for better living.[12] Rebecca West castigated *Marriage* for a different reason: Wells' conceptualization of Marjorie as a moral imbecile and his implicit claim that she represents all modern English women/wives.[13] I would argue that *Marriage*—ultimately an uneven novel— is dialogic in ways James did not perceive and that Marjorie and her plight are more thoughtfully conceived than West allowed.

As Wells constructs the wooing and marrying of Marjorie Pope, he explicitly envisions her continually having to choose between old and new texts. And importantly, up until the last scene of the novel, Wells does not simply disparage old texts to valorize new ones, nor *vice versa*. Early on, we do admittedly encounter a series of traditional texts which promise Marjorie thin fare: the carefully written, conventional jokes of Mr. Magnet; her father's pompous letters to the *London Times;* and the sweeping, sexist generalizations of a member of Trafford's club. Mr. Pope's attempt to make his family sit at his feet and listen to his latest missive—while all the sounds of the garden distract, while each member of the family squirms and interrupts—captures the way in which received wisdom is distinctly not received through much of the novel.

Carrying a different accent, however, are the framed religious texts Marjorie puzzles over in the rectory where she and her family vacation at the beginning of the novel. Left by the owners, these traditional texts stir Marjorie's mind with "intimations of a missed significance."[14] Initially using these texts and later the friendship between the Traffords and a close-knit Jewish family named Solomonson, Wells keeps posing the possibility that ancient, religious wisdom regarding the relations between men and women may actually have validity.

New texts and modern understandings enter the novel by way of Rag Trafford, a scientific new man who drops into Marjorie's life literally out of the sky. As they talk, he recalls Marjorie's keen performance in her exams on physical science at Oxford. Trafford, it turns out, had been one of the examining professors. Importantly, we learn that Marjorie has a mind that goes beyond the capacity to memorize others' words. Trafford wondered at the time of her exams, and wonders now anew, what will happen to this modern woman. Will she be "swallowed up" by "the old, old story?" (p. 146).

The form in which Trafford puts the question suggests, of course, the value of some new, new story. However, as with old texts, new texts are not univalent. Among the purveyors of new narratives are the social reform movements of the day, including feminism. But none seems able to offer adequate understanding to Marjorie and Trafford. Like other social reformers in the novel, the feminists tend to rally around clichés, albeit new ones. In earnest discussion groups, participants speak at cross-purposes, generally ignoring the difficult question that troubles the Trafford marriage: how can relatively thoughtful men and women best live together in the modern world, year in, year out?

As Trafford and Marjorie marry, have children, work through his career and her lack of same, they see-saw back and forth between times when old stories enrich and times when they stultify, periods when new stories inspire, periods when they do not. Marjorie and Trafford are stymied. Working with an image he will thoroughly revise when he writes *The Wife of Sir Isaac Harman*, Wells dramatizes the Traffords's difficulties partly by way of their housing. Marjorie's hunger for self-expression continually channels itself into expensive re-decoration projects. With fine insight, Wells constructs scenes that dramatize the compulsive quality of Marjorie's expenditures. A place where Marjorie might construct texts of her own, her desk is a nightmare image of misery and guilt, crammed as it is with bills and reprimands. Trafford himself is torn between devoting himself to independent research which promises no profit and keeps home and family on the margin of his life, and the alternative of plunging into the business world, creating for himself and his family a household of plenitude and wide horizons. Thus far, Wells is indicating the various traps and dilemmas Edwardian middle-class marriage scripted for hungry youth and eager brightness, regardless of gender.

Ironically, when Wells releases the Traffords from their mutual paralysis and sends them off to distant Labrador, the novel loses its balance. As a way out of the maze of promises and disappointments offered by both the old and new stories available in the culture, Trafford and Marjorie decide temporarily to exit the culture. They will get out of the house; they will articulate a brand new story-line for marriage. As Trafford says to Marjorie, we will "talk and think ourselves together—oh!—the old phrases carry it all—find God" (p. 470). Making arrangements for their children's well being, they set out for the wilderness. They will stay a year.

Feeling they must deal with an immense despair, at first they cannot talk. But then Wells constructs the novel's last movement, with its lifting of the sluices of silence and flow of new speech. Composed of two extended scenes, it is a remarkable climax, both for the richness of its vision of this modern wife's capacity to speak, and for the negative reaction that newly released capacity brings.

In the first scene, Trafford heads out from camp, gets badly mauled by a lynx, and must be tracked down and rescued by Marjorie. Wells emphasizes the stupidity of Trafford's unnecessary hunting; the extraordinary stamina and skill Marjorie displays in finding and tending him; and the pride she feels at her competence. Late at night, as Trafford lies unconscious in the temporary shelter she has constructed, Marjorie's voice holds the stage and speaks of all manner of things, axes, splints, wolf spoor, food and fever, men and women, cosmic distances, and self-discovery. Echoes of the Biblical texts that had earlier intrigued her resonate in her thoughts as she tries to understand herself and Trafford within all time, all space. And the understanding she gains relates not to female competence and male dependency, or *vice versa;* rather, it relates to human vulnerability and worth. Roofless, she thinks in new ways about human shelter.

> The wonder and the riddle of it. Here she and Trafford were! Phantasmal shapes of insubstantial fluid thinly skinned against evaporation and wrapped about with woven wool and the skins of beasts, that yet reflected and perceived, suffered and sought to understand; that held a million memories, framed thoughts that plumbed the deeps of space and time. (p. 515)

Reading this, one recalls Nancy Miller's comparison of the kind of heroic claims one finds in male and female plots of ambition: the masculine vaunt, "Nothing can happen to me," contrasts with the female cry, "if anything can go wrong, it will" or "at least I am morally superior to my victimizers."[15] Marjorie's words make an altogether different claim as she asserts the links between humans, male and female, and between their powers and their vulnerabilities. Not "Nothing can happen to me, the mighty male"; not "if anything can go wrong, it will, to me, the hapless female"; instead, the richly ambiguous, "Much can happen to us, fragile and full of potential as we mutually are."

Perhaps because Marjorie seems to have done what Trafford set out to do, "to talk and think [themselves] together" (p. 470), Wells' second extended scene reads as an intense reaction against this vision and the wifely voice that articulated it.[16]

Wounds dressed, leg set, Trafford spends the next few days going in and out of delirium. At first he merely mumbles, but as he gains strength, he gains eloquence. It is his turn to talk. And what is his view of things, his blending of ancient and new understanding? Well, it seems, Marjorie may be deep and great, but Trafford is "a deeper and bigger thing than [she]" (p. 558). As he puts it, "I reach up to something you don't ... You're in life—and I'm a little out of it. I'm like one of those fish that begin to be amphibian, I go out into something where you don't follow" (p. 558).

Marjorie's previous gift of speech falls silent. Though his speaking goes on for days, he, ever thoughtful, occasionally stops to ask if she is following. When she does occasionally add her views, she is "penitent," "so penitent," but eager to do better: "What shall we do with our lives and life? Tell me ... it's you who know" (pp. 540–41). They will go home, says Trafford. He will write. And she? She will strive to release him, ceasing at the very least to hold him back.

As a closing movement, these two scenes are astonishing in their discrepancies. There are staring contradictions. Having just repeatedly shown Marjorie lugging Trafford about, Wells has her apologize for being the burden he must carry on his back. Having just constructed his heroine as two things—a literal body who rescues and sustains another literal body, plus a richly languaged creature discoursing on the significance of human experience—Wells has his hero define woman as only mute, literal, physical life, while man, being "a little out of life," is a creature of language.

Bakhtin suggests that the process of "ideological becoming" occurs partly through a person's capacity to entertain a range of cultural voices, gradually assimilating those one finds persuasive. Eventually one claims certain voices or words as one's own, or at least half one's own.[17] Bakhtin's formulation is helpful in assessing Wells' progress through this sequence of novels. A genuinely uneven performance, *Marriage* entertains a range of cultural voices on the problems of modern marriage, but that is all it manages to do. The novel gives little indication that Wells has sorted through the many texts and voices he has included to find those that are persuasive, those which he will eventually assimilate and coherently orchestrate in *The Wife of Sir Isaac Harman*. Intervening between the two texts, however, is *The Passionate Friends*. As I see it, *The Wife of Sir Isaac Harman* reads as a thoughtful response to the unevenness of *Marriage*, while *The Passionate Friends* reads as a worried reaction. Tightly controlling the narrative voice in *The Passionate Friends*, Wells solves the discrepancies that plague the ending of *Marriage* by virtually silencing all potentially opposing voices.

Ostensibly, *The Passionate Friends* is a social protest novel. It attacks restrictive Edwardian divorce procedures, the lack of intellectual or economic opportunities for married women of the middle and upper classes, and the hypocrisy of a modern system of manners that encourages free social intercourse between the sexes but stands aghast at extra-marital liaisons.

The unifying subject of the novel is presumably jealousy. Recasting the Trafford flight to Labrador as a flight to adultery, *The Passionate Friends* denounces the current social order for the way it reinforces masculine jealousy and fosters the possession and circulation of women by men.[18] Lady Mary Christian is given the role of proud, rebellious, modern woman. She wants to belong to no man. Deciding that the best way to accomplish her freedom is to involve herself with two men, she marries the wealthy Justin and has a long affair with Stephen Stratton. But Lady Mary's solution inflames the jealousies of Stratton, Justin, and her conventional brothers. Parodying romance melodrama, Wells shows Justin and the Christian brothers eventually forcing Lady Mary to suicide. Wells' proclivity for name play is evident throughout. Wanting a modern kind of virginity, Lady Mary Christian seeks immaculateness through promiscuity. However, neither Old Testament Justin nor her Christian brothers will tolerate that practice. In the end, they make martyrs of both Stephen and Mary. *The Passionate Friends* closes with the image of sweet and beautiful possibilities strangled in the nets of masculine jealousy.

If this is a fair summary of the novel's social protest dimensions and what West called its brave "speculations" (*The Young Rebecca*, p. 83), then I would argue that an altogether different plot lies beneath the denunciation of masculine possessiveness. This underlying tale enacts the very circulation of silent, objectified women Wells had set out to protest.

Governing the dynamics of *The Passionate Friends* is the genre Wells chose for this novel. An epistolary text, *The Passionate Friends* exists as a long letter from father to son. Middle-aged Stratton is candid about the letter's aim. Having just experienced the death of his own father, he would have his young son read this letter, at some appropriate later date, and through it reaffirm the bond that exists between the Stratton men. As Stratton constructs his account, over the weeks and months, one realizes that there will be none of the interruptions we saw in *Marriage*, no entertaining of a range of voices. In particular, the son—and the reader—will hear the voices of women when and only when they reinforce Stratton's tale.

As did *Marriage*, *The Passionate Friends* imagines insight and wisdom coming through human conversation, through speaking, listening, writing, and reading.[19] But here, the gender roles are clear and consistent: women listen and read, men speak and write. Like the tamed Marjorie at the end of her adventure, from the outset, Stratton's wife Rachel and his mistress Mary beg their wise man to talk on. As Stratton reports one of his conversations with Rachel, he modestly says, "I think that for once I may have been eloquent ... Her dark eyes were alight with a beautiful enthusiasm for what I was trying to say ... Dumbly her eyes bade me go on."[20] Lady Mary's last wish, before going off to kill herself, is to hear Stephen talk about his work and life just a little bit more (p. 375).

Earlier in the novel, Stratton does intermittently give Lady Mary, though never Rachel, the floor. For example, he indicates the supposedly wide-ranging and brilliant debates they have by copying out, for his son, some of her old letters. But in this supposed debate about the mess of modern relationships—between the classes and the genders—Lady Mary mainly castigates Stratton for his naïvetè about the awful parasitism of women. While "men invent, create, do miracles with the world," women "translate it all into shopping" (p. 324). What is he going to do about this? He must have an answer, for "we women do not know" (p. 324).

The egregious lapses in self-awareness that mark Stratton's account finally come down to this: Wells has situated his narrator in a recording booth. Not only are the oppositional voices of the female characters screened out, but so too are any real challenges from the male characters. Justin and the Christian brothers are typecast as reactionaries. And Stratton's son? It was a series of male breaches that first set Stratton writing: the loss of his father; his need to punish his young son; his son's subsequent and frightening appendectomy.[21] As Stratton composes this epistle, he keeps trying to write away the possibility of a future breach. Reacting to his father's death, Stratton would save his son from such a loss: Stratton's voice, life, and character will remain with his son, for here it all is, vibrant on the page. Moreover, Stratton's son will be the perfect reader for this missive, for he is a replicate of narrator Stratton. The son will live and die a Stratton man. In *Feminist Dialogics*, Dale Bauer argues that the lack of a responsive interpretive community finally silences the new speech of the heroines she studies, Hawthorne's Zenobia, James's Maggie Verver, Wharton's Lily Bart, and Chopin's Edna Pontellier (note 16). Here it is a fictional *hero* who lacks an interpretive community, but the result, far from being a silenced protagonist, is a prolix and unconvincing one.

On a certain level, *The Passionate Friends* may exist as West saw it: a bravely speculative novel which traces out the conflict between a freedom-loving woman and the patriarchal social institutions that destroy her. But more fundamentally, it is a monologue on the ways women spoil men's lives and on the need for male bonds. In a novel protesting the circulation of silent women, the self-protective narrator works out his ideas in the absence of any genuine debate with women, or challenging men.

In the third novel of this sequence, Wells finally accomplishes a sustained rescripting of the old, old story of marriage. Whereas *Marriage* attempted to address the limited roles offered to husbands and wives by transporting the hero and heroine to a wilderness, and whereas *The Passionate Friends* on some level attempted to loosen the bonds of possessive monogamy through a vision of courageous adultery, *The Wife of Sir Isaac Harman* gets at both issues, while staying very much at home and exploring ways that difficult fidelity can enhance a multiplicity of responsibilities and relationships. In their distinct ways, *Marriage* and *The Passionate Friends* ultimately valorize wifely silence. In *The Wife of Sir Isaac Harman*, Wells constructs an increasingly articulate, activist heroine and, simultaneously, insists that the males who would gag her must cease their obstructionist ways. This reversal Wells accomplishes through a variety of elaborations on his figure of marriage as an exchanging of texts, the most interesting being his elaboration on the links between plots and housing.

As noted above, among the ways *Marriage* dramatizes the tensions in the Trafford marriage is through contrasting Trafford's and Marjorie's identification with their various homes. In *The Passionate Friends*, Wells situates Lady Mary between houses. Reading back from the perspective of *The Wife of Sir Isaac Harman*, one can imagine that the ease with which Lady Mary's voice is manipulated comes partly from Wells' having given her no ground to stand on. The males control all plots. In *The Wife of Sir Isaac Harman*, this will change. By the time Wells writes this third marriage novel, he has managed to assimilate those voices within the Edwardian women's movement he finds most persuasive. The result is a self-reflexive, feminist novel, exploring such issues as the gains and losses implied in women's rejection of romantic castles and cottages; the risk and attraction of homelessness; the value of communal homes; and the role of words in the structuring of human shelter. Beneath these issues is a complex inquiry into the ways a wife's speech and property may be linked, into the ways her plots intersect.

When wealthy Sir Isaac Harman is wooing the young Ellen, he gives her what is described as a Victorian task: to list in a rose-tinted book her "favorites" and "aversions" within a range of categories (colors, composers, flowers, etc.). Bored and distracted, she jots down whatever comes to mind. Wells makes good comedy out of Sir Isaac's slavish attention to these scribbles as the eager groom makes ready his and Ellen's first, grand house; but simultaneously Wells makes points about the powerful relationship between writing, reading, and praxis—between words and houses.

Asked to name her "Favorite Hero in Real Life," Ellen writes "Doctor

Barnardo." His name starts with a B, like her favorite composers Bach and Beethoven, and she vaguely recalls hearing of him as a good man. Later in the novel, Barnardo is described as an activist who provides housing for orphans. Ellen fleetingly recalls pictures, publicizing his philanthropies, in which "wistful little outcasts creep longingly towards brightly lit but otherwise respectable homes."[22] With its evocation of homelessness and its surprising opposition between "respectable" and "brightly lit," that image captures a risk and tension that Ellen Harman must learn to understand if she is to progress into speech, social activism, and a home of her own.

The marriage of Mr. and Mrs. Harman is launched from a most respectable mansion in Putney. Reversing the husband/wife associations set up in *Marriage*, however, Wells indicates that this house is mainly the husband's. A wealthy entrepreneur, Sir Isaac bought it, decorated it, and continues to tend it with enthusiasm and avidity. Populated though it is with her children and her servants, in this house Ellen is a silent, restless, incongruous "visitor" (p. 59).

Throughout the novel, other houses enter the text, reinforcing the imagery of silent, disaffected wives and respectable, nest-building husbands. Initiating one of the sustained contrasts between old and new texts, Wells has Sir Isaac come across Shakespeare's *Taming of the Shrew*. Fiercely scoring his "favorite passages" and leaving the text for Ellen to encounter, Sir Isaac would be Petruchio, master of his castle, his Kate (pp. 210–11). Brumley, popular writer and Ellen's would-be lover, takes her to Hampton Court and, caught up in another old tale, mentally scores his own favorite passages. In that Elizabethan setting, he imagines Ellen as a sleeping beauty who needs release from her husband's castle and transportation to his own exquisite cottage. As it now stands, that country cottage is an icon he has consecrated to the memory of Euphemia, his dear departed wife, silent subject of his most successful fictions. At this stage in the narrative, Brumley sees Ellen and Euphemia in essentially the same terms: silent subjects to fictionalize, absences that inspire icons.

From these and other plotted grounds of patriarchal power and respectability, Wells negotiates Ellen's various escapes. Whereas Ibsen's Nora walks out once and for all, Ellen traces a far more interesting pattern of insurrections, forgivenesses, defeats, and victories. This pattern comes to characterize her entire marriage to Sir Isaac. But there is one exit—occurring from Brumley's cottage, now owned by Sir Isaac—which is crucial to Ellen's progress. Sir Isaac has moved the family to the country, hoping that there Ellen will give up some of her new "idees." Having no money of her own, Ellen is virtually imprisoned, Sir Isaac playing Petruchio, she the frustrated

Kate. However, with the help of a sisterly friend, seamstress Susan Burnet, Ellen escapes. Where she goes and what she does comprise a major stage in Ellen's development and are, I would argue, all new material for Wells.

Ellen seeks out Agatha Alimony, the butt of numerous jokes on spinsters and suffragettes in Wells' previous fiction. Though satirized here as well, Agatha, like Susan Burnet, effectively aids Ellen. Agatha gives her the words and tools she needs to set up residence, temporary as it is, in the first home she can call her own.[23] From Agatha, Ellen finally hears the feminist analysis of marriage she herself has been trying to articulate. Under Edwardian law, marriage is a man-made contract and women are property. Once the vote is won, revision of that contract is first on the agenda (pp. 264–65). In the meantime, leaving one's home is foolish. "You mustn't run away ... You must fight in your home. It's *your* home ... it's not his" (p. 268). Ellen eventually will agree and from the Harman home take up the feminist fight. For now, however, she needs a temporary shelter. Through Agatha's suffragette newspaper—a text forbidden her under Sir Isaac's roof—Ellen reads of plans that evening to commit acts of civil disobedience and get arrested. Grabbing a poker from Agatha's fireplace, Ellen goes out to smash windows. In doing so, she gives Wells an evocative image that links the disrespectful with the well-lit.

The edifice Ellen attacks is a post-office. Breaking one of its windows, she creates a "thin-armed, irregular star" in what Wells describes as a rectangle of grimy, frosted, "milky dinginess" (p. 271). It is an image that comes to fascinate Wells. As he explains, if the technology of printing would permit, he would visually convey the reverberations of her act; he would give the reader a series of pages upon which that star-studded, broken window remains visible beneath the printed words of Ellen's arrest and the reactions of Sir Isaac and Mr. Brumley (p. 272). As the locus of light-bearing change, the star would shine behind the way the speeches of Ellen and Sir Isaac are respectively received at her trial. Sir Isaac is gagged: having been up all night writing a statement disassociating himself from his wife's act, he is not permitted to read it. Ellen, by contrast, is given the floor and delivers her defense with "simple dignity." She has "honestly assimilated" the feminist voices she has found persuasive (p. 273). The image of the star-shaped break in cloudy, respectable windows is then carried over into the next chapter which explores the "kindred spectacle" of Brumley's mind—"square and tidy and as it were 'frosted' against an excess of light"—being smashed open by Ellen's act (p. 276).[24]

But the "radiating gap" caused by Ellen's breaking of dingy windows is perhaps most richly used in the context of Ellen's eventual sentence: one month in prison. When Ellen first left the Harman/Brumley cottage, she had no clear sense of where she should go, nor what she should say or think about her situation. A different script might have sent her out into the wilderness, e.g., to Labrador, to come to enlightenment in existential loneliness. But as we saw with Marjorie, there is danger in such isolated storytelling, the danger of having no community to listen, interrupt, verify. In *The Wife of Sir Isaac Harman*, Wells imagines another destination for his escaping wife. He argues that outside the domestic walls that have encircled her, she finds herself with no wall from which to fight and defend herself, no wall to put her back against. As he envisions it, perhaps with the drifting and suicidal Lady Mary hovering in his memory, the escaped Ellen could too easily lack a plot on which to stake her claims. In a move that will become important in the last sections of the novel, Ellen finds that the one place to which she can escape, the one wall she can imagine putting her back against while she works out her stance, is a communal wall, the wall of the municipal prison. Not a lonely wilderness nor a claustrophobic, respectable house, the prison, populated with other lawbreaking feminists, becomes for Ellen a thoroughly disrespectful but distinctly well-lit shelter. There she can think, read, and discuss, wresting from the social dialogue of her times words she more and more can call her own.

Having served her time, Ellen is released and again astounds Brumley by evading his protection and heading straight for her Harman home. There, miracles do not occur, but revisions do. Joined by his mother, Sir Isaac listens to Ellen and tries to work with her in rescripting their marriage. And one aspect of the new script will be Ellen's engagement in the building of new communal housing for the single women who work in the Harman bakery and tea shops.[25] As the novel represents her work on the hostels, it carries Ellen into the last stage of her progress. She has risked homelessness; resided with a community of women at a site of rebellion and illumination; gone on to reclaim her own powerbase, her home; and is now ready to construct something genuinely new upon the gap between homelessness and respectable, patriarchal homes. The binary opposition between being set adrift with no one behind one and being trapped in a suffocating marriage turns out to be a false dilemma. No home/one home, no companion/one companion is answered by communal homes and multiple friendships—and all of the responsibilities and freedoms they imply.

As Ellen struggles to design the working women's hostels, we see Wells, for the first time in his marriage novels, imagining in positive terms an ambitious, articulate, politically active, feminist wife. In one scene, for example, Wells has Ellen reading out a series of rules and fines established

for the hostels by Sir Isaac and the dictatorial Mrs. Pembrose. She tears them
up in front of an assembly of the prospective renters, publicly explaining her
belief that these women might better write their own "rules" for living
together through dialogue and experience. The women are pleased. Ellen
commands here what Agatha commanded earlier, a female interpretive
community deeply appreciative of a feminist voice.

Not only does Ellen work hard for other women—with intelligence,
friendliness, and the commitment of a life time—but she does so at the
necessary modification of Mr. Brumley's insistent design for and upon her
life. Like Sir Isaac, Brumley tries to learn from post-prison Ellen. Like Sir
Isaac, he is a far from apt pupil. To the end of the novel, he sentimentally,
verbosely continues to offer her love and shelter. When she asks him, please,
for some real information on housing, e.g., on safety codes or zoning, he
does his best but keeps getting distracted by personal concerns (the sweep of
her hair, how he looks at the moment). In mocking patriarchal scripts, Wells
sets up Brumley as monologist *par excellence*. He writes endless letters and
speaks like "a University Extension lecturer" (p. 362). He is like "some open-
mouthed yokel at a fair who knows nothing of the insult chalked upon his
back" (p. 325). Permitted by Wells to walk around this yokel, as we never
could around Stratton, we see that the scrawled insult links Brumley with the
possessive Sir Isaac: "how he himself coveted and desired and would if he
could have gripped" the brave and struggling Ellen (p. 325).

Ellen never gives in to Brumley, and neither does the novel. In his will,
Sir Isaac stipulates that if Ellen marries again, all control of the hostels will
go to a Board of Directors. Ellen does not want that, nor, in the end, does
she want Brumley, or any man, on conventional terms. With the death of Sir
Isaac, she tastes freedom. When Brumley later comes to visit her, begging
her to marry him, she refuses, and Brumley runs sobbing into the woods.
Ellen takes up the chase, female tracking male. She finds him, and, with an
"irrational charity" is stirred by his longings, his love (p. 500). In the novel's
last, perhaps most surprising reversal of all, they make, after years of waiting,
a quick kind of love, with her on top. "She crouched down upon him and,
taking his shoulder in her hand, upset him neatly backwards, and, doing
nothing by halves, had [sic] kissed the astonished Mr. Brumley full upon his
mouth" (p. 502). Their likely future, implied earlier in the law offices of the
Harman solicitors, is neither a marriage nor an end to their long association,
but an arrangement with multiple possibilities, a genuinely passionate
friendship, an affair.

In concluding her introduction to *The Passionate Friends*, Glendinning
makes an apt claim for Wells: "often a maddening writer," he is "never a

bore" (n.p.). As I hope this discussion has demonstrated, on the topic of marriage he does indeed remain engaging. Representing marriage through the figure of difficult human conversation—a conversation threatened by power discrepancies, asymmetrical ambitions, jealousy, and possessiveness—he uses the figure to explore issues related to the silencing of the married woman, the comparative value of old and new social narratives, the potential for adultery successfully to critique monogamy, the place of friendship within marriage, and the need for women to assert ownership over their own plots. But an exploration it seems truly to have been, as *Marriage*, *The Passionate Friends*, and *The Wife of Sir Isaac Harman* progressively echo, challenge, and revise each other, replicating aspects of that very human conversation they seek to address.

On the basis of these three novels by Wells, can one argue that the modern British novel of marriage more often reflects the liveliness of the historical debate over the institution than delivers a sustained condemnation? No. At the least, this Wellsian trio invites us to revisit the question, to think again, in Chapman's words, about "Marriage Questions in Modern Fiction."

NOTES

The author wishes to express appreciation to the National Endowment for the Humanities for a research fellowship which allowed her to develop this essay as part of a larger project on Edwardian narratives of marriage and divorce.

1. *Experiment in Autobiography* (New York: The Macmillan Co., 1934), p. 392.

2. *Marriage Questions in Modern Fiction and Other Essays on Kindred Subjects* (London and New York: John Lane, 1897).

3. Carolyn G. Heilbrun, "Marriage Perceived: English Literature 1873–1944," in *Hamlet's Mother and Other Women* (New York: Columbia Univ. Press, 1990), pp. 112–33. Sandra M. Gilbert and Susan Gubar, *No Man's Land: The Place of the Woman Writer in the Twentieth Century*, vols. 1 and 2 (New Haven and London: Yale Univ. Press, 1988 and 1989).

4. *The Report of the Royal Commission on Divorce and Matrimonial Causes: Minutes of Evidence 1912–1913* (London: His Majesty's Stationery Office [Cmnd. 6478]) provides an invaluable record of the debate that was raging over marriage and divorce in the years before World War I. See too Lawrence Stone, *Road to Divorce: England 1530–1987* (Oxford: Oxford Univ. Press, 1990).

5. In "Uncle Wells on Women: A Revisionary Reading of the Social Romances," Bonnie Kime Scott approaches these three novels from a somewhat different perspective and posits a wider grouping under the rubric of "romantic fiction." She looks also at *Tono Bungay*, *Love and Mr. Lewisham*, *Ann Veronica*, and *Joan and Peter*. See Scott, in *H.G. Wells Under Revision*, ed. Patrick Parrinder and Christopher Rolfe (Selinsgrove: Susquehanna

Univ. Press, 1990), pp. 108–120. My own reading of Wells, women, and marriage has been greatly enriched over the years by conversations with Nancy Lynn Steffen-Fluhr. See her "Paper Tiger: Women and H.G. Wells," *Science Fiction Studies* 12 (Nov., 1985): 311–329.

6. Claude Lévi-Strauss, *The Elementary Structures of Kinship* (Boston: Beacon Press, 1969); Gayle Rubin, "The Traffic in Women: Notes on the 'Political Economy' of Sex," in *Toward an Anthropology of Women*, ed. Rayne R. Reiter (New York: Monthly Review Press, 1975), pp. 157–210; Nelly Furman, "The Politics of Language: Beyond the Gender Principle?" in *Making a Difference: Feminist Literary Criticism*, ed. Gayle Green and Coppelia Kahn (London and New York: Routledge, 1985), pp. 59–79.

7. Anthony West, *H.G. Wells: Aspects of a Life* (London: Hutchinson, 1984), pp. 6–7.

8. See Gordon R. Ray, *H.G. Wells and Rebecca West* (New Haven: Yale Univ. Press, 1974), Chapters 1–5.

9. See for example Wells' editorial exchanges with Dora Marsden in *The Freewoman*, vol. 1, nos. 15–18: (February 29, 1912): 281–83; (March 7, 1912): 301–02; (March 14, 1912): 321–23; and (March 21, 1912): 341–42. Needless to say, Wells' credentials as a feminist were contested at the time and continue to be so. See *The Freewoman* numbers above and, more recently, Scott's "Uncle Wells on Women"; Cliona Murphy, "H.G. Wells: Educationalist, Utopian, and Feminist?" in *H.G. Wells Under Revision*, pp. 218–25; and Susan M. Squier, "The Modern City and the Construction of Female Desire: Wells' *In the Days of the Comet* and Robins's *The Convert*," *Tulsa Studies in Women's Literature* 8 (Spring, 1984): 63–75.

10. *A Modern Utopia* (London: T. Fisher Unwin, 1925).

11. *Ann Veronica: A Modern Love Story* (London: T. Fisher Unwin, Ltd., 1925). For an analysis of the Edwardian "modern girl" novel, see Janice H. Harris, "Lawrence and the Edwardian Feminists" in *The Challenge of D.H. Lawrence*, ed. Michael Squires and Keith Cushman (Madison: Univ. of Wisconsin Press, 1990), pp. 62–76.

12. James's letter to Wells (October 18, 1912) and Wells' response are reprinted in *Henry James and H.G. Wells*, ed. Leon Edel and Gordon N. Ray (Urbana: Univ. of Illinois Press, 1958), pp. 166–68; pp. 217–20.

13. *The Young Rebecca: Writings of Rebecca West: 1911–1917*, ed. Jane Marcus (Bloomington and Indianapolis: Indiana Univ. Press, 1982), pp. 64–69.

14. *Marriage* (London: T. Fisher Unwin, Ltd., 1926), p. 24. Further citations are to this edition and will be indicated in the text.

15. Nancy K. Miller, "Emphasis Added: Plots and Plausibilities in Women's Fiction," in *The New Feminist Criticism*, ed. Elaine Showalter (New York: Pantheon Books, 1985), p. 346.

16. Constructing the scene so that Marjorie speaks only to the night air, with no one listening, raises issues concerning articulate heroines and interpretive communities that Dale Bauer thoughtfully explores in *Feminist Dialogics: A Theory of Failed Community* (Albany: State Univ. of New York Press, 1988). I will speak more of Wells' construction of interpretive communities below.

17. M.M. Bakhtin, *The Dialogic Imagination: Four Essays*, ed. Michael Holquist (Austin: Univ. of Texas Press, 1981), pp. 341–42; p. 345.

18. Focusing on masculine jealousy as a primary component of human marriage and citing Lang's work specifically, Wells follows the thinking of respected Victorian and Edwardian anthropologists Andrew Lang and J.J. Atkinson. See *Social Origins and Primal Law* (London, New York, and Bombay: Longmans, Green, and Co., 1903).

19. Also calling attention to the novel's representations of writing and speaking, William J. Scheick develops a different argument. See "Revisionary Artistry in Wells' *The Passionate Friends*," in *British Novelists Since 1900*, ed. Jack I. Biles (New York: AMC Press, 1987), pp. 29–39. See too J.R. Hammond's "Wells and the Novel," in *H.G. Wells Under Revision* for an interpretation that emphasizes the novel's indeterminacy (pp. 66–81).

20. *The Passionate Friends* (London: T. Fisher Unwin, Ltd., 1926), pp. 147–48. Further citations are from this edition and indicated in the text.

21. The appendectomy is not included in the 1986 Hogarth reprint. One finds it in earlier editions, e.g., the T. Fisher Unwin edition (pp. 13–16).

22. *The Wife of Sir Isaac Harman* (London: T. Fisher Unwin, Ltd., 1926), p. 172. Further citations are from this edition and indicated in the text.

23. In "Uncle Wells on Women," Scott discusses Wells' tendency to mock older and/or political women (in *H.G. Wells Under Revision*, p. 114). In general, Kime Scott's view holds, making *The Wife of Sir Isaac Harman* all the more noteworthy for the role it gives to Agatha Alimony. For an analysis of the depiction of the older single woman in a range of modernist writings, see Sheila Jeffries, *The Spinster and Her Enemies: Feminism and Sexuality 1880–1930* (London, Boston, and Henley: Pandora Press, 1985).

24. Ironically, Wells' imagery of smashed windows anticipates Virginia Woolf's later, similar imagery in "Mr. Bennett and Mrs. Brown." As Woolf employs the image, it refers to the destructive/constructive audacity of her Georgian peers (Lawrence, Joyce, Eliot, Forster, Pound, Strachey) as opposed to the conservative timidity of Edwardians Wells, Bennett, and Galsworthy. In Woolf, *Collected Essays*, vol. 1 (New York: Harcourt, Brace, and World, Inc., 1967), pp. 319–37.

25. Though one of the reviewers of Wells' novel finds trivial Ellen's interest in creating housing options for Harman's female employees (*The Dial* 57 (1914): 455), in fact the issue of safe and affordable housing for unmarried women is a constant concern through this period and the previous two decades. See, for example, Alice Zimmern, "Ladies' Dwellings," *Contemporary Review* 77 (Jan.–June, 1900): 96–104; Christabel Osborn, "Rowton Houses for Women," *Contemporary Review* 99 (Jan.–June, 1911): 707–17; "Women's Municipal Lodging Houses," *The Freewoman* 1 (Nov. 30, 1911): 26; and (Dec. 14, 1911): 68; and "Group Houses," *The Freewoman* 1 (Feb. 29, 1912): 291; and (Mar. 7, 1912): 312. See too Elizabeth Robins' play "Votes for Women" and her novel *The Convert*. In *Independent Women: Work and Community for Single Women*, Appendix B, Martha Vicinus gives a good overview of the way the issue played in the 1880s and 1890s (Chicago: Univ. of Chicago Press, 1985). While not focussing on *The Passionate Friends*, Jefferson Hunter provides thoughtful insight into the motif of housing in Wells and in Edwardian fiction in general. See *Edwardian Fiction* (Cambridge: Harvard Univ. Press, 1982), pp. 189–214.

WILLIAM KUPINSE

Wasted Value:
The Serial Logic of H.G. Wells's
Tono-Bungay

In a passage just before the midpoint of H.G. Wells's *Tono-Bungay*, one of the most telling examples of what would come to be called the Condition of England genre,[1] George Ponderevo's childhood friend Ewart, a hard-drinking, itinerant artist prone to spouting Nietzschean aphorisms, visits the factory where the narrator and his uncle Edward produce the novel's spurious, eponymous product. Speaking as "one artist to another," Ewart lectures Edward on aesthetic and economic value; indeed, in Ewart's sarcastic rendering, the two forms are inseparable (169). Praising the Ponderevo operation for its "poetry" of production, Ewart goes on to describe the artistry of the entire system of consumer culture that Tono-Bungay embodies: "And it's not your poetry only. It's the poetry of the customer too. Poet answering poet—soul to soul" (168). But if economic concerns have usurped the purportedly disinterested space of art, the notion of economic value itself has undergone a similar revolution. "The old merchant used to tote about commodities; the new one creates values," Ewart asserts. "He takes something that isn't worth anything—or something that isn't particularly worth anything, and he makes it worth something" (169). This ironic commentary by a minor character precisely identifies the major preoccupation of Wells's novel and marks the site of Edwardian anxiety

From *NOVEL*, vol. 33, no. 1. © 1999 NOVEL Corp.

informing the Condition of England novel: the apparent abandonment by "modern commerce" of established determinants of value and waste.

Just how quickly and absolutely these determinants have been abandoned in the realm of economics is suggested by examining Edward Ponderevo's wildly profitable patent-medicine scheme in light of the two most influential schools of economic thought of the time: the institutionally endorsed capitalism of Alfred Marshall's Neoclassical economics and the critique of capitalism offered by Karl Marx. Marshall's and Marx's definitions of value provide a contrasting set of coordinates against which to plot what Wells calls the "tumerous growth-process" of early twentieth-century consumerism (109). In its most virulent manifestations, this process encompasses such modern ills as overproduction, excessive domestic consumption, and colonial violence. But its more benign forms embody changes that may prove equally devastating, and they mark the extent to which a similar disruption of aesthetic value has also taken place. In this essay, I will suggest that the effects of this disruption include the dampening of what was formerly understood as authoritative cultural discourse through its framing by the "trash" of consumer culture and the redeployment of the literary text as marker of economically-defined national identity. Finally, I will argue that the novel's embodiment of Edwardian anxiety about this emergent waste-driven system of value also offers a way to understand the stylistic multiplicity of *Tono-Bungay* itself, a concern that has long troubled critics.

BEYOND MARSHALL AND MARX: EDWARD'S ECONOMIC FICTIONS

While criticism of *Tono-Bungay* has explored the text in depth as a commentary on the Condition of England, relatively scant attention has been devoted to the role of America in the larger social and economic system the novel attempts to describe. America is introduced as early as the section titled "Of Bladesover House," the name of the country estate where George Ponderevo's mother works as an upper-level servant and where George spends his uneasy boyhood. Having posited Bladesover as a "clue" to British national identity, George accords it an even greater, trans-Atlantic structuring value in his mature narration: "And America too, is, as it were, a detached, outlying part of the estate which has expanded in queer ways" (21). Expelled from Bladesover and fleeing the squalor of his subsequent home at Chatham with his cousins the Frapps, George begins an apprenticeship with his uncle Edward, who runs a chemist's shop in Wimblehurst. Upon their first meeting, George finds his uncle preoccupied with a desire for rapid economic gain he sees as intrinsically American. Insisting that "this place ... wants Waking Up!," Edward imagines "let[ting] a dozen young Americans loose" upon the shop (72). Parodying the example of much early twentieth-century fiction which positions America as the embodiment of capability and initiative, Wells's novel figures these characteristics as either military (Edward's wished-for platoon of American entrepreneurs) or mechanical: "America!" Edward sighs. "I wish to heaven, George, I'd been born American—where things hum" (72).[2] Though with a gesture of his hand Edward abruptly moves the locale of his fantasy back again to London, the economic strategies he propounds are characteristically American practices: "cover gambling" and "corners"—in other words, margin trading and industrial monopolies (73).

Margin trading—playing the market on credit, with only a small percentage of capital actually invested (in Edward's scheme just one percent)—would of course later bankrupt many American investors in 1929, just as it seems to have been the instrument of Edward's bankruptcy through his trading of Union Pacific (that Edward will be later forced to sell his shop "lock, stock, and barrel" suggests that he has committed more than his liquid capital [85]). Though his appreciation of the risks involved seem naïve— "Things go up one, you sell, realise cent per cent; down, whiff, it's gone! Try again!" (73)—Edward's statement is accurate in that he will, in typically American fashion, remake himself following his bankruptcy. The second scheme that he introduces in this preliminary discussion with George, cornering the market, will prove a similar failure for him when toward the end of the novel he attempts to corner the world's supply of the radioactive substance "quap." Unlike his early forays into margin trading, the quap fiasco, a last ditch effort to raise capital to shore up his sagging fortunes, will coincide with his total financial ruin. Here, however, cornering the market remains only an imaginative possibility, albeit a malevolent one. In the scheme he details, Edward recognizes that the success of monopoly capitalism depends not only on achieving complete control over a particular market—as for example John D. Rockefeller, whose industriousness George will later cite approvingly, did through his manipulations of Standard Oil— but finding the right market to control. While past monopolists have made fortunes controlling economies of scale—the examples he gives are wheat and steel—Edward envisions controlling the even more essential raw materials of medicine: ipecac, quinine, menthol, antiseptics, and the like. "Think of having all the quinine in the world, and some millionaire's pampud wife gone ill with malaria," Edward muses in a particularly transparent moment, reveling in the possibilities of legal extortion (73–74).

Thus far Edward's schemes, however irresponsible or craven they may be, are still in keeping with mid to late nineteenth-century economic theories of market value, though the latter of the schemes, "corners," pushes these descriptions of value to their limits. Two then-contemporary but disparate economic paradigms provide a useful backdrop for understanding Edward's efforts to force the market's hand: the Marxist account of the creation of capital, detailed in Volume I of *Capital* (1867), and Alfred Marshall's efforts to reconcile market equilibrium in terms of a combination of supply-side and demand-driven economics in *Principles of Economics* (1890).

Wells's relationship to Marx merits a special comment since, as G.R. Searle notes, Wells's privileging of physical rather than economic science as an "autonomous force ... was a damnable heresy from the Marxist standpoint" and Wells came under criticism from Marx's supporters throughout his career (262). Though Wells disagreed with the Marxist narrative of social change—just as he would later split with his own Fabian Society over its program for reform—Wells paints a relatively sympathetic picture of Marx in his encyclopedic *Outline of History* (1920), claiming him as the synthesizer of Trade Unionism and early Socialism: "It was the imagination and generalizing power of Karl Marx which brought these two movements into relationship" (2:407). Although he felt Marx overemphasized class antagonism and overlooked "the fact that labour everywhere has a common interest in the peace of the world,"[3] Wells agreed generally with Marx's account of labor as the source of surplus-value; labor is the middle term in Marx's General Formula for Capital, M-C-M', that special-case commodity which creates value as it is consumed (2: 408). But whereas Marx believed that the exploitation of labor's surplus-value would inevitably lead workers to seize the means of production, Wells advocated checking this exploitation through relatively modest government intervention. In his later thinking, Wells's understanding of the need to ensure that labor received fair wages focused on the buying power of those wages and led to his interest in monetary reform, and in particular to the endorsement of the policy recommendations of John Maynard Keynes, who served as a reader for a chapter of *The Work, Wealth and Happiness of Mankind* (1931). "To keep the maximum of people at work, content and hopeful, the issue of currency needs to rather more than keep pace with the increase in the production of commodities," Wells writes, echoing Keynesian doctrine (*Work* 401).

Keynes of course broke radically from the Marshallian economics in which he had been educated, but at the time of *Tono-Bungay*, Marshall's Neoclassical theories were the dominant economic paradigms of Edwardian

England. Though Marshallians advocated a laissez-faire economic policy (an approach George Ponderevo retrospectively rejects when he rails against the implicit government sanctioning of the "whole trend of modern money-making" [74]), Alfred Marshall's theory of value brought together the previously disparate notions of utility (demand) based and cost-of-production (supply) based economics. Thus despite Wells's distance from the policy recommendations that Neoclassical theory engendered, Marshall's work offers a means of establishing the primary features of Edwardian capitalism's prevailing economic paradigm. In his famous example, Marshall locates the value inherent in a given transaction in relation to the simultaneously functioning criteria of producer and consumer:

> We might as reasonably dispute whether it is the upper or the under blade of a pair of scissors that cuts a piece of paper, as whether value is governed by utility or cost of production. It is true that when one blade is held still, and the cutting is effected by moving the other, we may say with careless brevity that the cutting is done by the second; but the statement is not strictly accurate, and is to be excused only so long as it claims to be merely a popular and not a strictly scientific account of what happens.
>
>   In the same way, when a thing already made has to be sold, the price which people will be willing to pay for it will be governed by their desire to have it, together with the amount they can afford to spend on it. Their desire to have it depends partly on the chance that, if they do not buy it, they will be able to get another thing like it at as low a price: this depends on the causes that govern the supply of it, and this again upon cost of production. But it may so happen that the stock to be sold is practically fixed.... [In this case,] if a person chooses to take the stock for granted, and say that the price is governed by demand, his brevity may perhaps be excused so long as he does not claim strict accuracy. (348–49)

Marshall's theory represents a shift from previous theories of value in that it accounts for the lapse in time between the consumer demand for a particular item and the possibility of its production. Marshall sees these two drives as inextricably connected in an infinite feedback loop. This time lag can temporarily contribute to the scarcity of certain commodities, but eventually producers will respond to the demand, and the value of a given item will tend to reach an equilibrium. This equilibrium will always be temporary, however, since future disruptions in demand and corresponding supply are inevitable.

The first of Edward's schemes, margin trading, is easily described by both the Marxist and Neoclassical theories of value. In Marxist terms, Edward wishes to become a partial investor in a company's program of purchasing the labor of its workers and selling the results of that labor at a corresponding profit; in Marshallian phrasing, Edward wants to invest in a corporation in the hopes that the equilibrium achieved between its production costs and its utility value to its customers will be such that the profits generated—and thus its corresponding dividend and stock value—will be maximized. Edward of course complicates this process and his risk by investing money that has been extended to him on credit, but the basic role of capital is the same as in any investment.

A closer examination of the particular stock he chooses, however, suggests that for Edward, "margins" and "corners" may be part and parcel of an attempt to create value by forcing the hand of the market through any means necessary. In purchasing on margin, Edward seeks to cover his risk through his "scientific" and "verifiable" analysis of the peaks and troughs of Union Pacific's performance—significantly, an American corporation, and one whose history is fraught with attempts by its directors to corner the market of transcontinental shipping and passenger transportation.[4] The market responds in turn by proving itself unscientific and unverifiable, leaving Edward bankrupt. While it is difficult to ascribe an exact year to the "Wimblehurst Apprenticeship," Edward's boasting about his investment to George probably took place in the late 1870s or early 1880s; in fictionalizing the Union Pacific "bust," Wells may be alluding to the precipitous drop in the value of the company's stock that occurred in the autumn of 1882.[5] Charles Francis Adams, a former government director of Union Pacific who later became its president, describes this decline in a letter to the *Boston Advertiser* in December 1882. Examining the company in October and pronouncing it sound, Adams recounts returning to New York to discover a "veritable panic prevailing in respect to the stock." "It had fallen fifteen points and was still going down," Adams writes. Finding Wall Street teaming with "'bear' stories of enormous floating debts, falsified earnings, and overissues of stock," Adams uncovers what he claims to be a well-orchestrated conspiracy to depress the stock artificially:

> I have studied the several steps in one grand organized "bear" campaign. Had I time to follow it out I could make an account of no little interest. I could show the thorough knowledge the Wall

Street operators had of the way the stock was held, and how they based their plans upon this knowledge, so as "to shake the weak stock out." Unlike many other companies, the Union Pacific, with its 60,000 shares, was in no one's keeping. A great deal of the stock was floating about or carried on margin. There was a grand chance for a "bear compaign" and the bears knew it. (qtd. in White 61–4n4)

Here we see an American analogue to the fascination with and paranoia of information control that Thomas Richards indentifies as an integral part of the British Empire in *The Imperial Archive*.[6]" Cornerning the market" represents an attempt to secure value through the manipulative possibilities afforded by the possession of positive knowledge—in the case of Adams's Wall Street "bears," "the thorough knowledge ... of the way the stock was held," "floating about," or as in Edward Ponderevo's case, "carried about on margin." Similarly, Edward bases his investment on the assumption that through his "scientific" calculations, he possesses more accurate information than other investors. When he loses his fortune, he blames it on the incompleteness of his information: "I left out one factor" (83).

If artificially creating value through "corners" begins with cornering information on a service or commodity, the whole of the process depends on some very material activity. In this way there is a qualitative difference between the example of Union Pacific—both in its efforts to corner the trail market, and, if Adams's claim holds any truth, in the later attempts of Wall Street to manipulate its stock—and Edward's imagined scheme of cornering the medical supply market, in particular lifesaving drugs. To transpose Edward's drug scheme into Marx's General Formula for Capital, M-C-M', Edward desires to maximize the movement from his initial investment (M) to his return on investment (M'), by means of its circuit through a commodity (C) whose use-value is itself a source of value, or in the case of drugs, of life itself. While Union Pacific's efforts to corner the rail market rely on the fact that its customers have sufficient interest in moving their wares that they will pay an inflated price, this price presumably has an upper limit, and the company's profits still depend largely on the concealed surplus-value of the labor it purchases for the construction, maintenance, and operation of its rail lines. In contrast, Edward's imagined customers presumably will pay nearly any price for quinine or antiseptics. Thus Edward's scheme neatly circumvents the usual workings of M-C-M', in which the concealed component of the commodity which increases value is the surplus-value of the laborer. By artificially inflating M', Edward's strategic monopoly makes surplus labor value a negligible component of his particular equation. In Marshallian terms, Edward seeks to fix one blade of the scissors while he leverages the other, creating a situation in which the "stock to be sold" is not "practically," but effectively "fixed" and demand is unlimited, allowing Edward to command any price.

In his schemes of "corners" and "covers" Edward pushes the value theories informing emergent consumer and industrial capitalism to their limits, but he does not beak them. That his schemes are barely containable by the disparate paradigms of institutionally endorsed capitalism and capitalism's foremost critique suggests that Edward is reaching toward a definition of value for which neither school can fully account. These early schemes serve an important function in the novel by presaging a new embodiment of value, which will invoke aspects of marginal investment and market monopoly, yet will also depart from these concepts insignificant ways. I have sketched out the main points of Marshall and Marx in relationship to Edward's American-inspired schemes not only to establish the historical context of his early and unsuccessful forays in wealth-building, but even more so to mark Wells's account of an entirely new construction of value in which the notion of waste serves both a physical and structural role. As I will suggest, this construction of value from waste finds its purest embodiment in the elixir Tono-Bungay itself.

Reapplying the Marxist and Marshallian criteria reveals just how much Tono-Bungay departs from these economic paradigms. In attempting to solve the problem of how capital could be created within the totality of an exchange system, rather than having the vagaries of each instance of exchange of money and commodities cancel each other out, Marx postulated that the capitalist must find "in the market, a commodity, whose use-value possesses the peculiar property of being a source of value" (186). For Marx, as I have outlined earlier, that commodity with the peculiar property is labor. Edward, however, arrives at an entirely different but theoretically workable solution to Marx's famous problem by identifying another special-case commodity whose consumption creates value: namely, waste. Thus in the context of Edward's meteoric rise to capitalist fame, his formula for the creation of capital looks something like M-W-M', in which waste provides the middle term for capital's reproduction. This reworking of Marx's formula entails quite radical effects, most notably the exclusion, or more accurately the minimization, of labor's role in the circuit of wealth creation. For while Edward does employ workers in his patent medicine factory, labor appears as a negligible component of the factory's operations. When George finally signs on to Edward's scheme to secure the £300 a year his beloved Marion requires to marry him, his first assignment is to modernize the factory through a cost-benefit analysis. Fancying himself "a young lieutenant" and displaying something of the military efficiency of Edward's wished-for young Americans, George notes, "It was extraordinarily interesting to me to figure out the advantage accruing from this shortening of the process or that, and to weigh it against the capital cost of the alteration" (165). After a short time, George's technological improvements are so successful that once capital has been invested in novel machinery the factory requires almost no labor: "Our cases packed themselves, practically." The irony is that George's efforts reduce "waste and confusion" in the service of producing the same. In addition to mechanizing the factory, labor costs are reduced even further by employing poorly-paid "girls," rather than "expensive young men" (166).

If money is hardly being spent on labor, even less is spent on raw materials. George repeatedly insists that the hodge-podge of ingredients that make up Tono-Bungay are "trash," "rubbish," or even sewage (147, 156). In fact, the novel offers more than a hint of the suggestion that Tono-Bungay may contain not just figurative rubbish but actual industrial waste. During his visit to the Ponderevo factory, George's friend Ewart brainstorms a number of seemingly preposterous schemes for transforming waste into consumer products, such as marketing wood shavings as "Xylo-tobacco," a cure for influenza, or a breakfast cereal. Edward, however, who has already investigated the production of American cereals only to be disappointed to find them produced from actual (albeit spoiled) grain, again takes him at face value. Praised by Ewart as a man who'd "make cinders respect themselves," the elder Ponderevo muses that one "[m]ight make 'em into a sort of sanitary brick" (171). George's refusal to identify the exact formula, an omission performed parenthetically, thus suggests something more than his inability to violate trade secrets. Instead, it becomes the absent center of Wells's text, in fact a sort of pharmaceutical mock equivalent to Conrad's "the horror, the horror." "No!," George protests. "I am afraid I cannot give it away" (140).

But if the secret of Tono-Bungay is literally unspeakable, both George and Edward talk around the subject enough to give some sense of what it might contain. In describing the medicine's composition to George, Edward mentions several "vivid tonics" and "virulent substance[s]" (141). So in addition to any "rubbish" the product contains, which we might assume the Ponderevos could obtain at little or no cost, Tono-Bungay does require some raw materials which have at least a nominal cost.[7] George later reveals that the Tono-Bungay lozenges contain strychnine, which, while poisonous, is not free (163). At first glance, this description of Tono-Bungay's production seems to be in keeping with Marshall's account of how supply and demand reaches a temporary equilibrium. But Edward's scheme violates the Marshallian paradigm as neatly as it does the Marxist, since production costs are so minimal that the Ponderevo factory can accommodate any rise in demand . By production costs I mean both the labor costs that mechanization has nearly eliminated *and* the cost of raw materials, which remains stable not on a per item basis—this cost in fact *decreases*—but in terms of gross material costs, which are relatively constant regardless of gross output. "For we altered all our formulae," confesses George, "invariably weakening them enormously as sales got ahead" (163). By the time Edward's scheme has grown into a publicly-traded company, George will make this conglomeration of waste and dilution into an explicit formula for the unaccountable wealth the scheme generates: "£150,000—think of it!—for the goodwill in a string of lies and a trade in bottles of mitigated water!" Ever the realist, Edward argues that capital is its own justification; the investors, he asserts, have "never been given such value ... for a dozen years" (167).

Ultimately, what enables the Ponderevo's Tono-Bungay scheme to transcend Edward's earlier forays is its recognition of the role that public confidence plays in economic instruments. As Adams's letter to the *Boston Advertiser* reveals, the one factor Edward leaves out of his Union Pacific investment is the investors' wavering belief in the company's soundness, an uncertainty that might or might not have a material grounding, but that nonetheless has very real effects. By the height of the patent-medicine scheme, both Edward and George have come to a similar understanding that fiscal instruments are at root economic fictions dependent upon popular confidence. Edward embraces this discovery, chortling that "[w]e been making human confidence ever since I drove the first cork of Tono-Bungay," while George regards it with ambivalence: "It was all a monstrous payment for courageous fiction" (238). Professing distrust of confidences of any kind, George laments the investment of public faith in "fictitious values as evanescent as rainbow gold" even as he links his fortunes to the rapidly increasing wealth of the Tono-Bungay empire (239).

FAR FROM SOLID OBJECTS

The manufacturing of "confidence" in the form of bottles of "rubbish" represents only one facet of the destabilization of traditional determinants of waste and value. If *value-from-waste* represents the most immediate, alchemical possibility of the creation of initial consumer desire upon which Tono–Bungay's success depends, the notion of *waste-as-value* serves an equally important role in accounting for the insatiable appetite of the consumers who purchase mass commodities such as the patent medicine—an appetite not simply for more of the commodity but also for increasingly novel and innovative forms of it. In the case of Tono-Bungay, this drive for innovation leads to permutations of the formula: "Tono-Bungay Hair Stimulant," "Concentrated Tono-Bungay" for the eyes, "Tono-Bungay Lozenges," "Tono-Bungay Chocolate," "Tono-Bungay Mouthwash" (162–63).

But this process of incessant innovation—and the accumulation it entails—extends beyond the fictive utility of the patent medicine to the whole of England's process of residential development, industrialization, and technological advancement, and hence it connects the nameless Edwardian consumer to both the capitalist Edward Ponderevo and the scientist George Ponderevo. Financed with the growing proceeds from Tono-Bungay's sales, Edward Ponderevo's acquisitive streak soon becomes a full-fledged mania. His purchases are superseded by new acquisitions before they can even be appreciated. George recounts that a "curious feature of this time with him was his buying over and over again of similar things. His ideas seemed to run in series." These purchases include "five new motor-cars, each more swift and powerful than its predecessor," as well as a series of residences, from the house at Beckenham to the Chislehurst mansion to the ill-fated dream estate at Crest Hill, the "test of realisation" that Edward finally fails (289, 294).

While George wants to believe that his scientific undertakings lie outside the tainted world of commercial endeavor, a similar series characterizes his aeronautic and marine creations.[8] Faced with the failure of his marriage and dissatisfied with the financial success of Tono-Bungay, George tells his uncle of his decision to pursue his dream of flying: "I want some *stuff*, man. I want something to hold on to. I shall go amuk if I don't get it. I'm different sort of beast from you. You float in all this bunkum. I feel like a man floundering in a universe of soapsuds, up and down, east and west. I can't stand it. I must get my foot on something solid or—I don't know what" (217). Aside from an anticipatory jibe at the Ponderevos' joint venture with Moggs' Soap, George's lament is notable for its mixed metaphor; he wants to get his foot on something solid by building flying machines. Nothing could be less solid than his first navigable balloon, the Lord Roberts alpha, which explodes during an early test flight, yet George, driven by his desire for material realization, begins planning the Lord Roberts beta while still bedridden. In his description of his second aircraft, we see something of the successive approximation and gigantism which marks Uncle Edward's string of acquisitions: "It was to be a second Lord Roberts alpha only more so; it was to be three times as big" (328). While George will eventually abandon his aircraft after he and his uncle make a desperate crossing of the

English channel to exile in France, he simply exchanges one waste-driven series of realizations for another, replacing his genealogy of dirigibles with his latest passion, the design and manufacture of destroyers. Once again, George proposes his most recent invention as the final realization of his efforts, and though we never see the X1, George's proud assertion that the X2 is "my last and best!" suggests the abandonment of such a forerunner and foreshadows the development of an X3, since the X2 has been promised to an unidentified, non-European nation (216). This series of destroyers suggests that a waste-driven schema of successive approximations of value informs George's scientific endeavors just as it informed his uncle's homes and motorcars. Like the airships the destroyers hardly afford solid footing.

For both George's inventions and Edward's acquisitions, the privileged elements in the series are predecessors, which are either left behind (the house), collected (the motor-cars), destroyed utterly (both of the Lord Roberts aircraft), or entirely absent (the putative X1). In each case, the value of the most recent acquisition/innovation is described not so much for its inherent worth, but for its supremacy over its immediate antecedent. Value thus becomes defined in relation to waste, paradoxically making the discarded or superceded object the actual marker of value. This transformation of the most recent item in the series into the already-trashed object is not quite the same thing as the "planned obsolescence" of the cheap mass-produced item, though it encompasses this aspect of consumer-driven manufacture. Rather, it is more accurately described as a process of progressive discarding, in which commercial markets—like consumers themselves—are driven by a phantasmal object forever out of reach. In this schema—what *Tono-Bungay* terms "theory" or "social comparative anatomy" (107)—objects are valued not for what they stand for, but for where they gesture. As in the earlier case of the Ponderevo alchemy, which depended upon the derivation of value *from* waste, the definition of value *by* waste calls into question the wellness of a society which makes—or rather is incapable of making—such judgments.

ELEMENTAL DECAY: QUAP AND MULTINATIONAL CAPITALISM

While the notion of a waste-driven series underlies both Edward's capitalist schemes and George's scientific exploits, these two disparate ideological programs combine during the expedition to Mordet Island to steal the deposits of "quap," a strange radioactive substance. George, who earlier described his uncle's acquisitive compulsion as a "fever," himself succumbs to the "malaria of the quap" which he insists is "already in my blood," even before he has set eyes on the deposits (354). Like all off Edward's undertakings, the overriding purpose of the expedition in financial; Edward sees the exporting—or rather stealing, as George more accurately phrases it—of the quap as the remedy for his sagging fortunes. "[T]here's only one thing we got to do," he tells George. "Show value ... That's where this quap comes in" (333). As with Edward's prior enterprises, the quap project is based upon deception. In addition to the theft the adventure requires, the Ponderevo's plan depends upon their private knowledge—which they conceal even from Gordon-Nasmyth, the discoverer of the quap deposits— that quap contains significant amount of canadium, a scarce substance with immense commercial value in electric light filaments.

Though scholarship on *Tono-Bungay* has long dispensed with the early criticism of the novel which saw the quap interlude as an unnecessary diversion, Wells critics still have not fully described the manner in which a waste-driven definition of value connects the colonial violence of the Mordet Island adventure with the military tropes describing the growth of the Tono-Bungay empire within Britain. Focusing on the Conradian echoes of the quap episode, David Lodge's early commentary touches upon this structural analogy in examining the linguistic connection between George's description of Edwardian England and Mordet Island: "Coming from a decadent and disintegrating 'civilized' society he encounters in the primitive jungle a frightening tangible agent of decay and disintegration" (238). More recently, Thomas Richards suggests that "[b]y placing the quest for quap at the center of the novel, Wells also sees that the modern philosopher's stone has become the magical transformation of energy from high to low states of entropy" (94). Richards comes closer to identifying what I will argue is Well's crucial emphasis on the colonial hegemony inherent in the waste-based value schema that underlies both the marketing of Tono-Bungay and the Mordet Island fiasco when he describes quap as "the patent medicine of raw materials" (93–94). The relationship between the commercial colonization of Britain by a patent medicine empire and the exploitation of West African raw materials is of course an inverse one, but as Bryan Cheyette note, the rhetoric describing each process is nearly identical (xxxv–xxvii). Refiguring the notion of imperial romance, Edward Ponderevo speaks of the "romance of modern commerce," which he terms "conquest" "Province by province," he tells George, "[l]ike sogers," and indeed George himself understands this conquest as that of "soldiers" establishing the boundaries of empire, while at the same time laying waste to its subject population: "We subjugated England and Wales; we rolled over the Cheviots with a special adaptation containing eleven per cent of absolute alcohol; 'Tono-Bungay: Thistle

Brand'" (162). While this intramural militarism never extends beyond the niche-marketing of higher-proof Tono-Bungay to the Scots, it does locate consumption and waste at the center of both domestic and colonial imperialism. Furthermore, the comic subjugation of England and its territories anticipates the very real violence of the Mordet Island adventure, culminating in George's gratuitous murder of an African man, which he dismisses in his framing narration as the "most incidental thing in my life" (10).

Both the marketing of Tono-Bungay and the violence underlying the theft of the quap suggest a conception of national identity based on hegemonic relations of the expansion of domestic markets and the appropriation of foreign raw materials. Wells addresses this issue more than a decade later in *The Outline of History* when he offers a wry response to Ernst Renan's famous question: "What is a nation? ... We may suggest that a nation is in effect any assembly, mixture, or confusion of people which is either afflicted by or wishes to be afflicted by a foreign office of its own, in order that it should behave collectively as if its needs, desires, and vanities were beyond comparison more important than the general welfare of humanity" (951). England, however, does not have a foreign office on the fictional Mordet Island. As the Roumanian captain of the retired potato-boat the *Maud Mary* puts it, "Dis is forbidden country," though George looks forward to the day when the embargo will be lifted, and presumably such an office established (352). Edward, who always places his needs before those of others, has already made inroads into marshalling an army of foreign officers in the form of his Tono-Bungay "travellers," who are "opening up Great Britain at the rate of a hundred square miles a day" (163). Furthermore, the Ponderevos are themselves the foreign agency for "certain American specialties" (227). Thus the economic domination implicit in their domestic conquest and explicit in their African plundering invokes a notion of nationhood dependent upon the movement of multi-national capital, even as their representation of American products suggests their involvement in a competing economy that will ultimately pose a challenge to the security of British industry.

Though Edward's tottering fortune, weakened further by his need to keep up the work on Crest Hill, provides the ostensible motive for the voyage, George's scientific curiosity plays no small part in his decision to lead the expedition himself after Gordon-Nasmyth is injured. Through the lens of science, we are led to see the waste at the heart of a national identity based upon the model of multinational capitalism. Edward's interest in the quap is apparent from the moment Gordon-Nasmyth raises the subject: "*You're* different, and I know your books," he tells the explorer, waving away his uncle's dismissal of the plan. "What is it?" To which Gordon-Nasmyth explains, quap is "the most radio-active stuff in the world ... a festering mass of earths and heavy metals, polonium, radium, ythorium, thorium, carium, and new things too. There's a stuff called Xk—provisionally." This initial description is portentous because it describes exactly the waste-centered value schema informing the Tono-Bungay empire and, by extension, Edwardian consumer capitalism. That waste is inherent in this construction of value is suggested by Gordon-Nasmyth's account of a "festering mass," which he also describes as "a sort of rotting sand" that further lays waste to all that surrounds it: "the world for miles about it is blasted and scorched and dead:" (241). At the same time, his litany of quap's elemental constituents reveals that, on an atomic level, quap produces a familiar serial logic of superseded objects gesturing toward their postulated ultimate value. Prior to George's commissioning of a scientific analysis of the sample, Gordon-Nasmyth focuses on the early and the middle elements in the radioactive series. George remarks that the explorer is "still thinking of the experimental prices of radium and the rarity value of cerium," unaware that the sample contains significant quantities of valuable canadium (245). The text leaves undetermined the question of whether or not canadium is the provisionally termed Xk; more important is canadium's status as an unrealizable final object in a waste-driven series. The name Xk is significant, however, in that it locates this serial construction of value at the heart of matter itself, and in this respect I disagree with Lucille Herbert's dismissal of Lodge's earlier suggestion that "[t]he very name of the destroyer, 'X2,' recalls the name of the unidentified ingredient in quap, 'Xk'" (Lodge 242). Herbert claims that George's "aim in building the destroyer ... is to transcend individual, instinctive violence through collective violence, in the service of a still unidentified revolutionary community that may come into being," thus positioning the X2 as the "antagonist and not, as Lodge suggests, the symbolic equivalent of Xk" (147). It is difficult to see George's killing of the African man in purely individual terms, however, just as it would be difficult to understand Conrad's Kurtz as fully divorced from the collective violence of empire. Surely Well's rendering of the Mordet island scheme locates this violence at the heart of multinational capitalist exploitation, as the multiple resonances of the island's name ("more debt" and "*morte*" or "more death") suggest, just as it establishes capitalism as a waste-driven system—hence the hint of "*merde*" in Mordet.[9] Furthermore, George is hardly the only individual implicated in this violence; even if he carries out the killing in secret, some degree of complicity is shared by the captain and crew of the

Maud Mary, Gordon-Nasmyth, Edward Ponderevo, and even England itself, as the supposed market for the canadium. In this respect, the multiple connections Lodge draws among the quap, the X2, and the condition of Edwardian England seem as apt as ever.

Although Lodge's early criticism presciently identifies the decay and concomitant waste at the center of both Edwardian consumerism and Mordet Island's quap deposits, neither Lodge nor more recent critics focusing on decay in the episode, including Richards, have offered adequate commentary on the allegorical connection between the production and waste inherent in both George's scientific endeavors and the quap itself. Though quap seems the material manifestation of pure decay, Gordon-Nasmyth's initial description of the deposits suggests that quap is in fact the residual waste of the most fundamental kind of value-production. "What it is, how it got made, I don't know," Gordon-Nasmyth tells George Ponderevo. "It's like as if some young creator had been playing about there" (241). Himself a young creator, George's apprehension at his first sight of the quap deposits arrives in the form of his realization that every act of creating value involves a process of discarding, and his suspicion that matter itself might ultimately participate in the same waste-driven value system informing Edwardian England:

> To my mind radioactivity is a real disease of matter. Moreover it is a contagious disease. It spreads. You bring those debased and crumbling atoms near others and those too presently catch the trick of swinging themselves out of coherent existence. It is in matter exactly what the decay of our old culture is in society, a loss of traditions and distinctions and assured reactions. (355)

Worse yet, George speculates that the process of production—whether cultural, economic, or physical—might actually have an end, which would be nothing more or less than waste itself. "Suppose indeed that is to be the end of our planet; no splendid climax and finale, no towering accumulation of achievements but just—atomic decay!"(355).

A WASTE OF STYLES

If *Tono-Bungay* locates a relationship between supersession and waste at the heart of matter itself, the novel also suggests that this relationship might underlie the development of literary style and this connection is curiously rehearsed in the history of the text's criticism. For a long time scholarship on the novel preoccupied itself with discussion of Wells's supposed stylistic failures, a diagnosis that depends upon a misapprehension of *Tono-Bungay's* experimental structure and which further mutes the force of its ideological critique. This critical distraction was in no small part colored by the debate which erupted between wells and Henry James, in which the latter accused Wells and other writers of his day—among them Bennett and Galsworthy—of novelistic artlessness. In a two-part review in the *The Times Literary Supplement,* which ran in the spring of 1914, James described what he saw as the technique, or rather the lack thereof, of "The Younger Generation": "They squeeze out to the utmost the plump and more or less juicy orange of a particular acquainted state and let this affirmation of energy, however directed or undirected, constitute for them the 'treatment' of the theme" (133–34). Although Wells fared better than a number of novelists in James's essay, the elder writer took him to task for his excessive inclusiveness, or as James called it, "saturation". "The more he knows and knows, or at any rate learns and learns," wrote James, "the greater is our impression ... that he shall but turn out his mind and its contents upon us by any free familiar gesture and as from a high window forever open" (134). Wells fired back a number of shots, most notably his novel *Boon* (1915), which includes a section clearly aimed at James that parodies his writing as "a magnificent but ungainly hippopotamus resolved at any cost, even the cost of its dignity, upon picking up a pea which it has got into the corner of its den" (456). Wells, perhaps feeling that he had taken matters too far, apologized in a letter written shortly after his gift of a copy of *Boon* to James, at one point disparaging his own novel as "just a waste-paper basket" (*Correspondence* 430).[10]

Yet one wonders just how sincere this apology is, given the odd connection between James's description of the younger writer's prose as defenestrated rubbish, Wells's own dismissal of *Boon* as trash, and Wells's earlier assertion in *Tono-Bungay* that the style of the novel that George Ponderevo is supposedly writing—and which forms the bulk of *Tono-Bungay's* pages—is itself a form of waste.[11] At the beginning of the novel, George Ponderevo offers a disclaimer which anticipates Wells's concession to James: "I realize what a fermenting mass of things learned and emotions experienced and theories formed I've got to deal with, and how, in a sense, hopeless my book must be from the very outset" (12). Apologizing for his "method or want of method," George explains that he is attempting to render the messy totality of his life, and thus that both book and life will necessarily appear as pastiche: "a succession of samples," "something of an agglomeration," a "hotch-potch of anecdotes and experiences" (13, 9, 11, 12).

Given the irony and evident disingenuousness of this novelistic disclaimer, it is surprising that critics of *Tono-Bungay* were often quick to charge Wells with, to borrow George Ponderevo's words from a different context, a "want of style" (9). Mark Schorer's 1948 essay "Technique as Discovery" offered one of the earliest and most enduring critiques of Wells's stylistic shortcomings.[12] For Schorer, Wells's problem is that of his stylistic sampling, which Schorer argues

> flounders through a series of literary imitations—from an early Dickensian, episode, through a kind of Shavian interlude, through a Conradian episode, to a Jules Verne vision at the end. The significant failure is in that end.... As far as one can tell Wells intends no irony.... The novel ends in a kind of meditative rhapsody which denies every value that the book has been aiming toward. For all the kinds of social waste which Wells has been describing, this is the most inclusive, the final waste. (74–75)

While I disagree with both Schorer's evaluation of Wells's literary imitations as unintentional failures and his disparagement of the novel's ending, his identification of the succession of literary set-pieces marks a crucial point in the criticism of *Tono-bungay*, and I would like to suggest that the significant term in his commentary is "series." For just as a serially-defined, waste-driven value schema underlies the social, economic, and scientific commentary of Wells's novel—in the form of Tono-Bungay's spin-off products, Edward's acquisitions, George's air and seacraft, and, in the substance of quap, matter itself—so too does this notion of a series of discarded and soon-to-be discarded items undergird the serial presentation of *Tono-Bungay's* stylistic pastiches.

In fact, *Tono-Bungay's* assumption of various identifiable literary styles is equally notable for its eventual dismissal of these styles. The Dickensian overtones present in George's narration in "Of Bladesover House" give way to an entirely un-Dickensian class condescension expressed in George's attitude toward his cousins the Frapps and their circle which is never redeemed. The "Shavian interlude," by which Schorer seems to mean George's courting of Marion, renders Marion, unlike Shaw's Eliza Doolittle, without sympathy, and she remains essentially the same character when she and George part as when they meet. The Conradian adventure, which as Bernard Bergonzi has demonstrated, is among the most directly allusive of Wells's literary imitations, both parodies and reveals what it sees as the shortcomings of Conrad's style of imperial romance to account adequately for the machinations of consumer capitalism and scientific innovation driving the quap expedition.[13] Unlike Conrad's Kurtz, whose malevolence at least results in the production of ivory, Wells's George Ponderevo kills without actually delivering any quap—itself a parody of the ironic symbolism in *Heart of Darkness*, since it is intended to bring light to England in the form of "Capern's Patent Filament" (334). Given this pattern of quite deliberate failures, not of imitation but of the representational possibilities of successive fictional models, we should view *Tono-Bungay* as the tending closer to the vein of high modernism. Wells's practice of literary sampling neatly anticipates Eliot's strategy of high and low cultural ventriloquism in "The Waste Land," which was, after all, originally titled, "He Do the Police in Different Voices." Or perhaps a nearer affinity still can be found between Wells's novel and the "Oxen of the Sun" episode of *Ulysses*, which engages in an analogous process of assuming and dismissing an array of literary styles, ranging from Anglo-Saxon elegy to Milton, DeQuincey, Ruskin, and so on— or even the successively discarded narrative modes of *Ulysses* as a whole.

What is notable about Joyce's "Oxen of the Sun" is that, with the exception of the frame of Roman fertility chants and American evangelical exhortation, it focuses almost entirely on British writers, if by "British" we include such writers as the Scottish-born Carlyle and the Irish Synge. So too does Wells choose his samples largely from British literature, and it is significant that each of the writers he imitates is engaged in a critique of either British domestic or colonial policy, whether the treatment of the London poor (Dickens), the stultifying effects of class prejudice (Shaw), or the underside of Britain's colonial project (Conrad).[14] Given Wells's own program of critiquing the economic and social structures he saw as responsible for the decay of Edwardian England, we may understand his assumption and abandonment of these critical models as suggesting their ineffectiveness in the face of an inexorable and waste-driven British consumerism. Indeed, one of the anxieties that *Tono-Bungay* expresses is the possibility that the disinterested space of art, which might be idealized as affording a privileged site from which to voice social critique, would itself be co-opted by capitalism or an economically-centered nationalism. We see the latter of these fears embodied in Edward Ponderevo's purchase of the literary journal *The Sacred Grove*, which in its revamped format features essays on "The Genius of Shakespeare," "A New Catholic History of England," and an unpublished Pater letter, all framed by advertisements for "TWENTY-THREE PILL": "THE BEST PILL IN THE WORLD FOR AN IRREGULAR LIVER" (247). That the TWENTY-THREE PILL ad surrounds the table of contents on all sides—in addition to the ad copy at the top and bottom of the page, small facsimiles of the pill itself border the right and left hand margins—suggests that consumer capitalism has fully enclosed the ostensibly neutral spaces of literature, history, and criticism, all of which are now reduced to "the exalted pretensions of a vanishing age" (247). Wells's concern that literary texts might eventually be reduced to commercial symbols of nationalism manifests itself during George's journey down the Thames at the end of the novel. Sailing past London Bridge, which marks the border of the "essential London," George enters the port section of the Thames, where "monstrous" commercial development has overshadowed the remnants of forgotten townships (416–17). There he spots a trio of London Council County steamboats bearing the names *Caxton*, *Pepys*, and *Shakespear*. "One Wanted to take them out and wipe them and put them back in some English gentleman's library," observes George in a moment of nostalgia reminiscent of his furtive boyhood raids on the Bladesover library (418). Here the great names of English printing diarist history, and drama have been diminished to mere emblematic status; worse yet, they adorn the hulls of the purely domestic mercantilism of the city council.

As Shorer's commentary suggests, the last style assumed by *Tono-Bungay*—that of George Ponderevo's apparently transparent address to the reader in the chapter titled "Night and the Open Sea," posed something of stumbling block for early critics of the novel, but even more recent scholarship has yet to come to terms with the novel's close.[15] In these final pages, George comments on the waste and futility of his experience with Edwardian capitalism as he sets out on a parodic imperial voyage, travelling outward from the heart of London, headed for the open sea in his latest destroyer, the X2.

> It is, I see now that I have it all before me, a story of activity and urgency and sterility. I have called it Tono-Bungay, but I had far better have called it Waste.... I think of all the energy I have given to vain things. I think of my industrious scheming with my uncle, of Crest Hill's vast cessation, of his resonant strenuous career.... It is all one spectacle of forces running to waste, of people who use and do not replace, the story of a country hectic with a wasting aimless fever of trade and money-making and pleasure-seeking. And now I build destroyers! (412)

Schorer's pronouncement concerning the end of the novel that "[a]s far as one can tell Wells intends no irony" has proven puzzlingly persistent (75). Surely the juxtaposition of George's description of early twentieth-century

Britain as a moral, cultural, and economic waste land with his own militaristic inventions suggests an ample dose of irony, something George himself recognizes momentarily, even though he disowns this knowledge a few pages later when he resumes the demeanor of economic and moral disinterest that earlier allowed him to speak so confidently of his mistress. Science as a wished-for final object: "Through the confusion something drives, something that is at once human achievement and the most inhuman of existing things.... Sometimes I call this reality Science, sometimes I call it truth" (419). Yet subsequent critics, granting more weight to the latter passage than the former, continue to follow Schorer's line of reasoning. Herbert, reading the progression of the novel as a movement from individual to collective aims, no matter how destructive to individual life and freedom those larger aims may be, diagnoses this final section as "morally vicious" (154). Jeffery Sommers, who helpfully points out the demarcation between the novel and the "novel within the novel," nevertheless finds in *Tono-Bungay's* generic hybridity a subtly manipulative, if masterful move on Wells's part.[16] As a result of its conceit of a writer writing his life story, *Tono-Bungay* avoids the pitfalls of both autobiography and social treatise, argues Sommers, suggesting that "Well's 'propaganda' is not nearly so overtly 'propaganda' and thus is likely to be more effective" (77). And Linda Anderson's more recent commentary simply resituates the problem of the contradiction implicit in the wastefulness of the scientific truth embodied in the X2 to ambivalent space, refusing to attach this irony to either George Ponderevo or Wells by suggesting that "both readings are possible," and arguing that the "autobiographical mode" of *Tono-Bungay* deprived Wells of the customary narrative space from which he could suggest his characters' limitations. Thus according to Anderson, the "end of the novel indicates Wells's problems in achieving closure in any other way" (148).

I wish to argue, however, that the ending of the novel, far from being the kind of "final waste" that Schorer described and that subsequent critics have to some degree variously endorsed, is in fact a most artful form of cultural-ideological work, and represents the culmination of the process of stylistic assumption and abandonment that informs the body of the novel.[17] If the juxtaposition of humanist lament and scientifically-informed nihilism that comprises the novel's final section represents a "final waste," it is the waste that results when a willfully ironic strategy of cultural appropriation—what we might think of as a modernist aesthetic of stylistic recycling—finds nothing of culturally-resonant value left to appropriate. In citing the novel's ending as evidence of failed imitation, moral viciousness, covert propagandism, or structural incompleteness, critics have too often been swayed by Wells's professed lack of interest in literary technique and his various advocacies as a public figure. Frequently they accept the popular understanding of the Wells-James debate cited earlier, which presumes James the unequivocal victor, while ignoring Wells's more pointed statements about the craft of fiction—and his own novels—that he made later in his wife. Surveying his literary career in his *Experiments in Autobiography* (1934), Wells remarks that the "splintering frame [of the English novel] began to get into the picture," and that he himself "was feeling [his] way towards something outside any established formula for the novel altogether" (416, 418). By the same measure, I would like to suggest that we read Wells's now famous statement that *Tono-Bungay* was the nearest thing to "a deliberate attempt upon The Novel" by acknowledging that while "attempt" may signify "endeavor," it can equally suggest "assault" (*Experiment* 423).

Nor should we allow Wells's many public roles—among them educational advocate, Labour Party candidate, proponent of a world government—to overwhelm our reading of novel the often hasty writer toiled over with such deliberate care, since such a strategy risks conflating the public figure of Wells as author and the fictional device to *Tono-Bungay*'s narrator.[18] Indeed, the self-directed blindness and exuberant nihilism of "Night and the Open Sea" belong to George Ponderevo, not Herbert George Wells. Though Wells, as Herbert notes, could speak of war as "the most socialistic of all forces," he later envisioned what he saw as an inevitable phase in human history when humankind would reject "the increasing destructiveness and intolerableness of war waged with the new powers of science" and "the enormous waste caused by military preparation" (qtd. in Herbert 143, *Outline* 2: 585, 588). It would be as much a mistake to confuse the opinions of George Ponderevo and Wells as to conflate Stephen Dedalus and Joyce, yet the legacy of Wells's sometimes contentious politics and his literary self-deprecation continues to exert an undue influence on the criticism of *Tono-Bungay*. The Wells I wish to conclude with is a figure who moved deftly between the worlds of literature and politics, allowing the social and cultural waste he saw embodied in an England whose national identity had been reduced to a set of unsustainable consumer practices to inflect his narrative method, yet always keeping his distance from the narrator who inscribes and finally voices it. No less a fabulous artificer than Stephen Dedalus of Joyce's *Portrait*, George Ponderevo chooses silence, exile, and cunning over life in his native land, but just as readers now understand the exhortations of Stephen's diary entries as Joyce's fictional rendering of youthful hubris, so should we extend a similar credit to Wells and recognize George's parting words as a middle-aged version of the same. George, in fact, may be the closest thing we have to Stephen's spiritual forefather. "I go to encounter for the millionth time the reality of experience and to forge in the smithy of my soul the uncreated conscience of my race," boasts Stephen (275–76). George Ponderevo, only slightly less prone to exaggeration, finds Truth "in a thousand different figures, under a hundred names" (420). No less a forger than Stephen, and only a different sort of confidence man than his Uncle Edward, George hints at the provisionality of all constructions of value: "We are all things that make and pass"(421).

WORKS CITED

Anderson, Linda R. *Bennett, Wells and Conrad.* London: Macmillan, 1988.
Bergonzi, Bernard. *The Turn of a Century: Essays on Victorian and Modern English Literature.* London: Macmillan, 1973.
Cheyette, Bryan. Introduction. *Tono-Bungay.* By H.G. Wells. New York: Oxford UP, 1997. xiii–xlvi.
Edel, Leon, and Gordon N. Ray, eds. *Henry James and H.G Wells: A record of their Friendship, their Debate on the Art of Fiction, and their Quarrel.* Urbana: U of Illinois P, 1958.
Hammond, J.R. "The Narrative Voice in *Tono-Bungay*." *The Wellsian* 12 (1989): 16–21.
———. "The Timescale in *Tono-Bungay*. A Problem in Literary Detection." *The Wellsian* 14 (1991): 34–36.
Herbert, Lucille. "Tono-bungay: Tradition and Experiment." *Modern Language Quarterly* 33 (1972): 140–55.
James, Henry. "The Younger Generation." *Times Literary Supplement.* 19 Mar. 1914. 133–34.
———. *The Golden Bowl.* 1904. New York: Grove P, 1952.
Joyce, James. *A Portrait of the Artist as a Young Man.* 1916. New York: Penguin, 1992.
Lodge, David. *The Language of Fiction.* London: Routledge, 1966.
MacKenzie, Norman and Jean MacKenzie, *H.G. Wells: A Biography.* New York: Simon and Schuster, 1973.
Marshall, Alfred. *Principles of Economics.* 1980. 8th ed. New York: Macmillan, 1948.
Masterman, C.F.G. *The Condition of England.* 1909. London: Metheun, 1960.
Marx, Karl. *Capital,* 1867. Ed. Frederich Engles. Trans. Samuel Moore and Edward Aveling. New York: Modern Library, 1906.
Parrinder, Patrick, ed. H.G. Wells: *The Critical Heritage.* London: Routledge and Kegen Paul, 1972.
Richards, Thomas. *The Imperial Archive: Knowledge and the Fantasy of Empire.* London: Verso, 1993.
Schorer, Mark. "Technique as Discovery." *Hudson Review* 1.1 (1948): 67–87.
Searle, G.R. *The Quest for National Efficiency.* Berkeley: U of California P, 1971.
Sommers, Jeffery. "Wells's *Tono-Bungay*: The Novel Within the Novel." *Studies in the Novel* 17.1 (1985): 69–79.
Trottman, Nelson, *History of the Union Pacific.* 1923. New York: Kelly, 1966.

Wells, H.G. *Boon*, 1915, *The Works of* H.G. *Wells*. Vol 13. London: Unwin, 1925. 391–562.

————. *The Correspondence of* H.G. *Wells*: Volume 2. Ed. David C. Smith. London: Pickering and Chatto, 1998.

————. *Experiment in Autobiography: Discoveries and Conclusions of a Very Ordinary Brain (since 1866)*. New York: Macmillan, 1934.

————. *Outline of History*. 2 vols. New York: Macmillan, 1920.

————. *Tono-Bungay*. 1908–09. New York: Oxford UP, 1997.

————. *The Work, Wealth and Happiness of Mankind*. Vol. 1. Garden City, New York: Doubleday, 1931.

West, Anthony. H.G. Wells: *Aspects of a life*. New York: Random, 1984.

White, Henry K. *History of the Union Pacific Railway*. 1895. Clifton: Kelly, 1973.

NOTES

1. Prior to C.F.G. Masterman's "The Condition of England" (1909), which was itself heavily influenced by *Tono-Bungay* and which cites Wells's novel approvingly, the genre was commonly referred to as that of the industrial novel.

2. A telling example of this tendency occurs in Henry James's *The Golden Bowl* (1904). In an early scene in the novel, Prince Amerigo tells Fanny Assingham that the American "moral sense works by steam—it sends you up like a rocket. Ours is slow and steep and unlighted ..." (32). In addition to its mechanical moral efficiency, America also stands as the novel's symbol of entrepreneurial success, as embodied in the fortune which enables Adam Verver to endow his collection at American City.

3. Interestingly enough, however, in his *Experiment in Autobiography* (1934), Wells repeats his praise of Marx's "generalizing ability," but retracts his claim about Marx's originality: "Marx was an uninventive man with, I think, a subconscious knowledge of his own uninventiveness" (214).

4. Trottman discusses this issue at length in his *History of the Union Pacific* (1923); see also White.

5. *Tono-Bungay's* dates are inconsistent. In his mature narration, George refers to himself as being both forty and forty-five years old (178); Cheyette suggests that the latter age is correct (423n79). Despite this discrepancy, a rough time line can be established. We know that George's mature narration must take place after 1905, since he observes that the "great stupid rusty iron head of Charing Cross station ... came smashing down in 1905," but probably does not take place after 1908, the date of *Tono-Bungay's* initial serialization (108). We can assume that George's Wimblehurst apprenticeship extends from the time he is fifteen to nineteen; he reflects that the Grammar school education he received took place thirty years ago (90)—Wells himself worked in a chemist's shop at age fifteen (Cheyette xlvii)—and he is nineteen when he leaves to go to London (91). If his conversation with his uncle takes place somewhere in the middle of this period, this would put the date of the Union Pacific investment between 1878 and 1880. For further discussion of probable dates in the novel, see Hammond "Timescale."

6. Adams's professed knowledge of a Wall Street conspiracy is probably better described as either paranoia or propaganda rather than reliable information. As a result of the confidence his letter generated, many people continued to invest in Union Pacific stock, which in turn continued to drop. Adams was finally forced to take control of the

company in 1884, as White puts it, to "make good on the things he had said about it" (qtd. in White 64n4).

7. George reports that Tono-Bungay's original formula "cost about seven pence a bottle to make, including bottling, and we were to sell it for the cost of half a crown plus the cost of the patent-medicine stamp" (147).

8. Although at one point George remarks that "I was no doubt moved by something of the same spirit of lavish expenditure that was running away with my uncle," he believes that this lavishness actually removes him from the commercial circuit that taints Edward's endeavors: "I do not know how far it is possible to convey to anyone who has not experienced it, the peculiar interest, the peculiar satisfaction that lies in a sustained research when one is not hampered by want of money." For George, this disregard of expense affords contact with "[s]cientific truth," "the one reality" immune to "advertisement or clamour" (298–99).

9. Given Wells's interest in Dickens, we might also read "Mordet" as gesturing toward Mr. Merdle in *Little Dorrit* (1857), whose surname connects waste with fraudulent and unsustainable gain.

10. Norman and Jean Mackenzie give a concise account of the falling out between Wells and James in *H.G. Wells: A Biography*. Wells's son Anthony West offers a more personal commentary of Wells's relationship to James in *H.G. Wells: Aspects of a Life*. For an earlier and more detailed account the Wells-James relationship, see Edel and Ray.

11. Cheyette also comments upon this theme of waste in the novel and in the Wells-James exchange in his introduction to *Tono-Bungay*, but believes that "Wells came to agree with James's fierce criticism" (xxvii–xxviii).

12. For a useful summary of early criticism of Wells's style, see Lodge 215.

13. Bergonzi details these allusions, and makes a convincing claim that Conrad himself was the model for the Romanian-born, British naturalized captain of the *Maud Mary* (95–98).

14. It is difficult to understand what Schorer intends when he cites the "Jules Verne vision" at the end of the novel, unless he means the ending's thematic content; stylistically the concluding episode bears little in common with Verne. Most likely Schorer is following the convention of linking Wells and Verne by virtue of the shared genre of what was then termed scientific romance and now called science fiction. Both Wells and Verne disavowed any connection to each other, however—Wells because he felt the comparison limiting, Verne because he thought Well's fiction lacked a properly scientific basis.

15. Wells's contemporaries often read this section as the author's direct address to the reader, even if they profess otherwise. An unsigned review in the *Daily Telegraph* quotes from the section as evidence of "the sermon which Mr. Wells preaches" nothing that" even in a novel, he is never long out of the pulpit" (Parrinder 149). Charles L. Graves, in an unsigned review in the *Spectator*, remarks on Well's "general outlook" in the final section, which he finds "pessimistic" and morally suspect (Parrinder 153).

16. Sommers observes that "we must understand that '*Tono-Bungay*,' the novel written by George Ponderevo, has concluded with ... the chapter entitled 'Love Among the Wreckage,' and that it is Well's novel, *Tono-Bungay*, that concludes with the chapter, 'Night and the Open Sea'" (76).

17. Again, Cheyette also treats George Ponderevo's prose style within this context of waste. While he argues that George's narrative mode is an "attempt to distinguish himself from the language of society at large so as not to implicate himself in its lies" and further

comments on Wells's "aware[ness] of the playful potential within the modern novel" afforded by parody and pastiche, Cheyette does not in my mind fully establish the connection between the consumerist, technological, and literary paradigms underlying Wells's modernism. By referring to Wells's intertextual borrowings as a kind of "game playing," Cheyette's otherwise excellent evaluation mutes the comprehensiveness and force of Wells's cultural critique (xxvi–xxviii).

18. Cheyette notes that the time between *Tono-Bungay*'s conception and its initial serialization spanned almost five years (xiii). The tendency to equate the opinions of Wells's fictional characters with those of Wells himself persists throughout much of the history of Wells criticism. For an argument against an autobiographical reading of *Tono-Bungay*, see Hammond, "Narrative."

PHILIP COUPLAND

H.G. Wells's "Liberal Fascism"

'Is Mr Wells a secret Fascist?' was the ironic question posed in the British Union of Fascists' (BUF) paper *Action*. In fascist eyes Wells was a 'socialist' and, even worse, an 'internationalist', but against the certainty of that knowledge was the perplexing fact that there appeared to be Blackshirts playing the role of Wellsian revolutionaries in the Wells/Korda film, *Things to Come*. The author of the letter which prompted this enquiry regarding Wells's politics noted that 'the supermen all wore the black shirt and broad shiny belt of Fascism! The uniforms were identical, and their wearers moved and bore themselves in the semi-military manner of fascists.' A cinema audience, being familiar with the sight of Blackshirts on British streets for the previous three and a half years, would have naturally been struck in the same way, and 'Observer' wrote that 'all around me last night I heard people commenting on it'.[1]

The only way that the fascists could explain this apparent contradiction was to assume that 'Mr Wells had been caught napping'. John Macnab, reviewing the film for the BUF, mockingly enquired, 'Cap'n Wells, art tha' sleeping there below?'[2] However, this article will argue that the appearance of these mysterious men in black to build the world state was not the consequence of any slumbering inattention on Wells's part but reflected, on the one hand, the long-established Wellsian theory of how the world state

From *Journal of Contemporary History*, vol. 35, no. 4. © 2000 Sage Publications Ltd.

would be achieved and, on the other, important changes which Wells's thinking underwent in response to the specific political conditions of the early 1930s. As such this is a study in what I call the 'praxis of desire', in that it examines a theory of the ways and means whereby a desired end may be sought, in this case the Wellsian utopia of the world state or 'Cosmopolis'.

The praxis of desire is necessarily a dynamic thing, evolving response to changes in the political forces, theories and contingencies of the moment. Thus while, as Warren Wagar's penetrating analysis of Wells's 'Open Conspiracy' has shown, many aspects of Wells's thinking in this area long predated the 1930s, I would suggest that at the same time Wells was additionally and significantly influenced by the new political forces which appeared to be coming to dominance in the early 1930s.[3] In this respect he was not alone: in Britain during this period sections of the Labour Party departed both to the 'left'—the ILP—and the 'right'—Mosley's New Party and then BUF. Prominent intellectuals of the Labour movement, including Wells's old Fabian colleagues Sydney and Beatrice Webb and Bernard Shaw, and younger Labour figures including Sir Stafford Cripps and G.D.H. Cole, either embraced the authoritarian road to socialism or proposed the radical reform of parliamentary democracy. Labour intellectuals George Catlin and Raymond Postgate saw the need for, respectively, 'a voluntary aristocracy of asceticism' and 'an organization of storm-troopers or ironsides' as essential for their party in the new conditions.[4]

The question of whether the writer, social critic and utopian H.G. Wells had 'fascist' tendencies, secret or otherwise, is nothing new. At the time, Dmitri Mirsky and other communists were not slow to include him in their theory of fascism.[5] More recently, Wells the liberal and democrat has been defended against Wells the authoritarian and racist.[6] However, not only was Wells, as at least some commentators have shown, a man of complex contradictions but, as Leon Stover has argued, in Wells's thinking the forces of destruction and creation, darkness and light, are best understood as a dialectical unity.[7] The same paradigm, I would argue, when applied to Wells's theory of revolutionary praxis in the 1930s, shows how he was not forced to be *either* a liberal *or* an authoritarian, but could seek 'liberal' ends by means which were anything but.

The relationship between these two sides of Wellsism is well illustrated by the 'Liberal Fascism' which Wells called for in his addresses to the Young Liberals at their Summer School in Oxford in July 1932. The reason why he was there, Wells stressed, was to 'assist in a kind of "Phoenix Rebirth" of Liberalism'. 'Central' to this reborn 'Liberalism' would be what Wells called a 'competent receiver', by which he meant 'a responsible organisation, able to guide and rule the new scale human community'. The ' competent receiver' was also, Wells carefully explained, 'flatly opposed' to the norms of 'parliamentary democracy', being a 'special class of people' of the type anticipated in 'the Guardian of Plato's Republic'. 'Concrete expressions of this same idea' included '*the Fascisti* in Italy', Wells believed.[8]

For the 'modernized state' to come into existence, Wells asserted, would require 'the will and the ideas of public-minded, masterful people', formed into 'a militant organisation' which would 'release the human community from the entanglements of the past'. The alternative was for 'civilization' to be left to 'stagger down past redemption to chaotic violence and decadence'. Consequently liberalism, while seeking 'one prosperous and progressive world community of just, kindly, free-spirited, freely-thinking, and freely-speaking human begins', in a world of 'gangsters' also required 'a voice (and a backbone)'. One should add that this Wellsian 'liberal' utopia, with its renunciation of parliamentary democracy, private property and individualism was not the good society as liberals in the conventional sense would have understood it. Thus, in order to seek this 'prosperous and progressive' utopia, liberals had to 'move with the times', discard 'the sentimental casualness of nineteenth-century Liberalism' and transform themselves into 'a Liberal Fascisti'. In so doing, liberalism would become an organization to '*replace* the dilatory indecisiveness of parliamentary politics'. In the same way that 'the Fascist Party, to the best of its ability, *is* Italy now', so 'the Fascists of Liberalism must carry out a parallel ambition on a still vaster scale', Wells declared.[9]

As Wells made clear to his Oxford audience, his search for an active force to realize his utopian vision of the world state was nothing new—he had sought to turn the Fabian Society to that purpose 25 years earlier. Furthermore, during the second half on the 1920s Wells had postulated a means-to-utopia in the form of the 'open conspiracy' of *The World of William Clissold* (1926), an idea he went on to revise and develop through *The Open Conspiracy: Blue Prints for World Revolution* (1929) and then in what he described as 'definitive detail' in *What Are We To Do With Our Lives?* (1931). In this last version, the 'open conspiracy' was cast as an intellectual élite movement which would in time develop into 'a world religion'.[10]

There are suggestions that during the late 1920s the groundwork for Wells's later view of fascism was already in place. Writing of the Italian fascists in 1928, Wells mused that there was 'considerable reason to suppose that organized brotherhoods, maintaining a certain uniformity of thought and action over large areas and exacting a quasi-religious devotion within their members, are going to play an increasingly important part in human affairs'. Nonetheless, Wells had a fundamental objection to formally organized bodies of the fascist type in that they threatened to displace the solvent power of but effective life of a young Fascist or Nazi', the cult of personal leadership was a throwback to the automatic, unquestioning obedience demanded by monarchical authority. The member of the Wellsian élite owed allegiance only to the dictates of Wellsian 'common sense'.[11]

Reflecting this, he declared that 'the idea of the Open Conspiracy ever becoming a single organization must be dismissed from the mind'. Even at the moment of its final victory the open conspiracy would be a cultural movement without a centre, being a 'large, loose assimilatory mass of movements, groups and societies' which would finally 'swallow up the entire population of the world and become the new human community'. It was this model of the open conspiracy which appeared in the first edition of Wells's *The Work, Wealth, and Happiness of Mankind* in early 1932. This volume, together with *The Outline of History* (1920) and *The Science of Life* (1930) completed a project to bring 'together a complete system of ideas upon which the Open Conspirator can go' and included what Wells believed was 'an even more explicit statement of the Open Conspiracy plan'.[12]

In June 1932, pressing forward with his argument for the open conspiracy, Wells prepared a 'Memorandum on the World Situation' which he privately circulated among 'a number of public figures in Europe and America'. This sought international co-operation to act against the world economic malaise and to this end argued for 'some force that will jump political boundaries and operate in a world-wide manner'. However, this force was not to be a political movement but the 'few thousands' who could mould opinion through the media organizations of the world, and the heads of state 'who can make statements that will be respected and listened to throughout the earth'. As West notes, Wells 'did not get the response he hoped for, and no general debate took place'. Instead, the next month, in Oxford, Wells changed his approach and appealed to the Liberals to emulate the militarized vanguard party that he had hitherto rejected.[13]

Wells ended his Oxford speech by asking of the 'feeble giant of modern Liberalism': 'Can he be gingered up?'. H.M. Tomlinson's judgment of Wells's call to the Liberal leader 'Mr Ramsey Muir to be a Black Shirt, or a Nazi at the least' was that the Liberals were 'no more likely to resolve on New Jerusalem for England's green and pleasant land than are the guardians of the home for lost dogs'.[14] And so things turned out, but despite this disappointment, Wells by no means gave up his quest for such a force. Following his speech to the Liberals, Wells drew up a 'sketch of a possible revolutionary organisation' which, like the Open Conspiracy, would be outside established parties, but, unlike that earlier model, would replicate many of the characteristics of existing militarized political movements. As he wrote in the 1934 revised edition of *The Work, wealth, and Happiness of Mankind*, the world situation demanded a 'militant form of the open conspiracy', an 'overt and definite world organization of will and aim'. As has been shown, an authoritarian élite without scruples about using violence was a long-established aspect of Wells's theory of revolutionary praxis, but it was the notion of a formally organized political movement that was the novel element of Wells's approach in the early 1930s which led him to link 'fascist' means to 'liberal' ends. Unlike the old version of the Open Conspiracy, this new force would require 'ordered co-operation and discipline' and, graphically illustrating the nature of this 'new movement', Wells alluded to the 'various "arms", the infantry, air forces, "shock troops" ' into which its 'militant members' would be organized.[15]

Having so outlined the Wellsian revolutionary force, at the beginning of December 1932 Wells turned from the Liberals to the Labour movement. First canvassing the opinion of 'sixty to seventy sample people', Wells then issued his call in an article in *The Daily Herald*. Proclaiming the need for 'Common Creed or Left Parties Throughout the World', his article allowed that while the 'Class War' organizations of the left might create the conditions for revolution, the 'creative motive' in history was to be found 'in a variety of more or less disciplined and instructed associations' which included 'the various Fascist associations'. 'Such "efficiency" organizations' were 'a necessary factor for world revolution', Wells declared.[16]

Despite the comparative radicalism of the Labour Patty at the time, Wells's search for recruits for his new movement evoked 'very little response'.[17] However, while drawing another blank, he believed that his ideas were growing 'more precise'.[18] He also seemed to have more success with another organization around this time, as Kingsly Martin recorded in October 1932 that the Federation of Progressive Societies and Individuals (FPSI) had recently 'sprung up under Mr. Wells' inspiration'.[19]

With regard to the success of this engagement between Wells and the 'Progressives', it was true that the FPSI, some months after its inception by C.E.M. Joad, had redrafted its 'basis' into the clearly Wellsian form which then appeared in the organization's book, *Manifesto*, in 1934 and that Wells's *Daily Herald* article appeared in the same text as well. However, things were not necessarily as they seemed. A leading member of the organization later recalled that

> ... some months after the inception of the F.P.S.I. the society
> made a bid for the support of Mr H.G. Wells. Mr Wells
> responded to the tune of a donation of £20 and the grant of the
> permission to include his name in the list of vice-presidents ...
> but made the redrafting of the basis ... a condition of his support.

In light of this, the FPSI was 'presumably a Wellsian body'. However, J.B. Coates recalled that 'the original acceptance of the Wellsian basis was half-hearted' and Joad himself had opposed its acceptance, which had been secured by a single vote. In view of this, it was not surprising that 'as an organization pledged to propagate the Wellsian world view' the FPSI 'show[ed] a lukewarm spirits and a conspicuous lack of drive'. Although Wells continued as a nominal vice-president of the organization until he finally fell out with it towards the end of 1943, it seems likely that he disregarded the FPSI as a force towards world revolution much earlier. It was almost certainly the FPSI that Wells had in mind when he wrote of 'The New World Society' in his 1939 text, *The Holy Terror*, which, unlike 'Rud Whitlow' and his 'Purple Shirt', were 'barely cryptic nudists', 'extremely woolly vegetarians', 'flimsy people' and 'not the stuff revolutions are made of'.[20] Thus, despite considerable effort and an enviable access to the means of propaganda, Wells's attempts to mobilize his ideas via an effective political organization had failed utterly. Nonetheless, his writings provide ample indication of what he was seeking. In *The Shape of Things to Come*, Wells wrote that he had 'contrived to set out ... my matured theory of revolution and world government very plainly'. In this 'sociological novel' Wells began his narrative among the actual events of the contemporary world and then laid out an imagined history of a future of slump, chaos and then world war in the coming decades. It was out of the ruins of the old world that the vanguard of the new, the 'Modern State Movement', emerged. This élite, made up of the surviving airmen and technicians of the world, transformed it in accordance with the Wellsian blueprint with a 'pitiless benevolence' and few scruples. Finally, its work complete, this stern élite conveniently retired, leaving a society no longer needing a coercive state at all, as a place where 'liberty increases daily'.[21]

In this way Wells showed how 'fascist'—that is élitist, authoritarian and violent—means, could yield 'liberal' ends. *The Shape of Things to Come* was also understood by Wells as a discussion of 'contemporary revolutionary forces in the form of anticipating fiction'. Writing the year after the publication of *The Shape of Things to Come*, Wells saw it as a culmination of a dialectic between theory and events since his writing of *Anticipations* at the turn of the century: 'Step by step through that logic in events, the new pattern of revolution has been brought from Utopia and from the vague generalizations of the New Republic into contact with contemporary movements and political actuality', he wrote. Wells made clear that it events which had forced a major shift in his theory of revolution, writing of the interwar period that by the time of *The Shape of Things to Come,*

> ... the artificiality and unsoundness of those boom conditions had become glaringly obvious ... The Open Conspiracy of William Clissold was essentially speculative, optional and amateurish; the Open Conspiracy of De Windt which took possession of the derelict world, was presented as the logical outcome of inexorable necessity.[22]

This text thus also signalled changes in Wells's thinking on fascism. As late as 1930—as Michael Foot has pointed out in defending his hero against 'Fascist libel'—Wells had put forward an anti-fascist line in *The Autocracy of Mr.Parham*, which charted the rise and fall of 'Mr Parham' and the 'The Duty Paramount League' as, respectively, 'The English Duce' and 'The Fascisti of Britain'.[23] Three years later Wells was articulating a positive— albeit importantly nuanced—view of contemporary fascism.

Not without accuracy Wells portrayed the 1930s as seeing 'the conviction that Parliamentary democracy had come to an end spread everywhere'. However, rather than this being a disaster, this environment fostered the emergence of the crude prototypes of the 'Air Dictatorship' and 'Modern State Movement' which would remould the world into the Cosmopolis. Speaking in the voice of the text's historian of the future, Wells wrote of the reaction against democracy that:

> At its first onset this craving for decisiveness produced some extremely crude results. An epidemic of tawdry 'dictatorships'.... But there followed a world-wide development of directive or would-be directive political associations which foreshadowed very plainly the organization of the Modern State Fellowship upon which our present world order rests.[24]

Wells went on to specify the regimes which anticipated the new political order, writing that:

> The Fascist dictatorship of Mussolini ... had something in it of a more enduring type than most of the other supersessions of

parliamentary methods. It arose not as a personal usurpation but as the expression of an organisation with a purpose and a sort of doctrine of its own. The intellectual content of Fascism was limited, nationalist and romantic; its methods, especially in its opening phases, were violent and dreadful; but at least it insisted upon discipline and public service for its members.... Fascism indeed was not an altogether bad thing; it was a bad good thing; and Mussolini has left his mark on history.[25]

The ambivalence that Kemp detects in Wells's personal simultaneous rejection of and attraction to individual pre-eminence is also apparent in his attitude towards the fascist leader. Priestley recalled arguing 'in the later Thirties against both Shaw and Wells, who were declaring that Mussolini was a very great man, far greater than Napoleon', and even during the war years Wells threaded amidst his criticism of Mussolini the assertion that the Duce was 'immensely energetic, with the energy not of morbid concentration but physical abundance. He is what many men would like to be.' When seeking a contemporary parallel of the 'drive' of the 'chief figures of the Air Dictatorship' it was to 'Mussolini, the realizer of Italian Fascismo' with his 'single-handed accomplishment and ... disinclination to relinquish responsibility' that Wells turned.[26]

Bridging the gap in *The Shape of Things to Come* between the actual movements of the time and the fictional Modern State Movement, Wells wrote that 'millions of young men who began Fascist, Nazi, Communist ... became Modern State men in their middle years'. As this last quotation suggests, it was not only fascism which Wells saw as anticipating the vanguard movement he desired. He also noted that 'in Russia something still more thorough and broader came into operation after 1917' and approved of 'the modernity of many aspects of the early Bolshevik régime'. This echoed the fact that in his approach to the Liberals and the Labour movement the previous year he had called for 'a sort of Liberal Communist Party *or* a sort of Liberal Fascism'; 'a Liberal Fascisti, for enlightened Nazis ... a greater Communist Party'; and had grouped together the 'more or less disciplined and instructed associations from the Communist Party to the various Fascist associations'.[27]

'The Communist Party' and the 'Italian Fascisti' both shared Wells's approval to the extent that they represented 'that germinal idea of the Modern State, the Guardians in Plato's *Republic*'. However, this did not mean that he saw them as being equally close to the ideal Wellsian political movement. In this regard it is of the greatest significance that Wells's approval was of the '*early* Bolshevik régime' of Lenin for, by the early 1930s,

Wells had accumulated a weight of criticism of the communist movement that effectively displaced his former approval of Lenin's party. The early party had been acceptable because it replaced the mysticism of 'the version of deified democracy, the Proletariat' with an authoritarian élite. However, against this he saw the 'heavy load of democratic and equalitarian cant' which 'ordained that at the phrase "Class War" every knee should bow'.[28]

The ideal Wellsian revolutionary was the man (sic) of reason, a type in the modern period which included 'teachers of every class, ... writers and creative artists, ... scribes and journalists, ... doctors, surgeons and the associated professions, ... judges and lawyers generally, ... administrators, and particularly that most excellent type the permanent official, with technical experts, and finally, most hopeful, various and interesting of all, with the modern scientific worker'; whereas the communist doctrine of 'class-war', Wells believed, obstructed the employment of 'the most characteristically modern types in the community' and caused 'its inability to assimilate competent technicians, organizers and educators'. When he met Stalin in July 1934, the year after the publication of *The Shape of Things to Come*, prominent among the points Wells made to the Soviet dictator was that it was 'useless' to approach 'engineers, airmen, military-technical people' with 'class-war propaganda'. Without this group there could be no basis for the essential '*competent receiver*', communism might be able to seize power via the insurrectionary 'class-war' but would be able to do nothing with it. The 'weak point in communist proposals', Wells argued, was 'that they do not clearly indicate a competent receiver'.[29]

By raising the proletariat to supremacy, Wells saw that communism, rather than being progressive, was actually reactionary. Proletarians were not modern-minded but, possessed of 'their own distinctive modifications of the narrow peasant psychology' which reacted against 'the methods and machinery of modern production, against social discipline and direction', they were 'much more disposed to hamper and break up the contemporary organisation altogether than to reconstruct it'. In addition, Wells reacted strongly against the part that the peasant played in Soviet Russia. According to his pseudo-biological typology of human 'personas', the peasant was ineradicably acquisitive and superstitious and in the Soviet collectives Wells condemned 'the old sentimental unwashed sweating "democratic" side' of socialism, 'all natural virtue, brotherhood and kisses', 'Rousseauism pretending to love machinery and taking it to pieces out of sheer childishness, misusing it and destroying it'.[30] Strong hints to Wells's antisemitism were also apparent in his description of the Communist Party as 'that band of Russian Jews'.[31]

Wells's view of Stalin and of the direction the Soviet regime was taking
was also important. Wells believed that the early twentieth century had seen
the opening of 'the epoch of dictatorships and popular "saviours" '.[32]
However, not all forms of authoritarian rule were equal in his opinion.
Because Wells firmly and consistently believed that the cult of the leader
displaced the force of reason, what was important in the modern form of
dictatorship was not the person of the leader but the organization he led. On
the one hand, Wells believed that fascism in Italy was not reducible to
Mussolini, writing that 'if he were to die, Fascism would not have the least
difficulty in finding a … successor'. For all its emphasis on leadership,
fascism was 'only *apparently a* one-man tyranny'. On the other hand, 'the
persistent weeding out of his rivals and critics by Stalin' was 'rapidly reducing
the party control in Russia to a personal absolutism'. By this 'degenerative
process', the modern, and to Wells thus acceptable elements of Lenin's
original vanguard party were being exchanged for an old-fashioned form of
reactionary tyranny. 'Stalin, who has succeeded the scientific-spirited Lenin,
seems to possess all the vindictive romanticism of a typical Georgian', Wells
wrote. In this way Stalin belonged to the second reactionary 'class of
persona' which 'fundamentally … despises work', is 'fierce' and 'romantic',
and glories in 'waste', an ancient rather than modern form, being the
'disposition of kings, aristocrats, soldiers and ruling classes since the social
world began'.[33]

In the future history of *The Shape of Things to Come*, Wells projected his
conclusions about Stalinism into the future, writing that because of the
'ineradicable democratic taint of the Soviet system' there was 'the widening
estrangement of the Russian process from Western creative effort'. Wells
imagined a future in which 'at every point where constructive efforts was
made the nagging antagonism of the Class War fanatic appeared, to impede
and divide'. He dismissed the Soviet system as 'a politician's dictatorship,
propagandising rather than performing, disappointing her well-wishers
abroad'. It 'seemed to lead' but 'lied', he declared. Even at the moment when
the Communist Party basked in the reflected glory of the Red Army's
victories against fascism, it, along with Wells's other hate object, the Church
of Rome, was 'the right hand and the left hand of what is fundamentally the
same enemy' which fought 'mental liberation tooth and nail'.[34]

Fascism, although more free of 'democratic taint' and the 'elderly
methods of parliamentary democracy' was not pure either, being infected
with the 'poison of nationalism'. However, Wells's discussion of
'contemporary revolutionary forces in the form of anticipating fiction' found
that it was fascism rather than communism which offered a glimpse of 'the

shape of things to come.' The course of the world war which Wells prophetically imagined breaking out in 1940 demonstrated that 'the old enthusiasm for Revolution had faded out of the new Fascist pattern, more closely knit in its structure and dominated by an organisation of the younger spirits which claimed to be an élite'. Wells continued: 'Except for the fundamentally important fact that these Fascisti were intensely nationalist, this control by self-appointed, self-disciplined élites was a distinct step towards our Modern State organisations.' The Wellsian voice of the historian of the future approved of the fascits as:

> ... noteworthy ... for their partial but very real advance on democratic institutions, Amidst the chaos, that organized 'devotion of the young' on which our modern community rests was clearly foreshadowed.... The idea of disciplined personal participation in human government was being driven into the mentality of the new generation.
>
> Until something more convincing appeared, it had to crystallize, disastrously enough, about such strange nuclei as the theatrical Mussolini and the hysterical Hitler, it had to be patriotic because that was the only form in which the State then presented itself. But after these first crystallizations had been shattered and dissolved in the war ... the idea was still there, this idea of banded co-operation ready to be directed to greater ends. Youth had ceased to be irresponsible in all the Fascist countries.[35]

It was thus fascism which, of all extant political movements of the 1930s, came closest to the 'aggressive order of religiously devoted men and women who will try out and establish and impose a new pattern of living upon our race', which Wells appealed for in the final line of *The Shape of Things of Come*. Geoffrey Gorer noted in1935: 'Mr Wells thinks that he hates fascism; he is horror-struck as any liberal at its brutality, its barbarism, its philistinism, its illogicality and its narrow nationalism; but he puts all the blame on the last quality; if it was only international it wouldn't really be so bad.'[36]

It was not only in *The Shape of Things to Come* that Wells hinted that he saw his 'modern state movement' anticipated in the fascist movements of the day. It was a message that he also put forward in 1936 in the *Anatomy of Frustration*. Wells, speaking through the medium of a fictitious author, wrote that 'Steele' 'blamed the liberal type of mind for gentleness, for fastidiousness, for obscurity of thought and expression, for pedantry and needless dissensions, for mutual distrust'. Wells had written earlier of the

'Modern State Fellowship' of 'varied technicians' originally banding together in 'protective and aggressive gangs' and 'Steele' 'looked with envy at the working solidarity of the ... gangster régimes in various European countries'. Drawing on the 'experiences of Jesuit and Puritan, Communist and Fascist, for direction in the New Beginning', Wells imagined a 'New Model' of liberalism to replace the 'undisciplined and uncoordinated liberalism'. Once again, Wells distinguished between 'piecemeal-socialism' and fascism. Socialism had 'projected a new sort of society' but without the 'new sort of head' of the 'competent receiver', but at the same time 'the discursive human intelligence, in its subconscious realization of these ... deficiencies, was ... busy producing ... a series of rough experiments in directive control of such impatient, cruel and incalculable gang tyrannies, for example, as the Fascist and Nazi organizations.'[37] Two year later, in his novella *The Brothers*, in which two long-separated identical twins are reunited, of the two, it is 'Bolaris' on the 'right' who has sought to weld his party into an 'operative form'. The 'operative form' is synonymous with the *competent receiver* which, as Bolaris says to his socialist twin Ratzel, 'came from someone on your side'. In contrast, Ratzel and his followers are condemned as 'just a crowd of empty *antis*—without a creative idea in common'.[38]

   In *Things to Come*—in which the stages of the Wellsian revolution were turned into film for a mass audience—Wells once more drew the line between reactionary dictatorship and 'modern' fascism, directing that the character 'Boss' who comes to dominate the devastated 'Everytown' was 'not intended to be a caricature of a Fascist or Nazi leader. He is as much South American or Haytian or Gold Coast. He is something more ancient ... and more universal than any topical movements.' Wells also guarded against any suggestion of fascism in the salutations of the Boss's followers, directing that there was to be 'no hand lifting'.[39]

   Aside from these subtleties, which were lost on many critics and probably the majority of the audience, the major link between the 'Airmen' who bring the Wellsian revolution, and fascism, was their black uniform. Mellor has suggested that the costume of the Airmen deliberately drew on fascist 'iconography of the future' and indeed notes 'the transparent overlay of Raymond Massey/John Cabal/Oswald Mosley'. Whether this link was deliberately intended by Wells is unclear. Given the considerable attention that Wells devoted to the symbolism of scenery, props and costume in the film, these uniforms were certainly no accidental choice. Stover's interpretation that the shift from the black attire of the Airmen to the white of the rulers of the new Wellsian world symbolizes the 'destruction–construction dialectic' is convincing. At the same time, to suggest that Wells did not anticipate the inference that an audience would much more readily draw on seeing 'the New Airmen in their black costumes' implies that his powers were truly failing.[40] Whatever Wells's precise intention, the Airmen expressed the ideal of the militant, organized élite that he approved of in contemporary fascist movements.

In Wells's *The Holy Terror (1939)*, his final study of the ways of the Wellsian revolution before the war, there was no element of doubt concerning this linkage of fascism to Wellsian revolution. Wells based the action of the novel in the political scene of the England of the 1930s and it was not to the Communist Party of Great Britain to which he turned. Instead it was the BUF, albeit thinly veiled as the 'Purple Shirts' of the 'Popular Socialist Party', who under the leadership of 'Rud Whitlow' threw off their narrowly nationalistic ambitions to become a world state movement. Whitlow, as means to the Wellsian utopia, has been described as 'a paradox ... which no commentator has yet satisfactorily explained'. The story of *The Holy Terror* was perhaps paradoxical from a viewpoint of Wells as a conventionally democratic liberal or socialist, but rather than turning 'Wellsian ideas on their head', it was fully logical in relation to Wells's praxis of desire as laid out her.[41] By naming Whitlow the 'Holy Terror', Wells was probably articulating the same undesired, but regrettably necessary synthesis as he did with 'liberal fascism'. Whitlow is at one and the same time both 'The Stink" and the 'Superman'; contemptible and dangerous, but necessary; not important in himself as a leader, only as the mediator of the higher 'common-sense of mankind'; he, like the 'Modern State Movement' in *The Shape of Things to Come*, is a necessary transient evil. Wells also expressed the same qualified approval of Mussolini as in *The Shape of Things to Come*, making clear where he stood in relation to the ideal Wellsian figure to come: the Italian fascist leader was 'a minor Holy Terror, an opera-tenor Rud'.[42]

Returning to real politics, the actual BUF was launched at the very moment in 1932 when Wells was seeking a political movement to press forward his purpose. Nor was the idea to the BUF—which put itself forward as a 'Modern Movement' and as the handmaiden of 'the new world of science'— necessarily so strange in this role. Mosley, a wartime pilot, was happy to see himself described as an 'ex-airman', and many of his supporters were aviators, including Geoffrey Dorman, editor of *Aeroplane*, A.V. Roe, pioneer pilot and founder of the AVRO aircraft firm and P.P. Eckersley, RFC veteran, leading expert of the new technology of wireless, and a correspondent with Wells. Later on, and reflecting this interest in modern technology, the aircraft in *Things to Come* was a matter of some debate among 'air-minded' fascists in the pages of *Action*.[43]

Nor were Wells and Mosley strangers. Mosley later recalled playing Wells's 'childish but most enjoyable ball game in his house near Easton Lodge' and they co-existed in the same privileged social universe. Mosley dined alongside Wells in parties including Keynes and Harold Nicolson in May 1931 and Charlie Chaplain in October that year.[44]

In *The Autocracy of Mr Parham* published in mid-1930, Wells had paid Mosley ('Sir Osbert Moses') the compliment of singling him out from an unflattering portrait of the Labour Party by picturing him as 'pleading in vain with a sheepish crowd of government supporters for some collective act of protest' against 'Lord Paramount's' forced dissolution of parliament. Acting very much in the style of his fictional alter ego, Mosley resigned form his post as Chancellor of the Duchy of Lancaster on 20 May 1930 over the Labour government's rejection of his efforts spur it into action against the mounting crisis of unemployment. In February 1931 he resigned from the party itself to found the New Party. Before the formal launch of this new force, Mosley sent Wells a proof copy of its *National Policy* which, developed from the 'Mosley Memorandum' which Labour had rejected, appeared under the name of Allan Young, John Strachey, W.J. Brown and Aneurin Bevan. Mosley referred to Wells's open conspiracy in his accompanying letter, explaining that the *National Policy* 'represents our conversion to a point of view which you reached a year or so ago; that is to say that the only chance of successful progress in this country is in the co-operation with the more intelligent, at any rate, of the big business people'. Mosley anticipated that Wells would not 'agree with al we say' but was 'tremendously interested to hear what you think of the thing as a whole'. Later that year, when the Propaganda Committee of the New Party discussed the coming campaign for the Ashton-under-Lyne by-election in April, Mosley suggested that 'he would personally seek out G.B. Shaw, H.G. Wells and other intellectuals to seek their support'. No such support seems to have been give before the New Party's unsuccessful intervention at Ashton-under-Lyne, but later that year, on the day Wells had agreed to write 'an article on class distinctions' for the New Party's weekly *Action*, Harold Nicolson, its editor, wrote to Mosley that Wells had expressed 'serious interest about the policy' of the party.[45]

No such article ever appeared. Nicolson recorded that Wells was 'a trifle tipsy' at the time of his request, so perhaps, when sober, he withdrew his offer, or it may simply have been that the short life of *Action* allowed insufficient time. Alternatively, the explanation my lie in Wells's disenchantment with Mosley after meeting him approximately ten days later at the time of the crisis which led to the creation of the National Government. Both men were holidaying in the south of France at the time and Wells drove over from his home in Grasse to visit the Mosleys in Antibes. Vera Brittain, who recorded Wells's account of the meeting, wrote that the Mosleys, when asked for their response to the crisis 'seemed unable to think of anything except whether Mosley ... ought to sit on the front Opposition Bench & what should be the colours of the Mosley party'. 'So Wells', Brittain wrote, 'taking their mentality at the level it appeared incapable of surpassing, solemnly discussed with them the importance of "making a corner" in flame-colour before some other party appropriated it.'[46] Whether it was Mosley's parliamentarianism *per se* or his apparent preoccupation with its superficial details which disgusted Wells is unclear.

However, this episode did not mark the final break between the two men. Mosley recorded meeting Wells once more when—probably around the time of the launch of the BUF—the former was 'listening to marching songs for the new movement' and in August 1932, a short time before the formal founding of the BUF at the beginning October, Mosley wrote to Wells enclosing a pre-publication copy of *The Greater Britain*. At the time, Dino Grandi, the Italian ambassador to London, who was then deeply involved with Mosley, reported to Mussolini that Wells, although previously an enemy of fascism, was proposing 'un nuovo "fascismo"' as a solution to Britain's national ills. Mosley wrote to Wells that he had 'read with great interest a speech by you asking for a "Liberal Fascism"' and went on to explain that while 'the word "Liberal" had not much relation to' *The Greater Britain*, Mosley's proposals did represent 'an attempt to create a scientific Fascism which is free from the excesses and repression of the Continent'. As in his letter the previous year, Mosley once again linked his project to Wells's thinking, commenting that 'like most prophets, you will probably have the unpleasant experience of recognising many of your own teachings of the past reproduced and reshaped by less capable hands.'[47]

Given that both men shared a fervent enthusiasm for science and impatience with, and rejection of, parliamentary democracy, it should not be a surprise that Mosley sought to interest Wells in the new movement he was founding. What Wells's response was to Mosley's letter is unknown, but his reaction to a major BUF rally held in the Albert Hall in spring 1934 signalled an unambiguous rejection. Mosley's rally, held where Wells, four years earlier, had imagined Mr Parham holding a similar event, made that fictional episode 'seem preposterously sane and sound' in comparison. Of the Blackshirt leader Wells pronounced: "I have met Mosley intermittently for years, as a promising young conservative, a promising new convert to the

Labour party, with communist leanings, and finally as the thing he is. He has always seemed to me dull and heavy, imitative in his politics.' Wells attacked 'our own little black head, Mosley', not only on account of his intellect, but also imputed doubt about the fascist leader's war record, criticized his oratory and mocked his appearance. When writing *The Holy Terror* four years later, Wells attacked Mosley—if anything, even more fiercely—in the form of 'Lord Horatio Bohun' and, significantly, a successful coup against Mosley/Bohun was the prerequisite for the transformation of the "Purple Shirts' into a Wellsian vanguard. The years did not diminish Wells's animus against Mosley and, in 1942, amongst the 'bag of problems' which would face the Wellsian revolutionary, was 'Sir Oswald Mosley'. When Mosley was released from wartime internment on health reasons, a particularly hysterical piece from Wells in *The Daily Worker* spoke of Mosley as having 'the characteristic sadistic streak' of fascism and stated that 'to condone him is to condone essential evil', and proposed that 'shooting or hanging of a few of the more flagrant fascists, not for their opinions but for their activities, would have had a very wholesome effect'.[48]

Wells's splenetic response to Mosley may have been fuelled in part by the envy on the part of the rotund, squeaky-voiced and ageing Wells of what even many of his opponents allowed was the tall, eloquent and handsome Mosley. However, any such personal antipathy aside, there were fundamental intellectual reasons for the incompatibility of the two men's approaches and goals. Kingsly Martin, reviewing *The Greater Britain* in tandem with Wells's *After Democracy* in 1932, found that:

> Superficially there is a certain resemblances between their doctrines. Both Mr Wells and Sir Oswald Mosley describe themselves as revolutionaries: both regard our present Parliamentary system as a ludicrous anachronism, both aim at the formation of a corps of young people pledged to the fulfillment of a single social ideal. Sir Oswald declares that it would be dishonest to describe his movement as anything but Fascist.... Mr Wells is willing to describe the members of his new society as Liberal Fascists or Communist Revisionists or enlightened Nazis. They are both 'planners', both contemptuous of the old party game and of *laisser faire*.[49]

'But there', the review continued 'the resemblance ends abruptly.' While 'Mr Wells's society may not acknowledge allegiance to any unit smaller than the world ... Sir Oswald's Fascists are to be concerned solely with cultivating nationalism.' This was sufficient reason for an irrevocable incompatibility between Wells and Fascism. Thus, in *The Holy Terror* the 'Purple Shirts' had to lose their nationalism to become an acceptable Wellsian force with—for followers of an ideology centred on nationalism—an unconvincting ease.

Quite possibly Wells's reaction to Mosley and the BUF also signalled a moment when he came face of face with the uncomfortable actuality of things which were more easily accepted in the abstracted space of the imagination. However, even on the page unresolved tensions between Wells the 'liberal' and Wells the 'fascist' were visible. Shifting from the voice of the 'future historian' narrating *The Shape of Things to Come*, Wells commented in his own voice of a 'distaste … as ineradicable as it is unreasonable' aroused by the actions of the Airmen, and continued that 'but for "the accidents of space and time"' he would have 'been one of the actively protesting spirits who squirmed in the pitilessly benevolent grip of the Air Dictatorship'.[50] The reality of an actual fascist movement could only have been more distasteful to the 'liberal' side of Wells's personality.

Every theory of praxis reflects what are understood as the most practical means to achieve a desired end. However, pragmatism in pursuit of a desired utopia can only go so far before contradicting a political ideology's core aims and values and becoming self-defeating. Perhaps, in facing the reality of fascism, Wells might also have received the unwelcome intimation that his whole idea of a 'liberal fascism' was an impossible synthesis, akin, as John Hargrave wrote, to 'an attempt for tepid boiling hot water' or 'harmless poison gas'. Mosley described his intention to Wells as being to create a 'Fascism which is free from the excesses and repression of the Continent' but achieved the bloody scenes of the fascist rally at Olympia and a mean and vicious antisemitism. In all probability, a 'liberal' Wellsian utopia could also only be achieved by 'fascist' means in the space of Well's imagination and in its projections onto paper and celluloid. As R.H. Tawney noted of the contemporary scene: 'Mr Wells's vision of a world controlled by Samurai and airmen is the only utopia which has approached realization. It is still uncertain whether mankind can survive it.'[51]

NOTES

I should like to thank James Hinton and Warren Wagar for kindly reading and commenting on earlier versions of this article. All conclusions and any errors or omissions are, of course, my own.

1. *Action*, 28 February 1936, 8.

2. J[ohn] A. M[acnab], 'Things to Come', *The Fascist Quarterly*, 2, 2 (1936), 328–9.

3. W. Warren Wagar, *H.G. Wells and the World State* (New Haven, CT 1961), 164–205.

4. Sydney Webb and Beatrice Webb, *Soviet communism: A New Civilisation?* (no place of publication 1935); Bernard Shaw, *The Intelligent Woman's Guide to Socialism, Capitalism, Sovietism and Fascism* (Harmondsworth 1937), vol. 2 chaps 71–85; Gareth Griffith, *Socialism and Superior Brains: The Political Thought of Bernard Shaw* (London 1995), chap. 6; Peter Beilharz, *Labour's Utopias: Bolshevism, Fabianism, Social Democracy* (London 1993), chap. 3; R. Bassett, *Essentials of Parliamentary Democracy* (London 1964; first published 1935), part two; G.E.G. Catlin, 'Expert State *verus* Free State', *The Political Quarterly*, 3 (1932), 539–51; Raymond Postgate, *How to Make a Revolution* (London 1934), 194.

5. Dmitri Mirsky, *The Intelligentsia of Great Britain* (London 1935), 74–7; J.D. Bernal, *The Social Function of Science* (London 1939), 398; 'Christopher Caudwell' [Christoper St John Sprigg], *Studies in a Dying Culture* (London 1938), 73–95.

6. Anthony West, *H.G. Wells. Aspects of a life* (London 1984); David C. Smith, *H.G. Wells. Desperately Mortal* (Yale 1986); Michael Foot, H.G.: *The History of Mr Wells* (London 1995); Peter Kemp, *H.G. Wells and the Culminating Ape* (New York 1982); Leon Stover, *The prophetic Soul: A Reading of H.G. Wells' Things to Come Together with His Film Treatment, Wither Mankind? and the postproduction Script (Both Never Before Published)* (Jefferson 1987); John Carey, *The Intellectuals and the Masses: Pride and Prejudice among the Literary Intelligentsia, 1880–1939* (London 1992); Michael Coren, *The Invisible Man: The Life and Liberties of H.G. Wells* (London 1994).

7. Krishan Kumar, *Utopia & Anti-utopia in Modern Times* (Oxford 1991), 178–219; Leon Stover, 'Spade House Dialectic: Theme and Theory in "Things to Come"', *The Wellsian*, 5 (1982), 23–32; Stover, *The Prophetic Soul*, op. cit.

8. H.G. Wells, 'Project of a World Society', *The New Statesman and Nation*, 20 August 1932; H.G. Wells, *After Democracy: Addresses and Papers on the Present World Situation* (London 1932), 2–3, 9–11.

9. Ibid., 11–12, 17–18, 23–5; emphasis in the original.

10. Ibid., 5; H.G. Wells, *Experiment in Autobiography: Discoveries and Conclusions of a Very Ordinary Brain (Since 1866)* (London 1934), 746; H.G. Wells, *What Are We To Do With Our Lives?* (London 1935; first published 1931), 127.

11. H.G. Wells, *The Way the World is Going* (London 1928), 28; H.G. Wells, *The Anatomy of Frustration: A Modern Synthesis* (London 1936), 187; H.G. Wells, 'Grown Men do not Need Leaders' in *The Common Sense of War and Peace: World Revolution or War Unending* (Harmondsworth 1940), 7–12.

12. Wells, *What Are We To Do With Out Lives?*, op. cit., 20, 113, 127; Wells, *Experiment in Autobiography*, op. cit., 746.

13. West, op. cit., 129; Wells, *After Democracy*, op. cit., 234–47.

14. Ibid., 27; H.M. Tomlinson, 'Mr Wells has his Joke', *The New Clarion*, 13 August 1932.

15. Wells, *After Democracy*, op.cit., 31; Wells, 'Project of a World Society', op. cit.; H.G. Wells, *The Work, Wealth and Happiness of Mankind* (London 1934; revised edn, first published 1932), 809; Wagar, op.cit.

16. Wells to [Clifford] Allen, 17 December 1932, in David C.Smith (ed.), *The Correspondence of H.G. Wells: Volume 3 1919–1934* (London 1998), 456; H.G. Wells, 'Introduction: There should be a Common Creed for all Left Parties throughout the

World', 12–20 in C.E.M Joad (ed.), *Manifesto: Being the Book of The Federation of Progressive Societies and Individuals* (London 1934), 17–18.

17. Wells dismissed the readership of the *Daily Herald* as 'stupid'. See Wells to Joad, 14 December 1932 (Smith, op. cit., 455). In another letter he described what correspondence he had aroused by his article as 'idiotic' and commented that 'nobody else has taken notice of what I have said' (Wells to Allen, 17 December 1932, Ibid., 456). On Clifford Allen's unsuccessful attempts to interest Wells in participating in a public meeting to bring together 'progressive' opinion see Arthur Marwick, *Clifford Allen: The Open Conspirator* (Edinburgh 1964), 125–6; Martin Gilbert, *Plough My Own Furrow: The Story of Lord Allen of Hurtwood as Told through his Writings and Correspondence* (London 1965), 291–3; 307–9. Wells's involvement in the Next Five Years Group which emerged from Allen's efforts in 1935 was limited to allowing his name to be included in the list of the signatories to its programme (*The Next Five Years: An Essay in Political Agreement* [London1935], ix).

18. Wells, *Experiment in Autobiography*, op. cit., 748.

19. Kingsley Martin, 'Mr Wells and Sir Oswald Mosley', *The New Statesman and Nation*, 29 October 1932.

20. Jack Coates, 'Is the Progressive League Redundant?', *Plan*, 12, 5 (May 1945), 2–4; *Plan*, 11, 3 (March 1944); Wagar, op. cit., 198; H.G. Wells, *The Holy Terror* (London 1939), 73, 82.

21. Wells, *Experiment in Autobiography*, op. cit., 748; H.G. Wells, *The Shape of Things to Come: The Ultimate Revolution* (London 1936; first published 1933), 270, 312.

22. Wells, *The Anatomy of Frustration*, op.cit., 275, my emphasis; Wells, *Experiment in Autobiography*, op. cit., 749.

23. Michael Foot, 'In Defence of H.G. Wells', *The Times Literary Supplement*, 23 October 1995; H.G. Wells, *The Autocracy of Mr.Parham* (London 1930), 153.

24. Wells, *The Shape of Things to Come*, op. cit., 106.

25. Ibid.

26. Kemp, op. cit., 178–80; J.B. Priestley, *Margin Released: A Writer's Reminiscences and Reflections* (London 1936), 164; H.G. Wells *The outlook for Homo Sapiens* (London 1942), 111; Wells, *The Shape of Things to Come*, op. cit., 283.

27. Ibid., 321, 106–7; Wells, 'Project of World Society', op. cit., my emphasis; Wells, *After Democracy*, op. cit., 24–5; Wells, 'Introduction', op. cit., 18.

28. Wells, *The Shape of Things to Come*, op. cit., 107–8, my emphasis.

29. Wells, *The Work, Wealth and Happiness of Mankind*, op, cit., 315–326; Wells, *The Shape of Things to Come*, op. cit., 108; *The Stalin-Wells Talk. The Verbatim Record and a Discussion by G. Bernard Shaw, H.G. Wells, J.M. Keynes, Ernst Toller and Others* (London 1934), 8.

30. Wells, *The Work, Wealth and Happiness of Mankind*, op. cit., 184–5, 538.

31. Wells, *AfterDemocracy*, op. cit., 26. On Wells's antisemitism see: Bryan Cheyette, 'Beyond Rationality: H.G. Wells and the Jewish Question', *The Wellsian*, 14 (Summer 1991), 41–64; Kemp, op. cit., 181–3; Coren, op. cit., 211–19; Stover, *The Prophetic Soul*, op. cit., 50.

32. Wells, *The Work, Wealth and Happiness of Mankind*, op. cit., 540.

33 Wells, *The Way the World is Going*, op. cit., 28, my emphasis; Wells, *The Work, Wealth and Happiness of Mankind*, op. cit., 312, 540, 584, 614.

34. Wells, *The Shape of Things to Come*, op. Cit. 108–9; H.G. Wells, '42 to '44: *A Contemporary Memoir upon Human Behaviour during the Crisis of the World Revolution* (London 1944), 68.

35. Wells, *The Anatomy of Frustration*, op. cit., 275; Wells, *The Shape of Things to come*, op. cit., 109, 163.

36. Ibid., 333; Geoffrey Gorer, *Nobody Talks Politics: A Satire with an Appendix on Our Political Intelligentsia* (London 1935), 199.

37. Wells, *The Anatomy of Frustration*, op. cit., 89–90, 189–90; Wells, *The Shape of Things to Come*, op. cit., 122. Wells apparently preferred the fascist to the nazi regime. Writing of the 'very full and well-illustrated Italian (Fascist) Encyclopaedia', Wells described it as 'one of the many evidences of the higher mental level of the Fascist as compared with the Nazi regime'. Wells also noted the 'highly disciplined Fascist Legislature, in which Fascists only may be elected'. (Wells, *The Outlook for Homo Sapiens*, op. cit., 276; Wells, *The Work, Wealth and Happiness of Mankind*, op. cit., 613.)

38. H.G. Wells, *The Brothers: A Story* (London 1938), 44–7; emphases in original.

39. H.G. Wells, 'Wither Mankind? A Film of the Future' in Stover, *The Prophetic Soul*, op. cit., 137.

40. Elizabeth Coxhead, 'Things to Avoid', *The Left Review*, 2, 6 (March 1936), 275; F. McConnell, *The Science Fiction of H.G. Wells* (Oxford 1981), 213; David Mellor, 'British Art in the 1930's', 185–207 in Frank Gloversmith (ed.), *Class Culture and Social Change: A New View of the 1930s* (Sussex 1980), 189, 204; Christopher Frayling, *Things to Come* (London 1995), 17–18, 45–6; Stover, *The Prophetic Soul*, op. cit., 51–5, 77, 84, 90; Stover, 'Spade House Dialectic', op. cit., 28, 23; H.G. Wells, 'Wither Mankind?', op. cit., 157.

41. Brian Ash, *Who's Who in H.G. Wells* (London 1979), 265–7; see also Norman Nicholson, *H.G. Wells* (London 1950), 87; J.R. Hammond, *An H.G. Wells Companion: A Guide to the Novels, Romances and Short Stories* (London 1979), 217–19; Kemp, op. cit., 193–4; Smith, op. cit., 352. See also: Wagar, op. cit., 199; John Batchelor, *H.G. Wells* (Cambridge 1985), 142–3; Norman and Jeanne MacKenzie, *The Life of H.G. Wells: The Time Traveller* (London, revised edn 1987; first published 1973), 416–19; Coren, op. cit., 202. *The Holy Terror* is the one text which Michael Foot completely ignores in his otherwise comprehensive coverage of Wells's novels of the 1930s.

42. Wells, *The Holy Terror*, op. cit., 268–70, 437–41.

43. Oswald Mosley, *The Greater Britain* (London 1932), 125; Oswald Mosley, *Fascism: 100 Questions Asked and Answered* (London Undated; ca. 1936), preface; Myles Eckersley, *Prospero's Wireless: A Biography of Peter Pendleton Eckersley Pioneer of Radio and the Art of Broadcasting* (Romsey 1998); David Edgerton, *England and the Aeroplane: An Essay on a Militant and Technological Nation* (Basingstoke 1991); Colin Cook, 'A Fascist Memory: Oswald Mosley and the Myth of the Airman', *European Review of History*, 4,2 (1997), 147–62; Kemp, op. cit., 170–3. Fascist discussion of the aircraft in *Things of come* evoked a response from Nigel Tangye, 'aeronautical adviser to Mr Alexander Korda and Mr H.G. Wells' (*Action*, 24 October 1936).

44. Oswald Mosely, *My Life* (London 1968), 226; Harold Nicolson, *Diaries & Letters 1930–39* (no place of publication 1969), 70,91.

45. Wells, *The Autocracy of Mr Parham*, op. cit., 164; Robert Skidelsky, *Oswald Mosley* (London 1990; first published 1975), 199–282; Wells Archive, Mosley to Wells, 14 February 1931, I am grateful to the University of Illinois Library at Urbana-Champaign for copies of this and the letter cited below (note 47); Eckersley, op. cit., 335; Nicloson, op. cit., 85; Nicolson to Mosley, 14 August 1931 quoted in Nicholas Mosley, *The Rules of the Game* (London 1982), 195–6.

46. Vera Brittain, *Diary of the Thirties* 1932–1939: *Chronicle of Friendship* (London 1986), 92–3, entry for 5 October 1932.

47. Mosley, *My Life*, op. cit., 226; Public Record Office, GFM 36/141, Grandi to Mussolini, 13 August 1932 (I am grateful to Stephen Dorril for this reference); Wells Archive, Mosley to Wells, 31 August 1932.

48. Wells, *Experiment in Autobiography*, op. cit., 501, 782–3; H.G. Wells, *Phoenix: A Summary of the Inescapable Conditions of World Reorganisation* (London 1942), 56; *Daily Worker*, 7 December 1943; later published as a *Daily Worker* pamphlet: *The Mosley Outrage* (London 1943).

49. Martin, 'Mr Wells and Sir Oswald Mosley', op. cit., 517–18.

50. Wells, *The Shape of Things to Come*, op. cit.

51. John Hargrave, '"A Liberal Fascisti"', *The New Age*, 25 August 1932; Wells Archive, Mosley to Wells, 31 August 1932; R.H. Tawney, *Equality* (London 1964; first published 1931), 189.

PATRICK A. McCARTHY

Heart of Darkness *and the* Early Novels of H.G. Wells: *Evolution, Anarchy, Entropy*

I

Sitting on a boat in the Thames, his face almost invisible as darkness descends over England, Marlow tells his listeners of his trip into the alien and primitive African jungle. That land was, for Marlow, an impenetrable mystery:

> "... What was in there? I could see a little ivory coming out from there, and I had heard Mr. Kurtz was in there. I had heard enough about it too—God knows! Yet somehow it didn't bring any image with it—not more than if I had been told an angel or a fiend was in there. I believed it in the same way one of you might believe there are inhabitants on the planet Mars...." (27)[1]

We are not told exactly when Marlow speaks these words, but if he is speaking in the "present," that is, about 1898 or 1899, his audience might well hear in this remark an allusion to a book that appeared early in 1898, H.G. Wells's *The War of the Worlds*. Certainly many readers who first encountered *Heart of Darkness* in *Blackwood's Magazine*, beginning in February 1899, would have thought of Well's tale of a Martian invasion when they found a reference to "inhabitants on the planet Mars" in another story

From *Journal of Modern Literature*, vol. 13, no. 1. © 1986 Temple University, reprinted with permission of Indiana University Press.

of colonialism and exploitation. The reference would have been even stronger for having been phrased in terms of what one "might believe," for Wells had begun his novel with a similar question of belief: "No one would have believed in the last years of the nineteenth century that this world was being watched keenly and closely by intelligences greater than man's and yet as mortal as his own" (265). That contrast between great intelligence and mortality forecasts the deaths not only of Wells's colonists—the Martians— but of Conrad's Kurtz as well.

A single possible reference to *The War of the Worlds* might seem insignificant, but it gains in importance once we realize, first, that Joseph Conrad's high regard for H.G. Wells and his books might easily have led him to work along lines already developed by Wells, and second, that *Heart of Darkness* parallels Wells's fiction in several other specific ways. Conrad's acquaintance with Wells dated from 1896, when he learned that Wells was the anonymous reviewer of *An Outcast of the Islands*; writing to Wells in May 1896, Conrad noted that he had read *The Time Machine*, *The Wonderful Visit*, and *The Stolen Bacillus* (all first published in book form in 1895) and had ordered *The Island of Dr. Moreau* (1896).[2] Over the next two years the friendship grew, as Conrad indicated in a letter to Wells (September 1898): "I have lived on terms of close intimacy with you, referring to you many a page of my work, scrutinizing many sentences by the light of your criticism."[3] Conrad moved near Wells in October 1898 and the following month was writing to ask if he could borrow a copy of *The Invisible Man* (1897), his own copy having been stolen by "a god-fearing person" to whom he had lent it. The same letter contains a reference to the conclusion of *The War of the Worlds*.[4] In his letter of 4 December 1898, Conrad thanked Wells for the loan of *The Invisible Man* and called the novel "uncommonly fine." He extended his praise to include Wells's work in general: "I am always powerfully impressed by your work. Impressed is the word, O Realist of the Fantastic! whether you like it or not."[5] Later the same month, Conrad referred to *War of the Worlds* and *The Invisible Man* in a letter to Wells and praised Wells in a letter to Angèle Zagórska.[6]

It is not surprising, then, that when he began writing *Heart of Darkness* "sometime around 15 December"[7] Conrad would have felt the pull of Wells's imagination on his work. Indeed, several aspects of Conrad's story are reminiscent of Wells's scientific fantasies. The narrative situation, with a primary narrator whose story frames another character's description of a journey, had been used in *The Time Machine*; in addition, the reference to the core narrator (the Time Traveller, Marlow) as a man somehow apart from his auditors, the use of occupations as names for the auditors, and the break in the narration that reminds us of the basic narrative situation are all elements that link Conrad's story to that of Wells. More importantly, several of Conrad's themes—the moral ambivalence and degeneration of the self-appointed superman, the disastrous effects of a colonial policy based on the assumption of evolutionary superiority, and the relevance of the processes of entropy and atavistic regression to human affairs—are clearly set forth in Wells's novels of the time.

Several critics have noted parallels between the works of Conrad and Wells. Frank McConnell suggests that the anarchic "Professor" of *The Secret Agent*—a book dedicated to Wells—might be modeled after Griffin, the Invisible Man.[8] Frederick R. Karl describes *The Inheritors* as "an attempt ... to work along the line of Wells's new genre of science fiction and political fantasy," while Leo J. Henkin believes that the Dimensionists of *The Inheritors* are modeled after Wells's Martians.[9] Robert G. Jacobs finds reflections of Wells's treatment of time and invisibility in *The Inheritors* and, more strikingly, in *Lord Jim*.[10] Two other critics have called attention to connections between *Heart of Darkness* and Wells's short stories: Bernard Bergonzi says that "The Lord of the Dynamos" anticipates Conrad's African tale, and Robert M. Philmus, writing about "The Empire of the Ants," hints at possible points of contact with *Heart of Darkness*.[11]

Only two critics, however, have noted significant parallels between *Heart of Darkness* and Wells's science fiction novels. The first is Paul Kirschner, who suggests that the portrayal of Kurtz owes "a debt of imagination" to Wells's Invisible Man: like Griffin, Kurtz has "a dream of boundless power ... which becomes a nightmare." Both men are first apprehended as voices, and the image of Kurtz as a "gaping, voracious mouth" recalls the landlady's impression of Griffin when his muffler is removed: "it seemed to her that the man she looked at had an enormous mouth wide open,—a vast and incredible mouth that swallowed the whole of the lower portion of his face" (165).[12] The second critic, Cedric Watts, observes that Conrad "read, admired, and remembered" *The Time Machine*, whose image of the dying sun reappears in *Heart of Darkness*. He also relates Wells and Conrad through their treatment of atavistic regression, particularly in *The Island of Dr. Moreau*, whose protagonist, Prendick, sets the pattern for Marlow when he returns to Europe obsessed with the idea that man is essentially bestial and corruptible. Watts adds that "*The Time Machine* and *The War of the Worlds* may have had some slight influence on *Heart of Darkness* and *The Inheritors*."[13]

Although I believe that Watts understates his case, the question of "influence" seems to me less interesting that the extent to which parallels between the works reveal a shared vision, one at odds with the generally accepted idea that Wells and Conrad had little in common aside from an admiration for inventive and imaginative fiction. It is true, as Nicholas Delbanco observes, that the cluster of writers living in Kent and East Sussex at the turn of the century—Stephen Crane, Ford Madox Hueffer, and Henry James, along with Conrad and Wells—"staked no shared claim" and "denied rather than affirmed the rumor of cohesiveness."[14] It is also true, as Karl demonstrates, that between Wells and Conrad there were fundamental differences of opinion about the role of the writer and the nature and function of literary art.[15] Yet the differences between the two men came to dominate their relationship only in the years just before World War I: Wells's 1912 refusal to join the Reform Club, the attack on Henry James in *Boon* (1914), and Wells's defiant declaration to James that he "had rather be called a journalist than an artist"[16] are signs of the hardening in Wells's attitudes that also affected his relations with Conrad. In the 1890s, however, there was an affinity between Wells and Conrad that led to striking similarities in the ways they handled some of their most important social, psychological, and scientific themes, particularly the evolutionary theme, with its economic and political corollaries of laissez-faire capitalism and colonial expansion; the portrayal of a megalomaniacal mind, a mind that imagines that it is a law unto itself; and the pessimistic implications of the Second Law of Thermodynamics, which postulated a continual running down of the universe as a physical system. In the ways in which they responded to these characteristic late Victorian preoccupations, Wells and Conrad reveal a fundamental kinship with implications in the moral and aesthetic dimensions of their art.

II

Darwinian ideas and their relationship to human life and conduct were major elements in the intellectual climate of the Victorian age. Nor has the impact of evolutionary theory on Conrad and Wells been overlooked. Stanley Renner, who traces Darwinian themes in several of Conrad's works, finds in *Heart of Darkness* a particularly concentrated cluster of Darwinian motifs; Cedric Watts says that "*Heart of Darkness* has a more richly Darwinian atmosphere than any other major work of fiction"; and Ian Watt notes that "several aspects of evolutionary thought are present in *Heart of Darkness*."[17] Both Renner and Watt call attention to T.H. Huxley's 1893 Romanes Lecture, "Evolution and Ethics" (published 1894), as a likely source for Conrad's treatment of the ethical implications of Darwinism, but neither notes that Huxley's ideas might easily have reached Conrad through Wells. A former student of Huxley's at the Normal School of Science in South Kensington, Wells adapted Huxley's ideas to his own purposes in such essays as "Human Evolution, an Artificial Process" (1896) and "Morals and Civilisation" (1897), as well as in *The Time Machine, The Island of Dr. Moreau,* and *The War of the Worlds*.[18] In any event, the concerns and assumptions of Huxley's influential essay are essentially those of Wells and Conrad, and the way in which they adopt Huxley's view of evolution reveals one aspect of an underlying kinship between the two writers.

Huxley's lecture was in effect an answer to the appropriation of Darwinism as a defense for ruthless and exploitive behavior in human society. To some extent the position against which Huxley argued was a logical development of Darwin's own ideas: after all, Darwin derived the phrase "struggle for existence" from Thomas Malthus and "survival of the fittest" from Herbert Spencer.[19] In the fifth chapter of *The Descent of Man*, Darwin referred with apparent approval to the process of "natural selection" through which "civilized nations are everywhere supplanting barbarous nations, excepting where the climate opposes a deadly barrier"; he also deplored the way asylums, poor laws, and improved medical care interfered with "the process of elimination" and thereby allowed "the weaker members of civilized societies [to] propagate their kind," although he admitted that withholding assistance from the weak and needy would lead to "deterioration in the noblest part of our nature."[20] At the conclusion of *The Descent of Man* Darwin attempted, briefly, to separate moral development from physical evolution, noting that "the moral qualities are advanced, either directly or indirectly, much more through the effects of habit, the reasoning powers, instructions, religion, &c., than through natural selection"; but even then he traced "the social instincts, which afforded the basis for the development of the moral sense," to the operation of natural selection.[21]

In contrast, Huxley distinguished clearly between the physical laws underlying evolution and the moral laws that should guide human conduct. In "The Struggle for Existence in Human Society" (1888), Huxley noted that although society is "a part of nature," it nonetheless "differs from nature in having a definite moral object." The difference between the civilized man and the savage is that "The later fights out the struggle for existence to the bitter end, like any other animal; the former devotes his best energies to the object of setting limits to the struggle."[22] In "Evolution and Ethics" and in the Preface and prolegomena to the published lecture, Huxley enlarged upon this distinction. The evolutionary process leads to a species capable of maintaining its existence, and is therefore an important part of our heritage, but the moral development of mankind is, at this stage in history, at least as important as the struggle for existence. Hence:

> We cannot do without our inheritance from the forefathers who were the puppets of the cosmic process; the society which renounces it must be destroyed from without. Still less can we do with too much of it; the society in which it dominates must be destroyed from within. (viii)

And:

> Men in society are undoubtedly subject to the cosmic process ... But the influence of the cosmic process on the evolution of society is the greater the more rudimentary its civilization. Social progress means a checking of the cosmic process at every step and the substitution for it of another, which may be called the ethical process; the end of which is not the survival of those who may happen to be the fittest, in respect of the whole of the conditions which obtain, but of those who are ethically the best. (81)

Thus morality or human decency requires that we substitute other values for those demanded by natural law: "In Place of ruthless self-assertion it demands self-restraint; in place of thrusting aside, or treading down, all competitors, it requires that the individual shall not merely respect, but shall help his fellows" (82). Huxley condemns "the fanatical individualism of our time" as "a misapplication of the stoical injunction to follow nature," arguing that instead of submitting to the demands of our lower natures we should use our "intelligence and will" to "modify the conditions of existence," thereby "curbing the instincts of savagery in civilized men" (82,85).

Huxley's essay provided a much-needed corrective for an age when, as Avrom Fleishman says, "attempts to prevent the degeneration of Darwinist theory into an apology for economic amorality and nationalist aggressiveness proved ineffectual."[23] The debate was carried out again in Wells's and Conrad's fiction. In *The Time Machine*, for example, we see the possible results of capitalism when we travel eight hundred millenia into the future to the world of the Eloi and Morlocks, degenerate descendants of the moneyed class and the proletariat. "Individualism" in the form of unrestrained capitalism has resulted not in the "survival of the fittest" and the progressive evolution of the species, but in the splitting of the race into two species, one childlike and the other menacing, and neither one as morally, intellectually, or physically advanced as nineteenth-century man. Moreover, while the entire action of *The Time Machine* takes place within a small area near where London is now located, the descent of the Time Traveller upon the world of the Eloi is treated as comparable, in some respects, to a European exploration (or even invasion) of a land inhabited by a technologically backward people: hence the Eloi seem to believe that the Time Traveller is a kind of god who comes from the sun (18), much as the African natives of *Heart of Darkness* regard Fresleven and Kurtz as possessing divine power.

That uncontrolled social Darwinism may contribute to the atavistic regression of a people is one point Conrad makes in much the same way as Wells. Ultimately, exploitive competition *within* a species—as distinguished from interspecific competition—is self-destructive and cannibalistic. Indeed, cannibalism is a major theme in these works. In *Heart of Darkness*, for example, the cannibals on Marlow's boat represent a sort of innocent cannibalism, the result of a natural shortage of food; Marlow's comment that the cannibals "still belonged to the beginnings of time—had no inherited experience to teach them" (41) indicates that they have not evolved a moral sense to counter the aggressive instincts of primitive man. Nonetheless, Marlow praises the "inborn strength" that prevents the cannibals from giving in to hunger and eating the other passengers (42). Kurtz, on the other hand, is morally degenerate: his "cannibalism" represents an abandonment of all the ties that link human beings and a reversion to a completely egoistic self-assertion.[24] To the brickmaker, Kurtz is "an emissary of pity, and science, and progress" (25), and to himself it is obvious that "we whites ... 'must necessarily appear to them [savages] in the nature of supernatural beings"' (51), but Marlow sees him more accurately as a gigantic mouth attempting to swallow the earth and its inhabitants (60-61, 74). In his devouring and cannibalistic aspect Kurtz is superficially like the "brutes" whom he would "exterminate" (51), but his real affinity is with the other Europeans whose colonial policies bring chaos and destruction to the heart of Africa.

Conrad includes several specific indications of his Darwinian theme. A brief reference to the icthyosaurus (30) reminds us that in the struggle for existence some species become extinct; the vision of the jungle as being like "the earliest beginnings of the world, when vegetation rioted on the earth and the big trees were kings" (34) owes more to Darwin than to Genesis; and Marlow specifically describes his party as "wanderers on a prehistoric earth" (36). References to colonialism place it squarely in this Darwinian context:

"...They were conquerors, and for that you want only brute
force—nothing to boast of, when you have it, since your strength
is just an accident arising from the weakness of others.... The
conquest of the earth, which mostly means the taking it away
from those who have a different complexion or slightly flatter
noses than ourselves, is not a pretty thing when you look into it
too much...." (6–7)

This passage ironically turns the tables on the conquerors: conquest is a
matter of "brute force," yet it is often defended on the grounds that it is
necessary to suppress the brutish instincts in man and the "savage customs"
that those instincts lead to. In this sense, Kurtz's scrawled note, "Exterminate
all the brutes!" (51), might be seen as an expression of self-loathing: the
"brutes" are not merely the African natives but also Kurtz and the other
European colonists. Thus, as Conrad shows time and time again, the line
between Europe and Africa—between the Thames and the Congo—is
blurred. In the passage cited above, for example, the conquest specifically
referred to is the Roman invasion of England, another outcome of the
"natural" law of conquest. (Just after this passage Conrad indicates that
Marlow tells his story while waiting for the tide to turn, a fact that places the
narration squarely within the rhythm of natural cycles.) This inversion of the
colonial situation recurs later, when Marlow speculates on what would
happen "if a lot of mysterious niggers armed with all kinds of fearful weapons
suddenly took to travelling on the road between Deal and Gravesend,
catching the yokels right and left to carry heavy loads for them" (20).
Something far worse than this happens in *The War of the Worlds*, a book
whose action lends an ironic note to Marlow's ambiguous phrase, "the
conquest of the earth."

    Heart of Darkness tends to show that such apparently opposed entities
as London (civilization) and the Congo (nature) are in fact intricately
related.[25] The same structural pattern is central to Wells's early work, as
John Huntington has demonstrated in his study of the "two world" theme
and other examples of "opposition" in Wells.[26] *Heart of Darkness* seems to
displace the reader both geographically (moving from England to Africa) and
temporally (moving literally into Marlow's past and figuratively into man's
evolutionary past), yet the effect of these displacements is to return us to
contemporary England, a land that "has been one of the dark places of the
earth" (5) and that demonstrates its savage heritage through its political and
economic systems. Likewise, in *The Time Machine* we move literally into our
future and figuratively into our past, discovering the cause of our downward

evolution in the same ruthless and aggressive behavior—the same pattern of dominance and exploitation—that led to man's survival and progress in earlier ages. In fact, the Eloi and Morlocks present us with debased versions of two Victorian responses to evolution: the Eloi, like the Aesthetes of the 1890s, have retreated from the struggle for existence into what the Time Traveller calls "art and ... eroticism," which lead to "languor and decay" (25), while the Morlocks—descendants of the victims of capitalistic exploitation— have become like the Darwinian apologists for capitalism and imperialism and have reverted to cannibalism, using the weaker Eloi as cattle. The split here also echoes Huxley's warning about the twin dangers of weakness and ruthlessness—the dangers that lie in renouncing our evolutionary heritage, like the Eloi, and being dominated by it, like the Morlocks.

Although Marlow despises what Kurtz has done, he is in fact closely related to Kurtz, as we might suspect when Marlow becomes "no more to [his listeners] than a voice" (28)—anticipating Marlow's frequent description of Kurtz as a "voice"—or when Kurtz's illness and burial are followed immediately by Marlow's sickness and near-death. Likewise, the Time Traveller prefers to avoid facing his kinship with the "bleached, obscene, nocturnal" Morlocks (34), yet he is in some ways closer to these aggressive carnivores than to the passive, simple-minded, frugivorous Eloi: virtually his first words to his dinner guests, upon his return from the future, are "Save me some of that mutton. I'm starving for a bit of meat" (11). The superiority to the Eloi, in strength and intelligence, allows the Morlocks to live; his superiority to the Morlocks in precisely the same areas allows the Time Traveller to survive.

One of the impulses behind Huxley's Romanes Lecture was the attempt to demonstrate that while man was biologically related to the other animals, human society required an ethical sense that has no counterpart in animal society. Thus it was possible to be "on the side of the angels," in Disraeli's facile phrase, without rejecting evolution. Wells seems more pessimistic than Huxley, who concludes "Evolution and Ethics" with quotations from Tennyson's "Ulysses," but he implies the need for precisely the same distinction between biological and moral law. This issue of how human conduct ought to differ from that of other animals calls into question another of Wells's recurrent themes, the meaning of the term "human" in a Darwinian world. In *The War of the Worlds* a soldier says of the Martians, "It ain't no murder killing beasts like that" (288), implying that the Martians are like lower animals; yet at the outset of the novel the narrator says that the minds of the Martians "are to our minds as ours are to those of the beasts that perish, intellects vast and cool and unsympathetic" (265),[27] a statement that reverses the terms of the soldier's hierarchy. The "Beast People" of *The Island of Dr. Moreau*, animals artificially elevated to "human" status, present us with another, more complex, case, one that almost completely blurs the line between man and beast. In *The Time Machine*, the question is symbolized by the statue of a winged sphinx that the Time Traveller discovers when he arrives in the future. Since the statue calls to mind the story of Oedipus and the riddle of the sphinx, Huntington rightly notes that the sphinx's "literal combination of human and animal: woman and lion" raises a crucial issue;[28] he might well have added that the changes in human form described in the sphinx's riddle (four legs, two legs, three legs) parallel Wells's theme of evolutionary development and decline.

III

The evolutionary theme in Wells and Conrad carries a warning against the simple transfer of evolutionary principles into the realm of politics and economics. This warning is implicit in *The War of the Worlds*, a novel that David Hughes accurately describes as "an allegory of the conquest of a primitive society by technologically sophisticated colonists with no respect for native values or culture."[29] Wells depicts Mars as an older world with dwindling natural resources and compares the Martian conquest of earth to the "war of extermination waged by European immigrants" against Tasmania (266). The only justification for such action must be expressed in terms of the "struggle for existence" (266); yet when it is England rather than Africa or India that is invaded, the moral bankruptcy of such an argument becomes evident. The extraterrestrial invasion seems to bring into play the "natural" law of survival of the fittest, for at the end the Martians are defeated by their vulnerability to the microbes to which we are immune. The competition here, however, exists *between* species; that is, it is the kind of competition with which Darwin is concerned in *The Origin of Species*. Ruthless competition *within* a species, on the other hand, is often morally questionable, as when a newspaper vendor runs away while selling papers at a greatly inflated price, a scene that the narrator calls "a grotesque mingling of profit and panic" (318).

Ironically, the novel's most explicit spokesman for the ascendancy of evolution over morality is the artilleryman, a character whose ideas are often extreme or distorted reflections of Well's own positions. The choice for mankind, he says, lies between being oxen and returning to a wild state. Because the Martians are vampires (they drink blood because they have no digestive systems), they will raise tame humans, some of whom will adjust to their situation through religion or "eroticism" (371). The artilleryman here reflects Wells's contempt for religion and for late nineteenth-century decadence, and his vision of two types of future human beings—"big, beautiful, rich-blooded, stupid" tame beasts and "wild" and "savage" ones who live underground—obviously reflects the dichotomy of the Eloi and the Morlocks. One can even see a forecast of Wells's later contempt for "literature" in the artilleryman's statement that the kind of books that we need to survive are "not novels and poetry swipes, but ideas, science books" (372).

Despite his ruthlessness, the artilleryman is a dreamer who will never put his plans into action, for he is too lazy and too concerned with his own comfort to focus on the larger problem; hence McConnell calls him "a clownish version of the Nietzschean superman."[30] More sinister versions of the superman, Nietzschean or otherwise, appear in the title characters of *The Island of Dr. Moreau* and *The Invisible Man*, both of whom appear to have contributed to Conrad's portrayal of the egoistic and self-assertive Kurtz. In all three books, the problem is that the unrestrained individual will, despite its claim to a "natural" right to dominate and manipulate others, poses a challenge not only to conventional morality, but to the natural order on which it bases its assumption of moral right. In the end, the balance of the natural order is restored, bringing to a conclusion the anarchic rule of the self-styled superman.

Moreau, Griffin, and Kurtz are all "hollow men" with great intelligence but an underdeveloped or degraded moral center. There is in all three men a gap between power and moral authority, a gap which in Kurtz and Griffin is related to their "invisibility." Marc Shell has demonstrated that in Greek myth the man who sees others while remaining invisible to them is a powerful figure and a potential tyrant.[31] Invisibility is in fact a divine attribute, so that for a mortal to become invisible is to challenge the hierarchy of being. Conversely, the "invisible" figure who is discovered— Peeping Tom, the Wizard of Oz—loses his power. This happens in *The Invisible Man*, where Griffin's body becomes visible only after his death, and in *Heart of Darkness*, where our first view of Kurtz presents us with a dying man.[32] The connection between power and invisibility is made explicit in *The Invisible Man*, where Griffin describes the root of his desire to become invisible: "To do such a thing would be to transcend magic. And I beheld, unclouded by doubt, a magnificent vision of all that invisibility might mean to a man—the mystery, the power, the freedom" (221). As Roslynn Haynes has noted, this passage suggests Marlowe's Dr. Faustus, a character similar to Griffin in his "megalomaniac desire for power and profit," in his mistaken belief that he enjoys a sort of superhuman status, and in his contempt for others.[33] Griffin is perhaps even closer to Kurtz, who impresses himself on Marlow's imagination as an invisible and hollow man claiming possession over everything, claiming even the godlike right to decree whether others will live or die.

Because Griffin and Kurtz (and Dr. Moreau as well) deny the existence of any moral restraints on their power, they call into question the very source of moral authority. Invisibility is thus a function of anarchy (in this case, the substitution of private desire for public codes of conduct): it not only violates the natural order (invisibility being an aspect of the supernatural realm), but erases the line between ourselves and our surroundings, leaving the body without form or limitation. Indeed, chaos follows these invisible men: Griffin constantly violates doors and windows—boundaries set up for the protection of people against trespassers—and engages in arson and other acts of gratuitous destruction. Thus, while he sees himself as a superior man, distinct from the crowd, Griffin actually imitates some aspects of crowd behavior, as described by Elias Canetti;[34] in this way he becomes the emblem of anarchic man, the type of the crowd that he thought to distinguish himself from. This is hardly surprising, for while Griffin despises the common people, he adopts a device that we associate with the "unknown" or "invisible" people who get "lost in the crowd." To be invisible is to be powerful, but it is also to lose oneself, to be swallowed by the environment.

This happens again in *Heart of Darkness*, where those who are unseen are often of great concern: the possibly nonexistent natives in the bush are worrisome for the men on the French ship who shell the bush and call the invisible men "enemies" (14); the brickmaker is concerned with the unseen forces in Europe who direct the operations of the company; and Kurtz forces himself into Marlow's mind long before he is seen and long after he is dead. Here, too, the invisibility of the powerful man is also a sign of his surrender to the environment, in this case to the forest, which Conrad explicitly describes as a crowd: "Trees, trees, millions of trees, massive, immense, running up high" (35).[35] The wilderness, Marlow says, "had patted [Kurtz] on the head ... it had caressed him, and—lo!—he had withered; it had taken him, loved him, embraced him, got into his veins, consumed his flesh, and sealed his soul to its own by the inconceivable ceremonies of some devilish initiation. He was its spoiled and pampered favourite" (49). Setting out to conquer the wilderness—to suppress savage customs and bring order out of chaos—he regresses to a savage state, one made more horrible by the contrast with his former ideals. Kurtz's very lack of restraint, the hollowness and anarchy of his heart, leads to this capitulation to a primeval state (58–59,

67). Thus, when Marlow tells the manager that Kurtz had "No method at all" (63), Conrad does not need to remind his reader that the alternative to method is madness, a form of anarchy.

Kurtz is an extreme case, but the potential for this kind of regression seems to lie within everyone, at least in Marlow's view. What is needed are "external checks" on conduct (22) like those provided for Marlow's auditors:

> "... You can't understand. How could you?—With solid pavement under your feet, surrounded by kind neighbours ready to cheer you or to fall on you, stepping delicately between the butcher and the policeman, in the holy terror of scandal and gallows and lunatic asylums—how can you imagine what particular region of the first ages a man's untrammelled feet may take him into by the way of solitude—utter solitude without a policeman—by the way of silence—utter silence, where no warning voice of a kind neighbour can be heard whispering of public opinion? These little things make all the great difference. When they are gone you must fall back upon your own innate strength, upon your own capacity for faithfulness.... " (50)

The ethical impulse of which Huxley speaks is therefore a function of social engagement; it emerges from our relation to others, which require understood codes of conduct. When the normal restraints on conduct are dissolved—as they are, temporarily, for Griffin and Kurtz—the dream of the superhuman becomes the reality of the subhuman. That this theme is typically associated with disguise or invisibility in late Victorian literature might easily be demonstrated by reference to two other novels, Stevenson's *The Strange Case of Dr. Jekyll and Mr. Hyde* (1886) and Wilde's *The Picture of Dorian Gray* (1891): in the first, the "Hyde" identity is a means by which Dr. Jekyll can remain invisible or unknown while simultaneously satisfying his desires to control others and to cause destruction; in the second, Dorian Gray's real face, on the portrait, remains unseen. In both cases the anonymity or invisibility feeds the man's ego and contributes to his moral decay.

Another character removed from European society and freed of its restraints on conduct is Dr. Moreau. His island, where he surgically transforms animals into grotesque approximations of humanity, is a model of a European colony where Moreau—driven from England in a furor over the brutality of vivisection—reigns supreme. The parallels with *Heart of Darkness* are particularly striking: Kurtz aims to suppress savage customs, Moreau to suppress bestial instincts; both men are worshipped as gods, and both maintain their power through pain and fear; both stories are reported by men who, upon their return to Europe, undergo a Gulliver-like revulsion against common humanity; and like Fresleven—a crude version of Kurtz—Moreau is eventually killed by the "natives" in response to his own brutality. Moreover, Lee M. Whitehead's description of the Russian harlequin as "just as much a 'natural man' as the savages"[36] applies equally well to Moreau's assistant, Montgomery, whose flight from England after a moment's weakness makes him the most Conradian character in this novel: Montgomery's drunkenness and destructiveness (he sets fire to the boat which is the only means of escape from the island), and his tendency to blur the line between man and beast, show that his is another case of atavistic regression.

In his essay, "Human Evolution, an Artificial Process," Wells reworked Huxley's distinction between biological and ethical evolution, noting that modern man contains both "an inherited factor, the natural man, who is the product of natural selection" and "an acquired factor, the artificial man, the highly plastic creature of tradition, suggestion, and reasoned thought." Morality, Wells says, is "the padding of suggested emotional habits necessary to keep the round Palaeolithic savage in the square hole of the civilised state. And Sin is the conflict of the two factors—as I have tried to convey in my *Island of Dr. Moreau*."[37] In fact, the novel itself explicitly examines the terms of Huxley's argument. Prendick, the narrator, was once a student of Huxley's at the Royal College of Science, a fact that entitles him to a measure of respect from Moreau (84). On the other hand, Moreau rejects Prendick's (and Huxley's) concern with ethics, contending that "The study of Nature makes a man at last as remorseless as Nature" (116). Here, as so often, Moreau contradicts himself: his concern is to accelerate evolution in specific animals, to raise them above the bestial state, yet he resorts to brutality in the process. More importantly, his attempt to imprint the human form—and human conduct—on animals is only partly successful: Moreau reshapes their bodies and uses various strategies to enforce civilized behavior, but as he himself admits, "they revert. As soon as my hand is taken from them the beast begins to creep back, begins to assert itself again" (118).

In *Heart of Darkness*, the line between human and inhuman is constantly tested. For Marlow,

> "... the men were—No, they were not inhuman. Well, you know, that was the worst of it—this suspicion of their not being inhuman. It would come slowly to one. They howled and leaped, and spun, and made horrid faces; but what thrilled you was just

the thought of their humanity—like yours—the thought of your
remote kinship with this wild and passionate uproar...." (36–37)

Likewise, in *The Island of Dr. Moreau*, Prendick is startled by his response to
the Leopard Man, who is reverting to a wild state: "It may seem a strange
contradiction in me—I cannot explain the fact—but now, seeing the creature
there in a perfectly animal attitude, with the light gleaming in its eyes, and
its imperfectly human face distorted with terror, I realized again the fact of
its humanity" (130). Certainly the distinction between man and animal is
more complex than Moreau implies when he tells Prendick that "the great
difference between man and monkey is in the larynx ... in the incapacity to
frame delicately different sound-symbols by which thought could be
sustained" (114). Notice that the emphasis falls on *spoken* language: believing
that speech is the mark of humanity, Moreau ignores the expedient of
teaching his Beast People sign language, just as the same course of action was
ignored by those who tried to humanize the "wild boy" found in France in
1800.[38] To some extent Moreau is successful; Prendick even comments on
the "strangely good" English accent of one creature (104). It is also true that
the stream of "vile language" (76) spoken by the captain of the *Ipecacuanha*,
one of many signs of his brutishness, aligns him with the Beast People, whose
language becomes degraded as they regress into bestiality. Yet if language is
a sign of humanity, it is also an instrument of repression, as in the Law that
the Beast People memorize and chant or in Moreau's commands, which are
always threats.[39] Still another negative aspect of language is revealed by
Prendick, whose story that Moreau is alive and invisible convinces the Beast
People because "it takes a real man to tell a lie" (148).

A greater danger lies in the mesmeric effect of eloquence. A crude
example is the Law of the Beast People, a parody of the Decalogue and
religious law generally, which has a compelling, incantatory effect. Likewise,
Kurtz's use—or misuse—of language is one reason why he is so dangerous.
His language, which he uses to control others ("You don't talk with that
man—you listen to him," the Russian declares [54]), is essentially false: the
postscriptum "Exterminate all the brutes!" gives the lie to the "enthusiasm"
aroused in Marlow by the "burning noble words" of Kurtz's report (51). The
only other honest sentiment spoken by Kurtz is contained in his final words,
"The horror! The horror!"—words that echo in Marlow's mind as he tells his
own lie to the Intended (71, 75, 79). The final vision of horror undoubtedly
reflects Kurtz's recoil from his own empty eloquence, from the hollowness of
his words and of his life. It is as if he has seen that there is no *essential*
difference between his words and the language of the natives, described by

Marlow as consisting of "strings of amazing words that resembled no sounds of human language; and the deep murmurs of the crowd ... [which] were like the responses of some satanic litany" (68). Certainly the connection seems to be made by Marlow, for whom Kurtz and the others were "voices," the memory of which "lingers around me, impalpable, like a dying vibration of one immense jabber, silly, atrocious, sordid, savage, or simply mean, without any kind of sense" (49).

IV

The "immense jabber" of *Heart of Darkness*, the collapse of language into mere sound, both results from and contributes to the dissolution of all systems of morality and of understanding: private judgment and private meaning have been substituted for shared codes. The anarchic situation here recalls Raskolnikov's dream at the end of *Crime and Punishment*, where he imagines that all but a few people are killed by a plague. These survivors are infected with another sort of plague, microscopic parasites "endowed with intelligence and will" whose victims are mad and yet become convinced of their private judgments and beliefs. As a result, "each thought he was the sole repository of truth and was tormented when he looked at the others, beat his breast, wrung his hands, and wept. They did not know how or whom to judge and could not agree what was evil and what good." The result is chaos: insurrection, fire, famine.[40]

According to René Girard, "Raskolnikov is describing ontological sickness at the paroxysmal stage which triggers this orgy of destruction."[41] Elsewhere, Girard calls plague "a process of undifferentiation, a destruction of specificities" and notes that the "plague makes all accumulated knowledge and all categories of judgment invalid." Plague is typically represented as resulting in (or from) anarchy, which Girard calls "the social plague."[42] Canetti makes a related point when he observes that bacilli are "invisible crowds" whose "power to harm and ... concentration in enormous numbers in very small spaces is undoubtedly taken over from devils."[43] In any event, for Conrad, disease is more than a physical disorder: Europe's colonial policies are killing the native workers who have become "nothing but block shadows of disease and starvation, lying confusedly in the greenish gloom" (17), and it is primarily Kurtz's moral, rather than his physical, proximity that infects and nearly kills Marlow, whose contempt for common people upon his return to Europe demonstrates that he has not fully recovered from Kurtz's disease.

Kurtz's megalomania is shared by Griffin in *The Invisible Man*: when another scientist, Kemp, protests against his violations of the "common conventions of humanity," Griffin retorts that such considerations are "all very well for common people" (240). Like a giant bacillus moving unseen among the populace, Griffin can suddenly strike without warning. Even when he is killed he retains his germ-like property, for he has left behind books which infect their possessor with the dream of invisibility. Only one man knows of these books, and "none other will know of them until he dies" (262). Thus the plague of invisibility or megalomania is buried but not dead; it can resurface at any time and cause further destruction. [44] The point is reinforced by the epilogue to *The War of the Worlds*, a book in which the invasion from Mars is remarkably like the process of a disease: the narrator tells us that another invasion is always possible, even though the microbes on our planet have destroyed the invaders. The process here, however, is that of successful resistance to disease (the microbes are our planet's antibodies) and the development of immunity: we are now on guard against the Martians, and their invasion has performed a service for us by depriving us of "that serene confidence in the future which is the most fruitful source of decadence" (387).

The end of *The War of the Worlds* thereby involves a return to many of the ideas in its first paragraph, where Wells says that before the invasion men went with "infinite complacency" over the world, "serene in their assurance of their empire over matter" (265). In attacking the twin Victorian ideals of Empire and progress, Wells sounds the note of *fin de siècle* pessimism that recurs throughout these works and that obviously influences the repeated use of such plague-related themes as anarchy and moral decay. The pessimism would be less deep-seated if it were not in turn related to Lord Kelvin's Second Law of Thermodynamics, whose practical result is the process of entropy by which the energy once concentrated within a physical system becomes randomly distributed, causing the system to run down. If evolution could be used to support the idea of human progress, entropy just as obviously showed that all human effort was doomed.

In the late 1890s Conrad's letters contained several direct references to this entropic process. Writing to Cunninghame-Graham in December 1897, Conrad referred to "the curse of decay—the eternal decay that will extinguish the sun, the stars, one by one, and in another instant shall spread a frozen darkness over the whole universe."[45] A month later Conrad stated explicitly the relation between entropy and his pessimism about moral and political issues:

> The mysteries of a universe made of drops of fire and clods of
> mud do not concern us in the least. The fate of a humanity

condemned ultimately to perish from cold is not worth troubling
about. If you take it to heart it becomes an unendurable tragedy.
If you believe in improvement you must weep, for the attained
perfection must end in cold, darkness and silence.[46]

Randomness and disorder, moral relativity, physical decay—all of these
attributes of the plague are also associated with the entropic or dying
universe. Just as plague once seemed to threaten the immediate extinction of
all human life, so entropy promises the eventual death of the world, a death
memorably portrayed in *The Time Machine* (58–62). The connection between
plague and entropy is perhaps made clearest by the opening chapter of *The
War of the Worlds*, where the narrator traces the Martian invasion to the
"secular cooling" of the planet Mars (266): here, entropy at an advanced
stage in one part of the solar system produces a plague elsewhere in the
system.

The process of entropy, as it is described in *The Time Machine*, has two
important aspects: the cooling that results from the dying sun and the
blurring of margins (between day and night, land and sea) that indicates the
random dispersal of energy. These elements are reproduced in *Heart of
Darkness*, which is narrated on the margin between land and sea, at a time
between day and night; in the distance, "the sea and the sky were welded
together without a joint" (3). This passage obviously bears an ironic
relationship to the scene in which Marlow's attempt to repair the boat is
stymied by the lack of rivets, yet both situations are nonetheless versions of
anarchy and entropy: one suggests the obliteration of all differences, the
other the dissolution of all bonds.

The repeated image of the dying sun, specifically described in terms
taken from nineteenth-century astronomy, first occurs early in the story:

And at last, in its curved and imperceptible fall, the sun sank red,
and from glowing white changed to a dull red without rays and
without heat, as if about to go out suddenly, stricken to death by
the touch of that gloom brooding over a crowd of men. (4)

Here, the relation between entropy and pessimism is neatly reversed: the
"gloom" produced by the "crowd" (London) infects the sun, causing it to die.
Images of the setting sun, and the resultant darkness (or "impalpable
greyness" [71]), occur so frequently that we are not surprised to find Marlow
visiting the Intended at dusk, the time of Kurtz's death and of Marlow's
narration of his story.

There has always been a great controversy over the lie that Marlow tells the Intended—that Kurtz's last words were her name. Marlow's own judgment is made clear when he says that "There is a taint of death, a flavour of mortality in lies" (27). Marlow has been roundly criticized by critics like Garrett Stewart, who condemns the lie to the Intended as being related to "the lies of Western idealism [that] mislead us into death."[47] Yet the scene is altogether ambiguous and might just as reasonably be interpreted as a necessary lie, a redemptive illusion like that advocated by Relling in Ibsen's *The Wild Duck*. Marlow spares the Intended this confrontation with the ultimate darkness of the soul; he does not, I think, spare himself.

In a way, Marlow is following Huxley and Wells in focusing on the present illusion rather than the distant—and fearful—reality. Huxley admits that the direction of evolution will eventually be reversed and that nothing we do "can ever arrest the procession of the great year"; yet in the meantime we may use our "intelligence and will" to "modify the conditions of existence" (85). Wells's Time Traveller retreats from the dying world of the future to the living world of the present, saying (in a line that could easily be transplanted into Conrad's story), "A horror of this great darkness came on me" (62). After he returns, tells his story, and leaves again, the narrator—his alter ego—states explicitly the two possible attitudes toward the bleak vision of a dying world:

> He, I know—for the question had been discussed among us long before the Time Machine was made—thought but cheerlessly of the Advancement of Mankind, and saw in the growing pile of civilisation only a foolish heaping that must inevitably fall back upon and destroy its makers in the end. If that is so, it remains for us to live as though it were not so. (66)

McConnell observes that the two "voices" or attitudes expressed here "encapsulate between them [the] elementary tension between cosmic determinism and freedom of the will."[48] That tension is found also at the end of Huxley's essay—indeed, throughout the essay, for Huxley is concerned with the way human beings, the products of a cosmic process, must rise above that process, must focus not on what they *are*, but on what they *could be*.

Conrad's pessimism, it must be admitted, is deeper and more profound that of Huxley or Wells: there is in the later Conrad none of the simple enthusiasm for utopias that we find in the later Wells. Yet *Heart of Darkness* marks, or at least approximates, the point of Conrad's intersection with

Wells, and as bleak and deterministic as the novel often is, Marlow is not far wrong when he calls the Intended's misplaced faith "that great and saving illusion that shone with an unearthly glow in the darkness" (77), or when he says that to have told the truth "would have been too dark—too dark altogether" (79). Those who see too clearly into the darkness of the human condition and of the future—Marlow, Prendick, the Time Traveller—are often as misshapen by their experiences as Gulliver on his return from Houyhnhnmland. The miracle is that Marlow, in this state, had yet within him enough pity to tell a lie when it would have been easier, and in a sense more satisfying, to tell the truth. He reserves the truth for the Director of Companies, the Lawyer, the Accountant, and the narrator—all businessmen who will easily survive the shattering of one of their illusions, and perhaps, in the manner of Coleridge's Wedding Guest, will be better men for having learned the truth; but to tell the truth to the Intended would have been to give up on humanity altogether.

V

One might easily cite other parallels between *Heart of Darkness* and Wells's fiction—for instance, the odd fact that both the Time Traveller and Marlow throw away their shoes. My purpose, however, has not been merely to list parallels, nor even to argue for influence. There does seem to have been influence, enough of it so that if Wells had not written his books it is doubtful that *Heart of Darkness* would have appeared in anything like the form in which we now find it. My real argument, however, has been that comparisons with Wells's novels can illuminate ways in which Conrad responded to some of the dominant ideas of his time. It is no disparagement of Wells to say that his brilliant scientific fantasies were essentially simpler than *Heart of Darkness*, both in their narrative strategies and in their treatment of scientific and social themes. Yet they are valuable to us not for their own sake, but because of the relative directness that enables us to outline their dominant concerns; this outline, in turn, provides us with a viewpoint from which we might profitably analyze a more complex work like *Heart of Darkness*.

For what is at stake here is not merely how Conrad responded to Wells, but how both men responded to their age. We can discern their kinship in the way they handle certain related themes: entropy, atavism, anarchy, disease. The relationship among these apocalyptic themes is implied often in Wells's stories and in *Heart of Darkness*; likewise, the bleak, deterministic aspect of Wells—a reaction against the facile optimism of his age—resurfaces in Conrad. Energy and empire, science and progress—those great ideals of the Victorian age—are satirized in Wells's stories and treated with more complex irony by Conrad. The tone differs, but the essential attitude is much the same.

The situation was bound to change. Wells's emphasis on what he later called "life in the mass and life in general as distinguished from life in the individual experience"[49] was only one of several areas in which his writing differed significantly from that of Conrad. Wells believed that literature could, and should, be a form of journalism; he saw nothing wrong with playing the role of propagandist and was annoyed when the world failed to heed his advice—as we might gather from his desire that his epitaph read, "God damn you all, I told you so." Meanwhile, Conrad emphasized the inner life, and his works reflect an obsessive concern with irresolvable moral dilemmas. By the time Conrad dedicated *The Secret Agent* to Wells, the friendship was beginning to cool and the literary kinship was considerably weakened. Later, Conrad was to tell Wells, "The difference between us, Wells, is fundamental. You don't care for humanity but think they are to be improved. I love humanity but know they are not!"[50]

There is more than a grain of truth in this distinction, but it is only part of the story. For all of their later differences, Wells and Conrad were united by their Victorian (and anti-Victorian) inheritance. The proof of that shared inheritance may be found on virtually every page of *Heart of Darkness*. [51]

NOTES

1. Editions cited parenthetically in my text are *Heart of Darkness*, ed. Robert Kimbrough (rev. ed. W.W. Norton & Co., 1971) and *Seven Famous Novels by H.G. Wells* (Garden City Publishing Co., 1934).

2. *The Collected Letters of Joseph Conrad, Volume 1: 1861-1897*, eds. Frederick R. Karl and Laurence Davies (Cambridge: Cambridge University Press, 1983), p. 282.

3. G. Jean-Aubry, *Joseph Conrad: Life and Letters* (Doubleday, Page & Co., 1927), 1, 240.

4. Jean-Aubry, 1, 257

5. Jean-Aubry, 1, 259

6. Jean-Aubry, 1, 263–64.

7. Zdsilaw Najder, *Joseph Conrad: A Chronicle* (Rutgers University Press, 1983), p. 249.

8. Frank McConnell, *The Science Fiction of H.G. Wells* (Oxford University Press, 1981), pp. 48, 116.

9. Frederick R. Karl, *Joseph Conrad: The Three Lives* (Farrar, Straus and Giroux, 1979), p. 438; Leo J. Henkin, *Darwinism in the English Novel*, 1860–1910 (Russell & Russell, 1963), p. 256n.

10. Robert G. Jacobs, "H.G. Wells, Joseph Conrad, and the Relative Universe," *Conradiana*, I (Summer 1968), 51–55.

11. Bernard Bergonzi, *The Early H.G. Wells: A Study of the Scientific Romances* (Manchester: Manchester University Press, 1961), pp. 70–71; Robert M. Philmus, *Into the Unknown: The Evolution of Science Fiction from Francis Godwin to H.G. Wells* (1970); rpt. University of California Press, 1983), pp. 144–45.

12. Paul Kirschner, Conrad: *The Psychologist as Artist* (Edinburgh: Oliver & Boyd, 1968), p. 283.

13. Cedric Watts, *A Preface to Conrad* (London: Longman, 1982). pp. 86–87, 93–94, 184.

14. Nicholas Delbanco, *Group Portrait: Joseph Conrad, Stephen Crane, Ford Madox Ford, Henry James, and H.G. Wells* (1982; rpt. Quill, 1984), p. 26.

15. Frederick R. Karl, "Conrad, Wells, and the Two Voices," *PMLA*, LXXXVIII (October 1973), 1049–65.

16. *Henry James and H.G. Wells*, eds. Leon Edel and Gordon N. Ray (University of Illinois Press, 1958), p. 264.

17. Stanley Renner, "The Garden of Civilization: Conrad, Huxley, and the Ethics of Evolution," *Conradiana*, VII (1975), 109–20; C.T. Watts, *"Heart of Darkness:* The Covert Murder Plot and the Darwinian Theme," *Conradiana*, VII (1975), 139; Ian Watt, *Conrad in the Nineteenth Century* (University of California Press, 1979), p. 155. See also Watts, *A Preface to Conrad*, pp. 88–91. More recently, Redmond O'Hanlon has demonstrated the pervasiveness of the Darwinian theme in *Lord Jim*: see his *Joseph Conrad and Charles Darwin: The Influence of Scientific Thought on Conrad's Fiction* (Edinburgh: The Salamander Press, 1984).

18. Both essays are reprinted in *H.G. Wells: Early Writings in Science and Science Fiction*, eds. Robert M. Philmus and David Y. Hughes (University of California Press, 1975). The Darwinian theme in Wells has been discussed often; for two good examples, see David Y. Hughes, "The Garden in Wells's Early Science Fiction," and J.P. Vernier, "Evolution as a Literary Theme in H.G. Wells's Science Fiction," both in Darko Suvin and Robert M. Philmus, eds., *H.G. Wells and Modern Science Fiction* (Bucknell University Press, 1977).

19. Charles Darwin, *The Origin of Species by Means of Natural Selection* (D. Appleton, 1896), 1, 5, 77. Chapter 3 deals in Malthusian terms with the relation of population to natural selection. See also Ashley Montagu, *Darwin: Competition & Cooperation* (Henry Schuman, 1952), pp. 18–33.

20. Charles Darwin, *The Descent of Man, and Selection in Relation to Sex* (D. Appleton, 1896), pp. 128, 133–34.

21. Darwin, *The Descent of Man*, p. 618.

22. Thomas H. Huxley, *Evolution and Ethics and Other Essays*, volume 9 of *Collected Essays* (London: Macmillan, 1894), pp. 202–03. Further page references will be cited parenthetically.

23. Avrom Fleishman, *Conrad's Politics: Community and Anarchy in the Fiction of Joseph Conrad* (Johns Hopkins University Press, 1967), p. 51.

24. On Kurtz Cannibalism, see Tony Tanner, "'Gnawed Bones' and 'Artless Tales'— Eating and Narrative in Conrad," in Norman Sherry, ed., *Joseph Conrad: A Commemoration* (London: Macmillan, 1976), pp. 31–32.

25. Note Tanner, pp. 18–19: "one effect of *Heart of Darkness* is not to endorse either the West or the jungle but to erode some of the unexamined assumptions which make such either/or thinking possible."

26. John Huntington, *The Logic of Fantasy*: H.G. *Wells and Science Fiction* (Columbia University Press, 1982).

27. The phrase "intellects vast and cool and unsympathetic" relates the Martians to a possible future human race envisioned in *The Time Machine*, where the Time Traveller worries about what he will encounter in the future: "What if cruelty had grown into a common passion? What if in this interval the race had lost its manliness, and had developed into something inhuman, unsympathetic, and overwhelmingly powerful? I might seem some old-world savage animal, only the more dreadful and disgusting for our common likeness—a foul creature to be incontinently slain" (16).

28. Huntington, p. 45; see also David Ketterer, "Oedipus as Time Traveller," *Science-Fiction Studies*, IX 29 (November 1982), 340–41.

29. Hughes, p. 61.

30. McConnell, p. 140. Unlike McConnell, and unlike Bergonzi (107), I have avoided a specifically Nietzschean interpretation of Wells (and Conrad) because, although *Thus Spake Zarathustra* appeared in English translation in 1896, there is no clear evidence that either Wells or Conrad read Nietzsche at the time. In any case, they could have derived the same ideas from other sources, as David S. Thatcher implies when he says, "Nietzschean motifs appear in Wells's work long before Nietzsche was available in English—certainly before his ideas began to make themselves felt." *Nietzsche in England, 1890–1914: The Growth of a Reputation* (Toronto: University of Toronto Press, 1970), p.82

31. Marc Shell, "The Ring of Gyges," in *The Economy of Literature* (Johns Hopkins University Press, 1978), pp. 11–62.

32. Note Prendick's attempt, in *The Island of Dr. Moreau*, to convince the Beast People that the slain Moreau is not really dead but is invisible.

33. Roslynn D. Haynes, *H.G. Wells: Discoverer of the Future* (New York University Press, 1980), p.203. Kurtz also resembles Faustus, as Marlow(e) implies when he declares, "I take it, no fool [unlike Kurtz] ever made a bargain for his soul with the devil: the fool is too much of a fool, or the devil too much of a devil—I don't know which" (50).

34. Elias Canetti, *Crowds and Power*, trans. Carol Stewart (1962; rpt. Continuum, n.d.), pp. 19–20. One of Griffin's first acts after becoming invisible is to set fire to a house, an action that again associates him with crowds; see Canetti, pp. 20, 26, 27, 50, 75–80, 81.

35. Forests are among the crowd symbols described by Canetti, pp. 75–90; others that appear in *Heart of Darkness* include fire, sea, sand, and rivers.

36. Lee M. Whitehead, "The Active Voice and the Passive Eye: *Heart of Darkness* and Nietzsche's *The Birth of Tragedy*," *Conradiana*, VII (1975), 130.

37. H.G. Wells: *Early Writings in Science Fiction*, p.217

38. See Roger Shattuck, *The Forbidden Experiment*: *The Story of the Wild Boy of Aveyron* (Washington Square Press, 1981), pp. 158–59.

39. Canetti, pp. 303–33, argues that commands originated in threats of death and always retain some element of aggression.

40. Feodor Dostoevsky, *Crime and Punishment*, trans. Jessie Coulson, ed. George Gibian, 2nd ed. (W.W. Norton & Co., 1975), pp. 461–62.

41. René Girard, *Deceit, Desire and the Novel: Self and Other in Literary Structure*, trans. Yvonne Freccero (Johns Hopkins University Press, 1980), p. 282.

42. René Girard, "The Plague in Literature and Myth," "*To double business bound*": *Essays on Literature, Mimesis, and Anthropology* (Johns Hopkins University Press, 1978), pp. 136–38.

43. Canetti, p. 47.

44. Note the end of Albert Camus's *The Plague*, which stresses the ability of the plague bacillus to lie dormant for years and then reappear.

45. Jean-Aubry, 1,215. Watt, pp. 151–55, has a concise analysis of the impact of Conrad's thought. See also Watts, *A Preface to Conrad*, pp. 54, 86–88.

46. Jean-Aubry, 1, 222.

47. Garrett Stewart, "Lying as Dying in *Heart of Darkness*," *PMLA*, XCV (May 1980), 319.

48. McConnell, p. 88.

49. Preface to *Seven Famous Novels*, p. ix.

50. Cited by Edel and Ray, Introduction to *Henry James and H.G. Wells*, p. 28

51. I want to thank Robert Casillo and Hunt Hawkins for several suggestions that led to improvements in this essay.

Chronology

1866	Herbert George Wells born on September 21 to parents Joseph and Sarah Wells, at Bromley, Kent, twelve miles from London. H.G. is the youngest of the couple's four children. Joseph Wells ran a china and glassware shop he had purchased just as the couple started their family. Prior to owning the shop, Joseph Wells had worked as a gardener for an affluent family, where he met his wife, Sarah, who had been the maid.
1871	H.G. begins "dame school" in Bromley. Dame school was a name given to arrangements where neighborhood women taught small groups of children the rudiments of beginning education, such as reading, writing, and arithmetic.
1874	Transitions to Thomas Morley's Academy, where he remains through 1880.
1877	Joseph Wells falls and breaks his leg while gardening. The injury is severe enough to make working at the shop very difficult. The injury marks the family's return to financial jeopardy. (In the beginning of their marriage, Sarah and Joseph were homeless for a short period due to the high costs of paying debts left by Sarah's deceased parents.)
1880	Sarah Wells returns to housekeeping work to support the family. H.G. Wells begins a period wherein he changes schools several times as the family finances fluctuate.

1881	Wells leaves school to work in a druggist shop in Midhurst. Soon afterward, his mother, convinced that her son will make a good honest living as a draper, binds him to apprenticeship at Hyde's Drapery Emporium. Wells is miserable.
1883	After two years of increasingly dramatic entreaties to his mother, Wells one day walks the 17 miles to his mother's place of employment at Uppark and demands that she arrange for his release from the apprenticeship. He resumes his formal education soon afterward.
1884	A scholarship allows him to attend the Normal School of Science in South Kensington. Among others, he studies biology with T.H. Huxley, the eminent biologist and Darwin apologist, as well as the person who coined the term "agnostic," and the grandfather of later utopianist and social thinker Aldous Huxley.
1887	Wells fails his exams. He is also badly injured in a football match. He must convalesce for months, during which time he lives with his mother at Uppark. While so confined, he begins writing short stories. The same year, Wells's father sells the china shop and moves to Liss, Hampshire, to look for other work.
1888	Wells returns to London to work as a teacher. Continues writing stories.
1889-1891	Becomes a schoolmaster in Kilburn. The next year, takes a post at University Correspondence College while also teaching biology at Bookseller's Row, London. The lectureship at UCC will be his last conventional full-time job. During these years, he begins to publish short stories and to work as a freelance journalist, reviewer, and essayist.
1891	Marries cousin Isabel Mary Wells. According to the scholar John Hammond, Wells is fiercely physically attracted to Isabel, but she is not a match for him temperamentally or intellectually. The marriage is doomed. The couple do become close in later life, renewing their initial friendship.
1892	Wells meets Amy Catherine Robinson, the woman who will become his second wife, for the first time. He spends lots of time with her, discussing books, writing, politics, and the like, things he never can discuss in any depth with Isabel.

1893	Wells's poor health aggravates his already tenuous employment, and leads to the loss of his job. He begins to write full time, and before long, discovers he is making more money than would have ever been possible as a lecturer. Meanwhile, his mother is dismissed from her position at Uppark, so she joins her husband in Hampshire.
1894	Against all prevailing mores and wisdom of the time, Wells and Amy Catherine move in together. (He takes to calling her Jane, since he does not like either of her given names.) Publishing continues to go well. He starts writing *The Time Machine*.
1895	Publishes *The Time Machine, Select Conversations with an Uncle, The Stolen Bacillus and Other Incidents*, and *The Wonderful Visit*. He is officially divorced from Isabel, and he and Jane marry.
1896	Begins work on *The War of the Worlds*. Publishes *The Wheels of Chance* and *The Island of Doctor Moreau*.
1897	*The War of the Worlds* begins to appear in serial. Publishes *The Invisible Man* and *The Plattner Story and Others*.
1898	Wells experiences more health problems, including hemorrhaging while coughing. His writing continues, however. He begins to increase his circle of literary friends and associates.
1899	Publishes *When the Sleeper Wakes* and *Tales of Space and Time*.
1900	Builds Spade House, Sandgate, the place where, after a peripatetic decade or so, he settles and remains for the next ten years. Publishes *Love and Mr. Lewisham*.
1901	Birth of son, George Philip Wells, to Jane. Publishes *Anticipations* and *The First Men in the Moon*.
1902	Publishes *The Sea Lady* and *The Discovery of the Future*.
1903	Birth of son, Frank Richard Wells, to Jane. Publishes *Twelve Stories and A Dream* and *Mankind in the Making*. *Mankind in the Making*, along with other socialist and utopian writings, will attract the attention of London's Fabian Society, a socialist group. Wells joins, calls for radical change, and leaves in three years. According to John Hammond, Wells was "constitutionally incapable" of working with societies

and committees, given the writer's impatience, intellectual breadth, and zeal for ideas.

1904   Publishes *The Food of the Gods*. Meets Amber Reeves, daughter of two of Wells's ideological allies in the Fabian Society.

1905   Publishes *Kipps* and *A Modern Utopia*. His mother, Sarah, dies. Wells is deeply effected by the death. His mother was stern and their life together, especially in Wells's teen years, was tempestuous, and the writer discovered the depth of his affection for her only once she was departed. Hammond points out her appearance in several of Wells's works during his middle years.

1906   Publishes *The Future in America* (after conducting his first visit ever to the country in the same year) and *In the Days of the Comet*. Begins work on *Tono-Bungay*.

1907   Leaves Fabian Society. Publishes *Misery of Boots*.

1908   Finishes *Tono-Bungay*. Publishes *New Worlds for Old*, *First and Last Things*, and *The War in the Air*. Begins actual love affair with Amber Reeves.

1909   Publishes *Tono-Bungay* and *Ann Veronica*. Birth of daughter, Anna Jane, by Amber Reeves. Leaves Spade House, and relocates at Church Row, Hampstead.

1910   Publishes *The History of Mr. Polly*. Father, Joseph Wells, dies. While Wells is moved, and dedicated *The History of Mr. Polly* to his father's memory, the effect is not the same as the death of his mother five years before. In fact, the dissolution of the affair with Reeves leaves him more disturbed. But he soon begins an affair with Elizabeth Mary Beauchamp.

1911   Publishes *The New Machiavelli*, *The Country of the Blind and Other Stories*, and *Floor Games*.

1912   Moves to Easton Glebe. Publishes *Marriage*. Meets the writer Rebecca West for the first time.

1913   Publishes *The Passionate Friends* and *Little Wars*. Affair with Rebecca West begins.

1914   Publishes *The World Set Free*, *An Englishman Looks at the World*, and *The Wife of Sir Isaac Harman*. Birth of son, Anthony West, by Rebecca West.

1915   Publishes *Bealby* and *The Research Magnificent*.

1916	Publishes *Mr. Britling Sees It Through*. Travels to France and Italy, sees war zones, writes *War and the Future*.
1917	Publishes *God and the Invisible King* and *The Soul of a Bishop*.
1918	Publishes *Joan and Peter*.
1919	Publishes *The Undying Fire*.
1920	Visits Russia and meets Lenin. Afterward, writes *Russia in the Shadows*. Publishes *The Outline of History*.
1921	Publishes *The Salvaging of Civilization* and *The New Teaching of History*.
1922	Publishes *Washington and The Hope of Peace*, *The Secret Places of the Heart*, and *A Short History of the World*.
1923	Publishes *Men Like Gods*. Ends affair with Rebecca West, and starts new one with Odette Keun. Starts spending winters in Provence.
1924	Publishes *The Story of a Great Schoolmaster* and *The Dream*.
1925	Publishes *Christina Alberta's Father*.
1926	Publishes *The World of William Clissold*.
1927	Death of his wife, Jane (Amy Catherine). Publishes *Meanwhile* and *The Short Stories of H.G. Wells*.
1928	Publishes *The Way the World is Going*, *The Open Conspiracy*, and *Mr. Blettsworthy on Rampole Island*. Also publishes *The Book of Catherine Wells*, dedicated to his late wife. The book contained much of her writing.
1930	Publishes *The Science of Life* and *The Autocracy of Mr. Parham*. Sells residence in Eston Glebe and moves to Clarence Gate, London. Also maintains residences in Paris and Westminster.
1931	Publishes *The Work, Wealth and Happiness of Mankind* and *What Are We To Do With Our Lives?* Diagnosed diabetic. Also, death of first wife and cousin, Isabel.
1932	Publishes *The Bulpington of Blup* and *After Democracy*.
1933	Ends affair with Odette Keun and sells home in Provence, establishing London as permanent home. Publishes *The Shape of Things To Come*. Serves as international president of Poets, Essayists and Novelists (PEN).
1934	Publishes *Experiment in Autobiography*. Meets Stalin on visit to Russia.
1935	Meets Roosevelt on a visit to the United States. Publishes *The New America: The New World*. Changes residences for the last time, moving to Hanover Terrace, Regent Park, London.

1936	A film, *Things to Come*, is released.
1937	Publishes *Star Begotten*, *Brynhild*, and *The Camford Visitation*.
1938	Publishes *Apropos of Dolores*, *The Brothers*, and *World Britain*.
1939	Publishes *The Holy Terror*, *Travels of a Republican Radical*, *The Fate of Homo Sapiens*, and *The New World Order*.
1940	Publishes *The Rights of Man*, *Babes in the Darkling Wood*, and *All Aboard for Ararat*.
1941	Publishes *You Can't Be Too Careful*.
1942	Publishes *Phoenix* and *The Conquest of Time*.
1943	Publishes *Crux Ansata*.
1944	Publishes *'42 to '44: A Contemporary Memoir upon Human Behaviour*. Health problems mount.
1945	Publishes *The Last Turning* and *Mind at the End of Its Tether*. On August 13, H.G. Wells dies at his home. He is 79.

Contributors

HAROLD BLOOM is Sterling Professor of the Humanities at Yale University. He is the author of over 20 books, including *Shelley's Mythmaking* (1959), *The Visionary Company* (1961), *Blake's Apocalypse* (1963), *Yeats* (1970), *A Map of Misreading* (1975), *Kabbalah and Criticism* (1975), *Agon: Toward a Theory of Revisionism* (1982), *The American Religion* (1992), *The Western Canon* (1994), and *Omens of Millennium: The Gnosis of Angels, Dreams, and Resurrection* (1996). *The Anxiety of Influence* (1973) sets forth Professor Bloom's provocative theory of the literary relationships between the great writers and their predecessors. His most recent books include *Shakespeare: The Invention of the Human* (1998), a 1998 National Book Award finalist, *How to Read and Why* (2000), *Genius: A Mosaic of One Hundred Exemplary Creative Minds* (2002), and *Hamlet: Poem Unlimited* (2003). In 1999, Professor Bloom received the prestigious American Academy of Arts and Letters Gold Medal for Criticism, and in 2002 he received the Catalonia International Prize.

W. WARREN WAGAR is Distinguished Teaching Professor in the Department of History at the State University of New York in Binghamton. He is the author or editor of more than a dozen books, including *The City of Man, Memoirs of the Future*, and *H.G. Wells and the World State*.

COLIN MANLOVE is Reader in English Literature at the University of Edinburgh. He is the author of *Modern Fantasy: Five Studies* and *Christian Fantasy: From 1200 to the Present*.

KATHRYN HUME is Distinguished Professor of English at The Pennsylvania State University. Her books include *American Dream, American Nightmare: Fiction since 1960, Calvino's Fictions, Cogito and Cosmos,* and *Pynchon's Mythography, An Approach to* Gravity's Rainbow.

WILLIAM J. SCHEICK is the J.R. Millikan Centennial Professor at the University of Texas at Austin. He is the author of more than 20 books, including *The Half-Blood: A Cultural Symbol in Nineteenth-Century American Fiction; Three Contemporary Women Novelists: Hazzard, Ozick, and Redmon; The Splintering Frame: The Later Fiction of H.G. Wells; H.G. Wells: A Reference Guide;* and *The Critical Response to H.G. Wells.*

JOHN HUNTINGTON is Professor of English at the University of Illinois in Chicago. He is author of *H.G. Wells Reader: A Complete Anthology from Science Fiction to Social Satire, Logic of Fantasy: H.G. Wells and Science Fiction, Rationalizing Genius: Ideological Strategies in the Classic American Science Fiction Short Story,* and numerous articles on Wells and science fiction.

ROBERT SIRABIAN is Assistant Professor of English at Mississippi Valley State University.

PAUL A. CANTOR is Professor of English at the University of Virginia. He is the author of *Shakespeare's Rome: Republic and Empire, Creature and Creator: Myth-making and English Romanticism,* and the *Hamlet* volume in the Cambridge Landmarks of World Literature Series.

BRUCE BEIDERWELL is the Director of the Writing Program at the University of California at Los Angeles. He is the author of *Power and Punishment in Scott's Novels* and several articles.

JANICE H. HARRIS is Professor of English and Chair of the Department of English at the University of Wyoming. She is the author of *The Short Fiction of D. H. Lawrence, Edwardian Stories of Divorce,* and numerous articles.

WILLIAM KUPINSE is assistant professor of English at the University of Puget Sound.

PHILIP COUPLAND's Ph.D. thesis, "Voices from Nowhere: Utopianism in British Political Culture, 1929–1945," earned him the doctorate from the University of Warwick's Department of History. He is currently a Research Assistant at the University of Glasgow.

PATRICK A. McCARTHY teaches at the University of Miami. His books include *Ulysses: Portals of Discovery, Forests of Symbols: World, Text, and Self in Malcolm Lowry's Fiction, Critical Essays on Samuel Beckett*, and several others.

Bibliography

Aldridge, Alexandra. *The Scientific World View in Dystopia*. Ann Arbor: UMI Research Press, 1984.

Anand, Mulk Raj. "In Conversation with H.G. Wells." *The Journal of Commonwealth Literature* 18:1 (1983): pp. 84–90.

Anderson, Linda R. *Bennett, Wells, and Conrad: Narrative in Transition*. New York: St. Martin's Press, 1988.

Batchelor, John. *H.G. Wells*. New York: Cambridge University Press, 1985.

Bergonzi, Bernard. "Fictions & Facts: On H.G. Wells." *Encounter* 65 (July/August1985): pp. 31–32.

————, ed. *H.G. Wells: A Collection of Critical Essays*. New York: Prentice Hall, 1976.

————. *The Turn of a Century: Essays on Victorian and Modern English Literature*. London: MacMillan, 1973.

————. *The Early H.G. Wells*. Manchester: Manchester University Press, 1961.

Bloom, Robert. *Anatomies of Egotism: A Reading of the Last Novels of H.G. Wells*. Lincoln: University of Nebraska Press, 1977.

Borden, Richard C. "H.G. Wells' Door in the Wall in Russian Literature." *Slavic and East European Journal* 36 (Fall 1992): pp. 323–338.

Borrello, Alfred. *H.G. Wells: Author in Agony*. Carbondale: Southern Illinois University Press, 1972.

Brome, Vincent. *H.G. Wells: A Biography*. Westport: Greenwood Press, 1970.

Coleman, Arthur. "The Americanization of H.G. Wells: Sinclair Lewis' *Our Mr.Wrenn*." *Modern Fiction Studies* 31 (Autumn 1985): pp. 495–501.

Coren, Michael. *The Invisible Man: The Life and Liberties of H.G. Wells*. New York: Atheneum, 1993.

Costa, Richard Hauer. *H.G. Wells*. Boston: Twayne Publishers, 1985.

Delbanco, Nicholas. *Group Portrait: Joseph Conrad, Stephen Crane, Ford Madox Ford, Henry James, and H.G. Wells*. New York: Morrow, 1982.

Derry, Stephen. "H.G. Wells and the Expression 'Brain(s) Trust'." *Notes and Queries* 44 (September 1997): p. 353–354.

————. "*The Island of Doctor Moreau* and Stevenson's The Ebb-Tide." *Notes and Queries* 43 (December 1996): pp. 437.

Dickson, Lovat. *H.G. Wells: His Turbulent Life and Times*. New York: Atheneum, 1969.

Dryden, Linda. *The Modern Gothic and Literary Doubles: Stevenson, Wilde and Wells*. New York: Palgrave Macmillan, 2003.

Edel, Leon, and Gordon N. Ray, eds. *Henry James and H.G. Wells: A Record of their Friendship, their Debate on the Art of Fiction, and their Quarrel*. Urbana: University of Illinois Press, 1958.

Evans, Arthur B. "The Origins of Science Fiction Criticism: From Kepler to Wells." *Science-Fiction Studies* 26:2 (July 1999): pp. 163–186.

Foot, Michael. *H.G.: The History of Mr. Wells*. Washington, D.C.: Counterpoint Press, 1995.

Gardiner, John. "Lost Victorians." *History Today* 49:12 (Dec. 1999): pp. 18–19.

Grant, Barry. "Looking Upward: H.G. Wells, Science Fiction and the Cinema." *Literature/Film Quarterly* 14:3 (1986): pp. 154–163.

Hammond, J.R. *A Preface to H.G. Wells*. New York: Longman, 2001.

————. *H.G. Wells*. Essex: Pearson Education Limited, 2001.

————. *An H.G. Wells Chronology*. New York: St. Martin's Press, 1999.

————. *H.G. Wells and the Short Story*. New York: St. Martin's Press, 1992.

————. *H.G. Wells and Rebecca West*. New York: Harvester Wheatsheaf, 1991.

————. "The Timescale in *Tono-Bungay*." *The Wellsian* 14 (1991): pp. 34–36.

————. "The Narrative Voice in *Tono-Bungay*." *The Wellsian* 12 (1989): pp. 16–21.

————. *H.G. Wells and the Modern Novel*. Hampshire: Macmillan Press, 1988.

—————, ed. *H.G. Wells: Interviews and Recollections*. London: Macmillan, 1980.

—————. *An H.G. Wells Companion: A Guide to the Novels, Romances, and Short Stories*. London: Macmillan, 1979.

—————. *Herbert George Wells: An Annotated Bibliography of His Works*. New York: Garland Publishing, 1977.

Haynes, Roslynn D. *H.G. Wells, Discoverer of the Future: The Influence of Science on His Thought*. London: Macmillan Press, 1980.

Herbert, Lucille. "Tono-Bungay: Tradition and Experiment." *Modern Language Quarterly* 33 (1972): pp. 140–155.

Hillegas, Mark R. *The Future as Nightmare: H.G. Wells and the Anti-Utopians*. New York: Oxford University Press, 1967.

Holt, Philip. "H.G. Wells and the Ring of Gyges." *Science-Fiction Studies* 19 (July 1992): pp. 236–47.

Hughes, David Y. "Surfing the Intertext." *Science-Fiction Studies* 22 (November 1995): pp. 421–429.

—————. "H.G. Wells: Towards a Synthesis?" *Science-Fiction Studies* 18 (November1991): p. 431–436.

—————. "God, the Devil, and H.G. Wells." *Science-Fiction Studies* 16 (March 1989): pp. 103–108.

Huntington, John. *The Logic of Fantasy: H.G. Wells and Science Fiction*. New York: Columbia University Press, 1982.

Kemp, Peter. *H.G. Wells and the Culminating Ape*. New York: St. Martin's Press, 1982.

Laski, Marghanita. "Lives or Works? On H.G. Wells & Rebecca West." *Encounter* 69 (December 1987): pp. 82–84.

Leavis, L.R. "H.G. Wells, D.H. Lawrence, and Literary Influence." *English Studies* 79:3 (May 1998): pp. 224–239.

Lynn, Andrea. *Shadow Lovers: The Last Affairs of H.G. Wells*. Boulder: Westview Press, 2001.

MacKenzie, Norman, and Jean MacKenzie. *H.G. Wells: A Biography*. New York: Simon and Schuster, 1973.

McCarthy, Patrick A. "New Editions of H.G. Wells: A Mixed Bag." *Science-Fiction Studies* 29:2 (July 2002): pp. 247–252.

McConnell, Frank D. *The Science Fiction of H.G. Wells*. New York: Oxford University Press, 1981.

McKillop, A.B. *The Spinster & The Prophet: H.G. Wells, Florence Deeks, and the*

Case of the Plagiarized Text. New York: Four Walls Eight Windows, 2002.

Meisenheimer, Donald K. "Machining the Man: From Neurasthenia to Psychasthenia in SF and the Genre Western." Science-Fiction Studies 24 (November 1997): pp. 441–58.

Murray, Brian. *H.G. Wells*. New York: Continuum Press, 1990.

Newell, Kenneth B. *Structure in Four Novels by H.G. Wells*. Paris: Mouton, 1968.

Parrinder, Patrick, et al., ed. *H.G. Well's Perennial Time Machine: Selected Essays from the Centenary Conference "The Time Machine: Past, Present, and Future," Imperial College, London, July 26–29, 1995*. Athens: University of Georgia Press, 2001.

————. "George Orwell's Missing Obituary of H.G. Wells." *Notes and Queries* 47:3 (Sept. 2000): pp. 343–345.

————. *Shadows of the Future: H.G. Wells, Science Fiction, and Prophecy*. Syracuse: Syracuse University Press, 1995.

————. "Questionable Guides." *Science-Fiction Studies* 21 (November 1994): pp. 413–417.

———— and Christopher Rolfe, ed. *H.G. Wells Under Revision: Proceedings of the International H.G. Wells Symposium, London, July 1986*. Selinsgrove: Susquehanna University Press, 1989.

————. "Utopia and Meta-Utopia in H.G. Wells." *Science-Fiction Studies* 12 (July 1985): pp. 115–128.

———— and Robert M. Philmus, ed. *H.G. Wells's Literary Criticism*. Totowa: Barnes & Noble Books, 1980.

————, ed. *H.G. Wells: The Critical Heritage*. Boston: Routledge and Kegan Paul, 1972.

————. *H.G. Wells*. Edinburgh: Oliver & Boyd, 1970.

Partington, John S. *Building Cosmopolis: The Political Thought of H.G. Wells*. Burlington: Ashgate Press, 2003.

————. "*The Time Machine* and *A Modern Utopia*: The Static and Kinetic Utopias of the Early H.G. Wells." *Utopian Studies* 13:1 (2002): p. 57–68.

————. "The Death of the Static: H.G. Wells and the Kinetic Utopia." *Utopian Studies* 11:2 (2000): pp. 96–111.

Philmus, Robert M. "*A Story of the Days to Come* and *News from Nowhere*: H.G. Wells as a Writer of Anti-Utopian Fiction." *English Literature in Transition, 1880–1920* 30:4 (1987): pp. 450–455.

————. *Into the Unknown: The Evolution of Science Fiction from Francis Godwin to H.G. Wells*. Berkeley: University of California Press, 1983.

Poole, William. "Francis Godwin, Henry Neville, Margaret Cavendish, H.G. Wells: Some Utopian Debts." *ANQ* 16:3 (Summer 2003): pp. 12–18.

Ray, Gordon Norton. *H.G. Wells & Rebecca West*. New Haven: Yale University Press, 1974.

Reed, John Robert. *The Natural History of H.G. Wells*. Athens: Ohio University Press, 1982.

Scheick, William J., ed. *The Critical Response to H.G. Wells*. Westport: Greenwood Press, 1995.

———— and J. Randolph Cox. *H.G. Wells: A Reference Guide*. Boston: G.K. Hall, 1988.

Shelton, Robert. "The Mars-Begotten Men of Olaf Stapledon and H.G. Wells." *Science-Fiction Studies* 11 (March 1984): pp. 1–14.

Sherborne, Michael. *H.G. Wells*. Hampshire: Macmillan, 1987.

Smidt, Kristian. "T.S. Eliot's Criticism of Modern Prose Fiction." *English Studies* 76 (January 1995): pp. 64-80.

Smith, David C. *H.G. Wells: Desperately Mortal*. New Haven: Yale University Press, 1986.

Smith, Don G. *H.G. Wells on Film: The Utopian Nightmare*. Jefferson: McFarland & Co., 2002.

Sommers, Jeffrey. "Wells's *Tono-Bungay*: The Novel Within the Novel." *Studies in the Novel* 17:1 (1985): pp. 69–79.

Steffen-Fluhr. "Paper Tiger: Women and H.G. Wells." *Science-Fiction Studies* 12 (November 1985): pp. 311–329.

Suvin, Darko. "The Horizons of Wells's Numerology." *Science-Fiction Studies* 29:1 (Mar. 2002): pp. 148–149.

Wagar, W. Warren. *H.G. Wells and the World State*. Freeport: Books for Libraries Press, 1971.

West, Anthony. *H.G. Wells: Aspects of a Life*. New York: Random House, 1984.

Westfahl, Gary. "'The Jules Verne, H.G. Wells, and Edgar Allan Poe Type of Story': Hugo Gernsback's *History of Science Fiction*." *Science-Fiction Studies* 19 (November 1992): pp. 340–353.

Whiteman, Bruce. "Canadian Issues of Anglo-American Fiction: The Example of H.G. Wells." *The Papers of the Bibliographical Society of America* 80:1 (1986): pp. 75–81.

Williamson, Jack. *H.G. Wells: Critic of Progress*. Baltimore: Mirage Press, 1973.

Wills, Martin T. "Edison as Time Traveler: H.G. Wells's Inspiration for His First Scientific Character." *Science-Fiction Studies* 26:2 (July 1999): pp. 284–294.

Wood, James Playsted. *I Told You So!: A Life of H.G. Wells*. New York: Pantheon Books, 1969.

Wood, Joanne A. "Counter-Evolution: The Prosthetics of Early Modernist Form." *ELH* 66:2 (Summer 1999): p. 489–510.

Acknowledgments

"H.G. Wells and the Scientific Imagination" by W. Warren Wagar. From *The Virginia Quarterly Review*, vol. 65, no. 3 (Summer 1989). © 1989 by the Virginia Quarterly Review, the University of Virginia.

"Charles Kingsley, H.G. Wells, and the Machine in Victorian Fiction" by Colin Manlove. From *Nineteenth-Century Literature*, vol. 48, no. 2 (September 1993). © 1993 by The Regents of the University of California. Reprinted with permission.

"Eat or be Eaten: H.G. Wells's *Time Machine*" by Kathryn Hume. From *Philological Quarterly*, vol. 69, no. 2 (Spring 1990). © 1990 by The University of Iowa.

"The De-Forming In-Struction of Wells's *The Wonderful Visit* and *The Sea Lady*" by William J. Scheick. From *English Literature in Transition*, vol. 30, no. 4. © 1987 *English Literature in Transition, 1880–1920*.

"H.G. Wells: Problems of an Amorous Utopian" by John Huntington. From *English Literature in Transition*, vol. 30, no. 4. © 1987 *English Literature in Transition, 1880–1920*.

"The Conception of Science in Wells's *The Invisible Man*" by Robert Sirabian. From *Papers on Language & Literature*, vol. 37, no. 4 (Fall 2001). © 2001 by the Board of Trustees, Southern Illinois University.

"The Invisible Man and the Invisible Hand: H.G. Wells's Critique of Capitalism" by Paul A. Cantor. From *The American Scholar*, vol. 68, no. 3 (Summer 1999). © 1999 by the author.

"The Grotesque in Wells's *The Invisible Man*" by Bruce Beiderwell. From *Extrapolation*, vol. 24, no. 4 (Winter 1983). © 1983 by The Kent State University Press.

"Wifely Silence and Speech in Three Marriage Novels by H.G. Wells" by Janice H. Harris. From *Studies in the Novel*, vol. 26, no. 4 (Winter 1994). © 1994 by University of North Texas. Reprinted by permission of the publisher.

"Wasted Value: The Serial Logic of H.G. Wells's *Tono-Bungay*" by William Kupinse. From *NOVEL: A Forum on Fiction*, vol. 33, no. 1 (Fall 1999). © 1999 NOVEL Corp. Reprinted with permission.

"H.G. Wells's 'Liberal Fascism'" by Philip Coupland. From *Journal of Contemporary History*, vol. 35, no. 4 (October 2000). © 2000 Sage Publications Ltd. Reprinted by permission of Sage Publications Ltd.

"*Heart of Darkness* and the Early Novels of H.G. Wells: Evolution, Anarchy, Entropy: by Patrick A. McCarthy. From *Journal of Modern Literature*, vol. 13, no. 1 (March 1986). © 1986 Temple University. Reprinted by permission of Indiana University Press.

Index

Characters in literary works are indexed by first name (if any),
followed by the name of the work in parentheses.